a-z of psychod

Professional Keywords series

Every field of practice has its own methods, terminology, conceptual debates and landmark publications. The *Professional Keywords* series expertly structures this material into easy-reference A to Z format. Focusing on the ideas and themes that shape the field, and informed by the latest research, these books are designed both to guide the student reader and to refresh practitioners' thinking and understanding.

Available now

Mark Doel and Timothy B. Kelly: *A–Z of Groups & Groupwork*
David Garnett: *A–Z of Housing*
Jon Glasby and Helen Dickinson: *A–Z of Interagency*
Richard Hugman: *A–Z of Professional Ethics*
Glenn Laverack: *A–Z of Health Promotion*
Glenn Laverack: *A–Z of Public Health*
Jeffrey Longhofer: *A–Z of Psychodynamic Practice*
Neil McKeganey: *A–Z of Substance Misuse and Drug Addiction*
Steve Nolan and Margaret Holloway: *A–Z of Spirituality*
Marian Roberts: *A–Z of Mediation*
David Wilkins, David Shemmings and Yvonne Shemmings:
    A–Z of Attachment

Available soon

Jane Dalrymple: *A–Z of Advocacy*
Fiona Timmins: *A–Z of Reflective Practice*

a-z of
psychodynamic practice

Jeffrey Longhofer

 palgrave

First published 2015 by
PALGRAVE

Palgrave in the UK is an imprint of Macmillan Publishers Limited, registered in England, company number 785998, of 4 Crinan Street, London, N1 9XW.

Palgrave Macmillan in the US is a division of St Martin's Press LLC, 175 Fifth Avenue, New York, NY 10010.

Palgrave is a global imprint of the above companies and is represented throughout the world.

Palgrave® and Macmillan® are registered trademarks in the United States, the United Kingdom, Europe and other countries.

ISBN: 978–1–137–03386–4

This book is printed on paper suitable for recycling and made from fully managed and sustained forest sources. Logging, pulping and manufacturing processes are expected to conform to the environmental regulations of the country of origin.

A catalogue record for this book is available from the British Library.

A catalog record for this book is available from the Library of Congress.

Printed in China

*To Jerry – thanks for a lifetime of sharing,
loving, learning.*

contents

acknowledgements

One of the key ideas in this book is 'gratitude' (see entry, *envy, greed, jealousy, gratitude*). And I've learned over my lifetime, my training and my clinical practice to feel just how correct Melanie Klein was in her understanding of this most basic and complex of human feelings. It is to my many patients that I owe a most profound gratitude for teaching me about our deepest longings, frustrations and fears, our hopes and failures, our dreams and aspirations. You've taught me about respect and recognition, patience, working, loving, hating, living fully and dying. To my child patients I owe a special gratitude: you've taught me to temper my desire to know things beyond our grasp. You've helped me to stay close to the child inside, to play and to remain curious and open to surprise. Thanks to my many mentors and teachers at the Cleveland Psychoanalytic Center and the Hanna Perkins Center and School for the countless hours of mostly volunteer teaching, mentoring and supervising: Dr Thomas Barrett, Dr Vera Camden, Dr Scott Dowling, Mrs Erna Furman, Dr Anna Janicki, Dr Kay MacKenzie, Dr Murray Goldstone, Dr Sara Tucker and Mr Carl Tuss. I'm especially grateful to Catherine Gray, my editor at Palgrave. Catherine accepted this manuscript, nurtured it, sought thorough and thoughtful reviews and added to it invaluable insight. It is to my grandmother (see entry *parenting*), Inez Ellis Ray, that I owe my own early feelings of gratitude. It was with her that I learned to read with a special attention to detail, purpose and subtlety. Finally, there is no doubt a deeper kind of gratitude that escapes expression in language: it's felt in the body, the heart, the soul, the change of seasons and the sunrise. This is a gratitude I feel every single day for my life partner, friend and intellectual soulmate, Jerry Floersch. With Jerry I've learned to live with gusto and turn every moment, from dawn to dusk, into something extraordinary.

how to use this book

In this little volume, *A to Z of Psychodynamic Practice*, I offer an introduction to some of the key concepts that inform practice across a diverse range of theories. The aim here is to suggest ways of thinking about the important intellectual moves and controversies, and to situate where possible key ideas in psychodynamic practice in the broader scholarly debates and literature. In the Introduction I offer what might be called a philosophical history, that is, a history of key ideas as they connect and relate to unfolding debates in the social and behavioural sciences. I have attempted to accomplish for key concepts in psychodynamic practice what Raymond Williams achieves in his very well-known and widely cited book 'Key Words'. For Williams, 'Key Words' is not a dictionary or glossary of terms, or definitions or footnotes. I share with him an interest in how we come to have a common vocabulary and the various forms of enquiry that have led to relative consensus about what matters most in our formulations of suffering and flourishing. In the Introduction, I consider how that vocabulary is formed according to particular intellectual moves, commitments and institutional dynamics.

Each concept included in this volume has at one time or another entered my imagination, my thinking and my feeling; they have been forced upon me by the realities of clinical practice. Often I find myself at the end of a therapy hour writing a note to myself about the concepts that organize my thinking, and wondering how it is that a particular concept enters my imagination with the same or different sense of significance and difficulty. And if this were merely a problem of description or vocabulary, a book on key ideas would be largely irrelevant. This is important for two reasons. First, the meanings of the concepts have changed. Our understandings of the significance and nature of the Oedipal, for example, changed dramatically, even during Freud's life. Today, it is impossible to summarize and digest the viewpoints and controversies that surround the Oedipal event, crisis or complex. The terms change as we see new connections in clinical material and as clinical material is served up to ideas from other fields (i.e. phenomenology). Second, these new connections are often only implicit in the developing conceptual vocabulary.

The key ideas selected for this volume are among the most controversial and enduring and, for these reasons, they present a particular challenge. They require careful consideration not only of how they have been revised over time but also the issues and problems presented by their revision. Each concept has been chosen because I believe it is significant to our current practice and thinking. The key ideas in this volume are of many types. While some are quite descriptive, others are deeply theoretical. Some are among the most important conceptual tools for thinking about psychodynamic theory and practice. Together these ideas are meant to provide students and professionals a vocabulary not only for thinking with, and across, the concepts but also for linking to current controversies, even beyond the psychoanalytic canon.

The concepts are organized alphabetically. I have assumed that some readers of this volume will find it useful as a resource to examine particular ideas. You will find the alphabetical organization of the book easy to navigate. Some readers will no doubt find it useful to pursue a single concept and will use the volume as a kind of quick reference. Others will want to exploit the many links among and between the concepts. You will find that many of the concepts in this book relate to one another in integral ways and a fuller understanding of them may require navigating across conceptual domains. If you are new to psychodynamic theory and practice, you might want to read the Introduction, where you will find many of the most important ideas identified. Other readers will no doubt want to pursue particular ideas relevant to a problem in practice. You will for this reason find at the end of most entries a brief list of bullet points, 'Points for Reflection and Practice'.

The navigational logic is organized by key idea in the table of contents. Under each entry in the text, you will find a list of related concepts (directly under the key concept heading). These concepts also appear as key ideas and can be found in the table of contents. In short there are several navigational strategies: (1) you can work from the Table of Contents; (2) you can work from the Index;

(3) or you can work from the linking key concepts enumerated under each key idea subject heading. Where some concepts are known by more than one word or term, cross referencing is used. There are also several Appendices: (1) timeline; (2) brief biography of Freud; (3) list of dictionaries, reference works, introductions, encyclopaedias; (4) list of the major defence mechanisms; (5) Erik Erickson's developmental stages; (6) list of relevant biographies, histories and related resources. Finally, following each concept you will find, KEY TEXTS. These readings have been carefully selected for those wanting to pursue particular ideas in greater depth.

Finally, there is a tendency for most professions to limit their engagements with the literature to their own tribe (e.g. psychoanalysis, object relation, Jungian, ego, drive, self-psychology, group). When we come to live in these silos, we often miss how others are working on similar problems or using similar methods. You will see that I have throughout this text, where possible and appropriate, engaged with thinkers and literature from other fields of knowledge and have often included these ideas in the KEY TEXTS. This is not meant to be an intellectual history or a history of ideas, nor is it a history of the men and women who founded and propounded the movement. Throughout this book I use the terms 'psychoanalysis' and 'psychodynamic' interchangeably.

introduction

This brief introduction is meant to provide a background for understanding the key concepts in this volume and for knowing how
and why psychodynamic/psychoanalytic theory and practice have
been, and will always be, controversial and in a necessary tension
with myriad versions of empiricism (i.e. what is, is what we see),
positivism (i.e. causality is understood as the statistical regularity
among events, see key concepts, *evidence-based practice, positivism
critical realism, social constructivism*) and the academies that promote
epistemological (i.e. ways of knowing based upon sensory experience and statistical regularity among visible events) hegemony
(Houston, 2005). Stanley Houston writes that, 'The problem arises
when evangelical proponents of these approaches [evidence-based]
begin to deride other (i.e. psychodynamic) perspectives as unsci-
entific. Thus, evidence derived from qualitative sources, from local
context, and professional experience is sometimes accorded a low
rank in the notional hierarchy of esteemed research measures ... For
instance, the idea that we can explain a person's actions with reference to unseen mechanisms, say in the person's unconscious mind,
is seen to be misleading because there is no way of proving their
existence' (Houston, 2005, pp. 7–8).

For practitioners it is important to know why psychodynamic
ideas have created such passionate and sometimes irrational debate.
It is strange that psychoanalysis, an area of human enquiry that
trades in a world of ideas about the irrational, should elicit from
so many such extraordinary and often irrational polemics (Crews,
1998; Grünbaum, 1979; Jiménez, 2009) and from psychoanalysts
reactions sometimes equally polemical and troubling. Today there
is a passion for making psychoanalytic ideas conform to standards
of positivist (i.e. statistical/quantitative methods) methods, where
explanation is reduced to, or conflated with, prediction (Shedler,
2010; Shedler and Weston, 2004).

It is especially important in our current era, the age of the brain (as declared by recent US presidents and widely embraced by many in the natural and cognitive sciences), where it is now assumed that all roads lead to the neurotransmitter or the deeper molecular structure of the brain (Rose and Rose, 2010, 2013), that we understand the relevance of key ideas and what psychodynamic thinking has to offer in this climate of biological/brain determinism. Steven Rose (2006), a neuroscientist, offers the following about our current fascination with, and investment in, the brain, 'Not merely such long-runners as intelligence, addiction and aggression, but even political tendency, religiosity and likelihood of mid-life divorce are being removed from the province of social and/or personal psychological explanation into the province of biology. With such removal comes the offer to treat, to manipulate, to control' (p. 66).

As we have become more and more enmeshed in descriptive and symptom-based (see entry, *symptom, symptom formation*) diagnosis (see entry, *diagnosis and the DSM*), we become further and further removed not only from the lived experience of pain and suffering but also from the broader meanings that symptoms convey (Laurent, 2014). These concerns, however, are not situated only in our current age of the brain and other forms of biological reductionism. We have since the beginning of the human genome project (Venter *et al.*, 2001) suffered from increasing atomism (Keller, 2010, 2011). Richard Lewontin (2011), Agasiz Professor of Genetics at Harvard and a major critic of genetic reductionism and the human genome project, summarizes the problem: 'We are conscious not only of the skin that encloses and defines the object, but of bits and pieces of that object, each of which must have its own "skin." That is the problem of anatomization ... We do not have simply an "endocrine system" and a "nervous system" and a "circulatory system," but "neurosecretory" and "neurocirculatory" systems that become the objects of inquiry because of strong forces connecting them. We may indeed stir a flower without troubling a star, but we cannot stir up a hornet's nest without troubling our hormones' (http://www. nybooks.com/articles/archives/2011/may/26/its-even-less-your-genes/).

Genetics, according to Lewontin, 'may be able to discover the function of a particular gene in isolation, perhaps one day even map a static vision of the human genome; but the random variation in the development and growth of any organism at the level of the cell, what is commonly referred to as "developmental noise," constitutes an open system at work – the organism – thus introducing variation that cannot be predicted from the genetic structure' (1991, p. 27). In open systems the human sciences (i.e. psychotherapists, social workers, psychologists, economists, anthropologists, sociologists) must confront one of our most vexing problems: as we practically engage with the world, moment-to-moment, the world is changed. And as practitioners, it is our hope that in these open systems our actions make a difference and cause change to happen. New meanings are made, new possibilities are envisioned, and new projects are formed and implemented.

What makes our understanding of human action, emotion and thought so complicated is that we operate in open systems, where 'mechanisms operate and have effects other than those they would have in experimental situations, due to the co-determination of these systems by other mechanisms' (Collier, 1994, p. 36). In his conceptual vocabulary, Freud called this over determination. For Freud reductionist views of human behaviour and consciousness could not adequately account for human consciousness as complexly shaped by diverse and sometimes even contradictory experience, even those not remembered. And for Freud, 'reasons' were causal. In 'The Interpretation of Dreams', he writes that 'there are no limits to the determinants that may be present' in the consciousness of a human being (Freud, 1900, p. 999). Similarly, he writes in 'Studies on Hysteria': 'There is in principle no difference between the symptom's appearing in a temporary way after its first provoking cause and its being latent from the first. Indeed the great majority of instances we find that a first trauma has left no symptom behind, while a later trauma of the same kind produces a symptom, and yet the latter could not have come into existence without the co-operation of the earlier provoking cause; nor can it be cleared up without taking all the provoking causes into account' (p. 157).

While Freud was not exceptional among neurologists interested in the complex and multiple causes of symptoms, he was unique among late-nineteenth-century theorists arguing that multiple causation was more likely the rule, not the exception.

Also, for Freud, there was the very difficult problem of 'Nachträglichkeit' ('afterwardness'). This concept, not listed among the key words in this volume, is important to understanding the rela-tionship between time and psychic causality. It describes for Freud and others the complex dynamic between significant life events and the ways they ultimately become meaningful and are later invested with renewed causal efficacy. With this concept important debates in the history of psychoanalysis have been pursued. Among the questions: (1) How to avoid assuming that the psychic cause of events is to be inevitably located in a distant past (i.e. early develop-ment)? (2) How do we allow in our theory for the ways that psychic events are reimagined and reinvested with meaning long after their occurrence (i.e. their afterward effects)? In sum, it is impossible to imagine that there are simple and clear relationships between past events and their current meanings and psychic significance. It is in this way that past events and their meaning are transformed and made significant in any present moment.

Our current practice world is also dominated by a kind of ideology calling for special and singular kinds of evidence (see entry, *evidence-based practice*) and manualized (i.e. standardized, one-size fits) approaches to practice (Cartwright, 2007, 2011). And the expec-tation is to provide a kind of evidence that we would not expect from many in the natural and physical sciences (e.g. we know the existence of gravity, for example, not because we see it but because it has effects which can be explained by abstract theory). Nancy Cartwright, a philosopher of science and major critic of the rand-omized control trial (RCT), the so-called gold standard for estab-lishing the basis for effective treatment and evidence, writes: 'The fact that RCTs are a deductive method underwrites their claims to be the gold standard. But RCTs suffer, as do all deductive methods, from narrowness of scope. Their results are formally valid for the group enrolled in the study, but only for that group. The method itself does not underwrite any strong claims for external validity, that is for extending whatever results are supposed to be established in the test population to other "target" populations. This is impor-tant to keep in clear sight in comparing RCTs with other methods' (2007, pp. 11–20).

It is also an age dominated by what many have dubbed the 'phar-maceutical-industrial complex'. The industry sells drugs for every-thing, promising elixirs for our everyday pains and struggles, and in reducing the practice of psychiatry to the application of drugs, the meaning of pain and suffering is reduced to a 15-minute med check and the elision of a search for meaning. David Healy (2012), a psychiatrist and major critic of our pharmaceutical world, writes:

> In one sense measurements from mood scales to lipid levels involve new ways of looking at ourselves, and as such they can claim the mantle of scientific progress. But if they lead to over-looking context or other dimensions of an individual's function-ing – dimensions that may not be open to measurement or that are simply not being measured – rather than being modestly scientific by measuring what we can and attending also to what we cannot measure, we risk being pseudoscientific. Scientific measurement and quantification succeed when they force us to look ever more closely at things while allowing us to see them in their wider contexts. By stripping away context, mindless meas-urement does exactly the opposite. This mindlessness is doing to medical practice something similar to what an exclusive focus on manufacturing goods driven by the target of increasing GNP is doing to the environment and the quality of life. (p. 15)

There is no doubt that Freud's influence on the human sciences, humanities and psychiatry has been far-reaching and long lasting. While not without controversy, Freud's ideas are widely circulated and used across an array of disciplines. In reading the key concepts in this book, it is impossible to escape the reach of Freud's thinking: into the humanities, philosophy, medicine and psychiatry, anthro-pology, sociology, and history and political theory (Elliott, 1992, 2007; Frosh, 1987; Rustin, 1991). There can be little doubt that one of the reasons that the theory, not unlike Marxism, has such a broad reach is that it is always incomplete, reaching for elabora-tion and extension. It is a daunting task to enter the vast literature produced by Freud, his followers, his critics, and those involved in the continued development of his thinking, so I will simplify this task by turning to philosophy of science.

One way of understanding the many and complex turns psycho-analytic ideas have taken is through the philosophy of social science (Clarke, 2005, 2007; Will, 1980, 1985). Philosophers of social science ask questions about what is real, knowable, or about the nature of being human. These are sometimes called 'ontological' questions. They also ask, how do we know what's real? And these are called 'epistemological' questions. Many in the philosophy of social science have criticized psychoanalytic theory and practice based upon naive empiricism (i.e. what is is what we can see) and because much of modern science, including physics, would not stand the test of empiricism, I have decided to give little attention here to those ideas. While philosophers of mind have altogether abandoned (Kim, 2011) attempts to defend behavioural conceptions of mental life and functioning, in clinical practice and research, behaviourism remains a formidable force. Noam Chomsky (1959) offered a very early and still today cogent and compelling critique of Skinner's behavioural empiricism. He writes in that widely cited essay,

> It is important to see clearly just what it is in Skinner's program and claims that makes them appear so bold and remarkable. It is not primarily the fact that he has set functional analysis as his problem, or that he limits himself to study of observables, i.e., input-output relations. What is so surprising is the particular limitations he has imposed on the way in which the observables of behavior are to be studied, and, above all, the particularly simple nature of the function which, he claims, describes the causation of behavior. One would naturally expect that prediction of the behavior of a complex organism (or machine) would require, in addition to information about external stimulation, knowledge of the internal structure of the organism, the ways in which it processes input information and organizes its own behavior. These characteristics of the organism are in general a complicated product of inborn structure, the genetically determined course of maturation, and past experience. Insofar as independent neurophysiological evidence is not available, it is obvious that inferences concerning the structure of the organism are based on observation of behavior and outside events. Nevertheless, one's estimate of the relative importance of external factors and internal structure in the determination of behavior will have an important effect on the direction of research on linguistic (or any other) behavior, and on the kinds of analogies from animal behavior studies that will be considered relevant or suggestive. (Chomsky, 1959, p. 27)

I believe it is useful to array the many psychoanalytic ideas along a continuum from realist naturalism (i.e. ontology) to complete idealism. In radical naturalism, for example, one might argue that the drives (see entry, *drive*) are simply present, in nature, ready to be expressed but constrained by the parental and social surround. Here the drives are seen as an essential reality (i.e. ontology) and the psyche is motivated by complex dynamics of energic forces. Freud's intellectual world, recall, was rooted in electromagnetism and Newtonian physics: charges, forces, drives, impacts (see Appendix 2, Brief Biography of Freud). Others argue quite differently (Mitchell, 1988; Loewald, 1971, 1979, 1988; Whitebook, 1996). For them, the drives are an emergent property of interaction between caregivers and infants. Here, the drives are not materially and naturally given but rather the outcome (or emergent property) of relational dynamics and social constructions (see entries, *drive* and *positivism and critical realism*). It is important, here, to note that there is a recent and very relevant literature in the philosophy of social science on emergence (Elder-Vass, 2010). Andrew Collier, a critical realist philosopher of social science writes of emergence, 'emergence theories are those that, while recognizing that the more complex aspects of reality (e.g. life, mind) presuppose the less complex (e.g. matter), also insist that they have features which are irreducible, i.e. cannot be thought in concepts appropriate to the less complex levels – and that not because of any subjective constraints on our thought, but because of the inherent nature of the emergent strata' (1994, pp. 110–111).

Joel Whitebook, in his review of the work of Cornelius Castoriadis, argues that the drives exist in a space or tension between the psyche and the soma. Castoriadis uses Freud's term 'Anlehnung' (to lean on) to describe this more complex dynamic; in short, the psyche (and the drives) are rooted in the soma but not reducible to it. The oral drive requires the materiality of the mouth and breast, but the drive itself is not the mouth but the result of the psyche leaning on the breast. Otherwise drive states would vary only according to body states and their vicissitudes would be determined solely by biological difference. Hans Loewald, in his essay 'On Psychic Structure Formation' makes a very similar argument:

> Following a formulation of Freud's – to which he himself and other analytic theorists have not consistently adhered – I define

instinct (or instinctual drive) here as a psychic representative
of biological stimuli or processes, and not as these biological
stimuli themselves. In contradistinction to Freud's thought in
'Instincts and Their Vicissitudes' (1915, pp. 121–122), however,
I do not speak of biological stimuli impinging on a ready-made
'psychic apparatus' in which their psychic representatives are
thus created, but of interactional biological process that find
higher organization on levels which we have come to call psychic life. Understood as psychic phenomena or representatives
instincts come into being in the early organizing mother-infant
interactions. (2000, p. 208)

For Castoriadis, while the bodily organ is an external condition
'without which the drive and its related fantasies cannot exist' the
drives cannot be reduced to the organ. Put differently, the drives are
necessarily and always rooted in the organ but not reducible to the
organ. Castoriadis writes,

Mouth and breast, like the anus and faeces, like the penis or
vagina are neither causes nor means, and certainly not 'signifiers' in some univocal relation to a signified which would always
and everywhere be the same, nor even the same for the same
subject. We must learn to think otherwise; we have to understand that the idea of anaclisis, of leaning on, is just as original
and irreducible as the idea of cause or the idea of symbolizing.
The privileged somatic data will always be taken up again by
the psyche, psychical working out will have to 'take them into
account', they will leave their mark on it – but which mark and
in what manner cannot be reflected in the identitary frame of
reference of determinacy. For the creativity of the psyche enters
in here as radical imagination, as the emergence of representation (phantasying) and the alteration of representation, thereby
rendering absurd the idea that the breast or the anus are the
'cause' of a phantasy as well as the idea that the oral or the anal
can be assigned once and for all to a universal and complete
determination-determinacy. (1975, p. 178)

David Will (1980, 1985), in several very important essays, locates
psychoanalytic ideas in a contemporary philosophy of social
science called critical realism (these philosophers of science have

reconceptualized explanation – not in terms of general laws that is, covering laws of positivism, but in the powers and tendencies of things, including people). Will, among other things, offers the language of emergence to describe how psychoanalytic theory works and defends the notion that reasons can be causes (Collier, 1995). About reasons as cause, Roy Bhaskar (see entry, *positivism and critical realism*) argues that the mental world cannot be simply reduced to physical events or mechanism; if this were possible, reasons would be irrelevant to causal explanation. Simply put, the reduced level would explain everything without the need to refer to reasons (Bhaskar, 2010, pp. 164–165).

I argue that our sometimes different and competing psychodynamic accounts (i.e. drive, ego, object, self, relational) are not different theories at all, but differing accounts of levels in a stratified reality, each with powers and liabilities, each with its own emergent properties. Drive theory, for example, refers to the complex dynamic between bodies and minds: the psyche and the soma. And while the psyche is rooted in the soma, it obviously has its own powers and liabilities with its own emergent properties. Just as the brain is a contingent (not determined or necessary) and emergent property of the body, the mind is also a contingent and emergent property of the brain. The drives, as argued above, emerge in a complex social and interactional world. It is for this reason that Freud avoided scientistic language in preference for a more humanistic conceptual (Bettleheim, 1983) vocabulary; many, for example, are surprised to learn that Freud never used the terms 'ego', 'id' and superego. These were introduced by his translators and were meant to give them a gloss of scientific acceptability. His translator, Srachey, described psychic energy in electromagnetic terms: 'cathexis' and 'decathexsis'. And some in child development have talked about the fusion of drives: the aggressive drive fused with the libidinal (Furman, 1985). When all goes smoothly in the course of early development, fusion of the drives produces a kind of neutral or usable energy. Some might describe this as the sublimation of instinctual impulse, that is, the transformation of raw emotional energy, sexual and aggressive, into creativity. These are all ontological questions: questions about what is real and knowable. Others, such as Loewald, take the drives to be emergent properties rather than natural kinds (Zachar, 2000).

Elaborations of Freud's ideas have been many and diverse, too many to elaborate in this brief introduction. And many of his staunchest critics came from his own inner circle. In the fall of 1912, Jung, president of the International Psychoanalytic Association, in a series of lectures in New York, challenged many of Freud's fundamental understandings of sexuality, the origins of neuroses, dream interpretation (see entry, *dream*), and the unconscious (see entry, *conscious (unconscious, preconscious)*). And most of these objections were ontological. Jung writes,

Fairness to Freud does not mean, as many fear, an unqualified submission to a dogma; one can very well maintain an independent judgement. If I, for instance, acknowledge the complex mechanisms of dreams and hysteria, this does not mean that I attribute to the infantile sexual trauma the exclusive importance that Freud apparently does. Still less does it mean that I place sexuality so predominantly in the foreground or even grant it the psychological universality which Freud, it seems, postulates under the impression of the certainly powerful role which sexuality plays in the psyche. Concerning Freudian therapy, it is in the best case one of the possible, and perhaps does not always offer what one theoretically expects.

Anna Freud, on her father's 80th birthday, offered him the gift of a book, her own book, 'The Ego and the Mechanisms of Defense' (Dyer, 1983; Stewart-Steinberg, 2012; Young-Bruehl, 1994). Anna was especially interested in the role of the ego and its defences. After Freud introduced the structural theory in 1923 (see entries, *ego* and *defence mechanisms*) many theorists turned to what has been called a functionalist view of the ego and impairments of function (i.e. the essential and fundamental functions were reality-testing, impulse-control, judgement, affect tolerance, defence and synthetic functioning). Much of this new theorizing focused on strengthening the functions against pressures from the id and superego (Schafer, 1999). For Heinz Hartmann, the healthy ego requires a sphere of autonomous function, that is, functioning outside the realm of psychic conflict. For Hartman the autonomous functions of the ego (e.g. memory, motor coordination, and reality-testing) should function outside of conflict. And the aim of psychoanalysis, therefore, was to expand the conflict-free sphere. And it is in this way that psychoanalysis promotes adaptation and regulation of the relation between the ego and the environment. In the 'Essays on Ego Psychology', Hartman (1964) writes, 'It is via the study of the ego and its functions that psychoanalysis will reach its aim of becoming a general psychology. For a long time, the study of drives and their development was the core of psychoanalytic psychology, and to it was later added the study of the defensive functions of the ego. A next step pointed to extending the analytic approach to the manifold activities of the ego which can be subsumed under the concept of the "conflict-free sphere"' (p. x).

For Paul Gray, a more recent contributor to the literature in ego psychology, therapy should not, really cannot, be aimed at replacing the once punitive superego of the analysand with the more benign one of the analyst. For Gray, this approach is rooted in an older history of hypnotic technique and should be abandoned in favour of therapeutic action aimed at promoting autonomy. For Gray, therapeutic action results from shared observation of analyst and patient and understanding of intrapsychic activities and resistance to drive derivatives allowed into consciousness. For Gray (1990), the goal of psychoanalysis is the production of increased capacity for rational autonomy, which results in the ability to observe mental states and processes as they emerge moment-to-moment and determine how patients want to live with them.

For Erik Erikson, the ego functions as more than a mediator between the superego and the id. It is necessary for the establishment and maintenance of a sense of identity, a sense of purpose and place in life, a sense of uniqueness, belonging and wholeness (see Appendix 5 for a summary of Erikson's stages of identity development). According to Erikson, identity crises begin with lack of direction, a sense of being unproductive.

For Jacques Lacan the ego is object, not subject (see entry, *ego*). It is not the site of autonomous agency or the true 'I'. This ego-as-object is the basis of Lacan's critique of Anglo-American ego psychology. For Lacan, the ego cannot be strengthened or managed through promotion of autonomous and 'conflict-free' functions. The ego, for Lacan, is always compromised and inherently neurotic.

Finally, throughout this volume, you will see reference to *object*, object relations theory, and *attachment* theory. I am persuaded that this group of theorists, heavily influenced by the thinking of Klein and Fairbairn, are related in many ways (Mitchell, 1981; Clarke, 2005, 2007). Object-relations theory shifts the focus of attention from intrapersonal structures or agencies and conflicts (i.e. id, ego, superego) to how the internal world is constructed from ways of relating to internal and external objects, in reality and in fantasy. The attachment theorists, especially, shift attention to the real and external ways of relating and the formative influence habits of relating have on the building up of psychic structure (i.e. mental models, internal working models). Klein places the mother–infant relationship at the centre of development and significantly influenced the work of John Bowlby and Donald Winnicott. Klein's 'play technique', treated the content of child play as symbolic unconscious material subject to interpretation just as were dreams and free associations with adults.

In this little volume I hope you'll find these ideas and others addressed in ways that will deepen your understanding of this rich and diverse body of knowledge.

adolescence

SEE ALSO attachment; developmental stages; diagnosis and the DSM; drive; ego; emerging adulthood; gender

While Freud wrote very little in depth about adolescence, he did pay close attention to it phylogenetically, in terms of psychosexual development, and in his frequent use of the term puberty. Remarkably, in the 'Cambridge Companion to Freud' (Neu, 1991), adolescence is mentioned only twice and then only in passing. In the 'Standard Edition' (Freud's collected works), adolescence is mentioned only three times while puberty appears 240 times. For many *psychodynamic* theorists, adolescence is marked by three key developmental moments and potential outcomes. First, there is a change in the sexual impulse, resulting in the discovery of *object* love. There is at this moment also a very *real* danger of what the Laufers (2011) call 'developmental breakdown' (see entry, *developmental stages*): a rejection of the emerging sexual and adult body alongside potential conflicts over *gender*. Anna Freud, similarly, understood that adolescent struggles simultaneously satisfy and balance inner impulse (i.e. the wishes of the id), against the demands of reality and the *ego* (see entries, *ego* and *drive*).

Second, there is disengagement from parental ties. This, for some theorists, is described as a second individuation (Blos, 1967). For Blos, individuation is realizable only with resolution of adolescent conflicts and in separation from internalized infantile object dependency. At one extreme, adolescents make sharp breaks from parental worlds and imagos and, at the other extreme, others remain intensely attached and find it nearly impossible to form relationships outside the family. Between these extremes most remain meaningfully attached to parents while forming rich and intense ties to others in their social surround. Third, there is an affirmation of identity and subjectivity. And recent research shows the importance of understanding how early *attachment* relationships *affect* later adolescent development and relations with important others: parents, peers, and romantic partners (Smetana *et al.*, 2006).

Erik Erikson, strongly influenced by Anna Freud's thinking on adolescence, argued that during adolescence one must establish a 'personal identity' in order to avoid 'role diffusion and identity confusion' (see Appendix 5). Ego identity is achieved with growing self-knowledge and a growing sense of how one fits into the larger social order. Moreover, because identity is not simply transmitted to the individual by the cultural surround (nor is it merely the outcome of maturational events), it must be acquired through sustained effort; in short, adolescents must actively seek answers to questions about where they've come from, who they are, and what their future holds. However, this is not easily accomplished without culturally mediated rites of passage, rituals, and other forms of social *recognition* marking life course transitions. Anthropologists (Bucholtz, 2002; Korbin and Anderson-Fye, 2011; Schlegel and Hewlett, 2011) have described the complexity of adolescent experience and the diverse ways in which adolescents undergo periods of ritual transition marking changes in status and roles. And with culturally marked moments in life, the possibility for role confusion is significantly diminished (i.e. less uncertainty about one's place in society).

With role confusion comes identity crisis and adolescents at these moments struggle with the quite common identity question: Who am I? If successful at this stage, adolescents feel 'fidelity', a sense of loyalty to the social world, without compromising important values, along with the ability to recognize and manage the inevitable social contradictions, imperfections, and inconsistencies. Answers to these questions, in turn, may result in a sense of continuity and sameness. Erikson pays close attention to values developed during adolescence, particularly, fidelity, which he argues results in stable identity. 'The adolescent mind is essentially a mind of the moratorium, a psychosocial stage between childhood and adulthood, and between the morality learned by the child, and the ethics to be developed by the adult' (Erikson, 1950, pp. 262–263).

A more recent theorist of adolescent development, Janet Sayers, a British Kleinian, describes boy craziness, or male valorization, through which, she argues, our androcentric culture is maintained and reproduced. For adolescent boys, unlike girls, 'internal' conflicts (see entry, *conflict and compromise formation*) are intensely acute: 'they experience divisions of mind and body, truth and falsehood, past and present, fantasy and reality, love and sex. Adolescent girls, on the other hand, experience a division of love and hate toward their mothers and others. Their conflicts, unlike boys, are 'external' and relational. Girls experience their mothers as gender models and as having achieved only secondary status in the world: cause for both celebration and resentment on their parts for becoming like their mothers' (p. 104). Both sexes, however, escape the torment of these divisions through, as Sayers (1998) puts it, 'boys crazily aggrandizing themselves or others as gods, heroes, or saviors' (p. 104). She continues, 'Boys look to heroes, rock stars and super-heroes, or fantasize themselves as heroes, thus firmly reinforcing male-dominated culture; girls look to romance with boys as a way out of their conflicted feelings, thus reinforcing male-dominated culture' (p. 104).

Some argue that in Western culture, in order for boys to become boys, they must separate from their mothers and that culturally mediated and necessary separations produce subsequent difficulties in relating to women (Benjamin, 2013; Rubin, 1983).

For social scientists, adolescence (e.g. Arnett and Tanner, 2006; James, 2007; Mead, 1954; Schlegel and Hewlett, 2011) has always been a source of controversy and cultural critique. Many look for a golden age of childhood, others seek to show that childhood is ever changing and responding to ideological, economic, and political climates. The anthropologist Margaret Mead (1954) sought to show with her ethnographic data from Samoa that adolescence was not a stage of development inevitably fraught with conflict, disturbance, and struggle. And more recently, Jeffrey Arnett and Tanner (2006), the principal theorist of a new stage *'emerging adulthood,'* argues that 'The timing and meaning of coming of age – that is, reaching full adult status – is different today than it was 50 or 100 years ago, different in fact than it has ever been before' (p. 4). For Arnett, 'the social and institutional structures that once both supported and restricted people in the course of coming of age have weakened, leaving people with greater freedom but less support as they make their way into adulthood' (p. 4). Emerging adults (see entry, *emerging adulthood*), according to Arnett, enter a world dominated by deinstitutionalization and increased individualization, and a growing expectation that life course transitions must be matched with greater commitments of personal resources and agency.

For others, especially in the more recent field of childhood studies (sociology, anthropology, history), childhood and adolescence are seen as singularly cultural and historical constructions; 'social constructivist' arguments (see, for example, James, 2007), in their strong form, deny the possibility of universally shared adolescent experience. These accounts, however convincing, tend to altogether ignore the material determinants of child and adolescent development (i.e. biological maturation) and the many common and universal ways children experience bodily change. This cultural relativism, moreover, fails to account for the important ways in which developmental moments are made profoundly personal and felt to be essential to the self and intractable, even when they've been socially constructed. In short, it must not be assumed that what is culturally constructed is not also experienced and felt as essential, immutable and determined aspects or qualities of being and self-hood. Adolescence, as with all developmental stages, is not like a light switch to be turned on and off as cultural winds change.

For Ken Corbett (2009), Freud offered a developmental theory of childhood and adolescence that inevitably produced a normative *Oedipal* narrative. For Corbett, Freud 'foretold' masculinity through the case of Little Hans and by so doing produced a limited narrative and understanding. The result, through exclusion, was the 'Ur-boy of psychoanalysis'. Beginning with the story of Little Hans, we come to know a 'a boy to be a boy through his phallic preoccupations and castration fears, enacted alongside and through his desire for his mother and his rivalry with his father, which in time resolve via the boy's separation from his mother and his *identification* with his father' (p. 19; emphasis added). For Freud, rivalry and aggression override the counter narrative, which reveals an underlying affective world of dependence and desire: 'A theory of masculinity that is forged solely through competition with paternal authority, with little regard for the interplay of identifications, desire, and mutual recognition ... is largely a theory of phallic *narcissism*-qua-masculinity' (p. 49; emphasis added).

Finally, it is not uncommon, in our current pharmaceutical age, to treat normal adolescent development as a disease, as 'symptoms' to be managed with anti-depressants and anti-*anxiety* drugs, rather than necessary to becoming fully and richly human. This entails toleration of fluctuating mood and affect due to both the new body and the mournful sadness resulting from movement into the world of peers and away from the security of familial and familiar relationships.

points for reflection and practice

- It is important in clinical practice with adolescents to consider how they bring anxieties about their 'new bodies,' along with assaults to esteem and mournful sadness about body changes.
- Work with adolescents requires careful consideration of the boundaries with parents. In meeting with parents, it is important to consider their availability and capacity to support and actively engage their adolescents as they negotiate increased autonomy and self-reliance; they must also learn to know that they may need to be available for support during periods of transition
- It is especially important for therapists to help parents support adolescents as they test and explore normative standards for behaviour. *Listening* to their expressions of concern for peer approval and pressure and helping them define their own values is crucial.
- Some parents come to psychodynamic psychotherapy with lots of questions and doubts about the effectiveness of the approach. It is useful for clinicians to be aware of outcome research and meta-analytic studies which demonstrate effectiveness. The Anna Freud Centre in London (Fonagy and Target, 1996), in collaboration with the Yale Child Studies Center conducted outcomes research using data on 763 youth treated with intensive and nonintensive treatment. The findings (reported in 1996) show that for children with severe emotional disorders, long-term intensive treatment was more effective than short-term therapies, or a combination of therapy with medication. A more recent meta-analytic study corroborates these findings (Midgely and Kennedy, 2011).

KEY TEXTS

- Arnett, J., and Tanner, J. (eds) (2006) *Emerging Adults in America: Coming of Age in the 21st Century* (Washington, DC: American Psychological Association), pp. 3–19
- Erikson, E. (1950) *Childhood and Society* (New York, NY: W. W. Norton & Company)

- Erikson, E. (1968) *Identity: Youth and Crisis* (New York, NY: W. W. Norton & Company)
- James, A. (2007) 'Giving Voice to Children's Voices: Practices and Problems, Pitfalls and Potentials', *American Anthropologist*, 109 (2): pp. 261–272
- Laufer, M., and Laufer, M. (2011) *Adolescence and Developmental Breakdown: A Psychoanalytic View* (London, UK: Karnac Books)
- Sayers, J. (1998) *Boy Crazy: Remembering Adolescence, Therapies and Dreams* (London, UK: Routledge)

affect

SEE ALSO **affect regulation; attachment; drive; mentalization**

Early in his thinking on affect, Freud described it as variable quantities of excitation: symptoms develop when affect-laden experiences are repressed. Much later Silvan Tomkins (1995) argued that affects could be sorted into fundamental and discrete categories governed by mechanisms over which the individual had little control. Building on the work of Tomkins, Paul Ekman (1993) and others identified what they believed were basic, universal, essential and innate emotions. These included surprise, happiness, anger, sadness, fear, and disgust. For Jesse Prinz (2004), a contemporary philosopher of emotion, the dichotomy between innate, basic or nonbasic emotions is unsustainable. He writes, 'First, while there is a difference between basic emotions and nonbasic emotions, it is not a structural difference. All emotions are fundamentally alike. Second, the standard list of basic emotions, thought by many to be universal across cultures, are not basic after all. We don't have names for the basic emotions. All emotions that we talk about are culturally informed' (2004, p. 69).

Daniel Stern (2009) differentiates categorical affects from 'vitality affects' and for him, affective experience is intersubjectively produced principally though not exclusively through 'affect attunement' in the mother/infant dyad. For Brian Massumi (2002), affects are differentiated from feeling and emotion: feelings are personal and biographical, emotions are social, and affects are prepersonal. There is much debate about whether the so-called basic emotions comprise a 'natural' kind and whether some are more basic than others. Finally, there is an important literature, research and practice, on how affects are regulated (i.e. *affect regulation*).

Affect is often differentiated from emotion, feeling or sentiment. Sometimes it refers to observable manifestations of feeling (i.e. facial expression, gesture, tone of voice, tears). Affects may also be seen as incongruent with feeling, that is, one's affect may conceal hidden feelings: a smile may obscure a deeper sense of anger or disappointment. For *psychodynamic* theory, the key ideas and research concern the complex and dynamic relationships among emotion, belief, and desire and between emotion and action and the role of cognitive (or *ego*) antecedents, the significance of bodily arousal and physiological expressions and the relationship to pain and pleasure. Affect is made especially complex because it refers simultaneously to bodily and mental states. And some argue that the normal range of affect, called the 'broad affect', is partly determined by cultural context.

How do these mental states, affects, feelings, and emotions, differ? In everyday language, the terms are often used interchangeably (Kleinginna and Kleinginna, 1981). There is little agreement among the disciplines about the differences and many use the terms – emotion, affect, and feeling – without making finer distinctions. And in recent years, the study of affect and affect regulation has been taken up by a broad array of disciplines with an equally diverse set of ontological assumptions (i.e. what emotion is): philosophy, literary theory, media studies, neuropsychoanalysis, social work, psychology, sociology and anthropology. Nevertheless, there are some things we know for sure about emotion and feeling: (1) we feel even before we learn a language, or meaningful verbalization of feeling; (2) emotions will determine how we engage with, and take action with, objects and people in the external world; (3) our engagements with others will always involve emotional states; (4) emotions are sources of motivation (Stanghellini and Rosfort, 2013). Spezzono (1993), a psychoanalyst, argues that affects are the foundation for relationships: 'affects give rise to relationships, and drives evolve out of the interplay between them.' The central and most radical argument of psychoanalysis is that human psychological life is, at its core, human affective life' (p. 113).

In recent years, there has been growing interest in the relationship between cognition and emotion. Richard Ryan (2007), in an editorial for the journal, 'Motivation and Emotion', describes the change: 'After three decades of the dominance of cognitive approaches, motivational and emotional processes have roared back into the limelight ... More practically, cognitive interventions that do not address motivation and emotion are increasingly proving to be short-lived in their efficacy, and limited in the problems to which they can be applied' (p. 1).

Matthew Ratcliffe (2005), one of our contemporary and most important philosophers of emotion, writes that feelings in philosophy are 'usually restricted to the role they play in emotions. Emotions, for the most part, are ways in which specific objects, events or situations are perceived, evaluated or felt. But all specific intentional states presuppose general structures of intentionality, ways of finding oneself in the world that determine the space of experiential possibilities' (p. 61). Ratcliffe calls the various ways we find ourselves in the world 'existential feeling'. And for him, the location of a feeling can be differentiated from what it is a feeling of: 'Thus accounts of bodily feeling which assume that what is felt must be the body are mistaken. Existential feelings are bodily feelings that constitute the structure of one's relationship with the world as a whole' (p. 61).

points for reflection and practice

- Evaluation and assessment should include the role of affect regulation in producing or limiting goal-directed activity and in recovery from negative life events and stressors.
- Research shows that voluntary self-regulation of negative affect is essential to treatment outcomes and chronic inability to regulate affect is commonly associated with mood and bipolar disorders.
- Special consideration should be given to the processing of *shame* for self-regulation and the role of shame in the capacity to tolerate treatment.

KEY TEXTS
- Green, A. (1999) *Fabric of Affect in the Psychoanalytic Discourse* (London, UK: Routledge)

- Johnston, A. and Malabou, C. (2013) *Self and Emotional Life: Philosophy, Psychoanalysis, and Neuroscience* (New York, NY: Columbia University Press)
- Jones, J. M. (1995) *Affects as Process: An Inquiry into the Centrality of Affect in Psychological Life* (Hillsdale, NJ: The Analytic Press)
- Ratcliffe, M. (2005) 'The Feeling of Being', *Journal of Consciousness Studies*, 12 (8–10): pp. 45–63
- Rusbridger, R. (2012) 'Affects in Melanie Klein', *International Journal of Psychoanalysis*, 93 (1): pp. 139–150
- Schore, A. (2003) *Affect Regulation and the Repair of the Self* (New York, NY: W. W. Norton & Company)
- Stanghellini, G. and Rosfort, R. (2013) *Emotions and Personhood: Exploring Fragility-Making Sense of Vulnerability* (Oxford, UK: Oxford University Press)
- Stein, R. (1999) *Psychoanalytic Theories of Affect* (London, UK: Karnac Books)

affect regulation

SEE ALSO **affect; attachment; mentalization**

Psychoanalysts, neuroscientists, and *attachment* theorists have turned attention to *affect* regulation and the relational world. Attachment theorists (Fonagy *et al.*, 2002; Fonagy, 2007; Fonagy and Target, 2003), in particular, are interested in how *mentalization* (i.e. effectively using mental representations of the emotional states of self and other) is connected to the developing capacity for affect regulation (i.e. conscious and unconscious ways of maximizing pleasant emotion and minimizing unpleasant emotion appropriate to the social surround) and to disruptions in later life. Neuroscientists argue that the brain structures necessary for affect regulation mature late in development (Schore, 2003), and that these mechanisms and functions are necessary for the formation and maintenance of interactions between the self and the social surround. Self-regulation, then, is not only experience-dependent; it is also rooted in intersubjective states essential to the brain's regulatory potential.

In the dyadic relation between child and caregiver there is an ongoing and rapid synchronization of affect, called 'affect synchrony', which produces steadily increasing measures of joy and excitement.

In what Fonagy and his colleagues (2002) call mentalization, the attuned, empathic caregiver uses his or her own sensory world and stimulation in a synchronized way with those of the infant's: as a child's mood changes, so does the mental state of the caregiver: the infant learns that arousal with an attuned caregiver will not lead to disorganization beyond the capacity for coping; and that the caregiver will be predictably present to restore calm. When aroused and out of control, the infant will seek the caregiver for soothing and for return to a normal state. These affect-laden, face-to-face, moment-to-moment transactions, moreover, contain social and cognitive information. Mutual regulation and interaction also include ruptures and repair: where negative affect is reintegrated in the dynamic of interaction, positive affect follows. Negative affect is increasingly managed and tolerated and relational stress is regulated. Together the child and caregiver move with greater ease between positive and negative affect states. This synchronization enables ongoing appraisal and intersubjective communication about nonverbal and psychobiological states, including negative states, of the child and caregiver.

Schore (2001, 2003, 2005) looks at affect regulation in the early years of life and specifically at the development of the right orbital frontal cortex and its central role in processing socio-emotional information and in coupling and regulation of the sympathetic and parasympathetic aspects of the autonomic nervous system.

points for reflection and practice
- The goal in therapy, for Schore and others conducting research on affect, insecure attachment and emotional dysregulation, is to develop new capacities for the management of attachment distress.
- Research shows that voluntary self-regulation of negative affect contributes significantly to well-being, and the chronic inability to regulate affect is commonly associated with major mood disorders, *depression* and bipolar disorder.
- Research shows that it is important to understand the normal processes of affect regulation so that treatment can, especially with mood disorders (e.g. bipolar disorder), be aimed at severe mood swings.

- Harder and Folke (2012) offer important insights into the role of affect regulation and attachment on early development and intervention in *psychosis*.

KEY TEXTS
- Fonagy, P. *et al.* (2002) *Affect Regulation, Mentalization, and the Development of the Self* (New York, NY: Other Press)
- Kandel, E. (1999) 'Biology and the Future of Psychoanalysis: A New Intellectual Framework for Psychiatry Revisited', *American Journal of Psychiatry*, 156 (4): pp. 505–524
- Schore, A. (2003) *Affect Dysregulation and Disorders of the Self* (New York, NY: W. W. Norton & Company)

alpha and beta elements (and functions)

SEE ALSO **container/contained; illusion; mentalization; projection; projective identification; reverie**

Wilfred Bion, a British psychiatrist and psychoanalyst, borrowed from the *object* relations theorist, Melanie Klein, *projective identification* (PI), to think more generally about mental functioning and cognition. For Bion, projective identification refers to much more than powerful fantasies in the infant's mental world. It is also an early, necessary, and principal means of communication. It is through *projection* of primitive mental states, what Bion called 'beta elements', from the mind of the infant into the mind of the mother, that these states are processed and made comprehensible and the infant comes to know their own thinking and mental lives. The baby, in early life, lacks a thought-thinking apparatus sufficient to metabolize (i.e. use and integrate) early mental experience. These states he called beta (b) elements: bodily feelings and emotional states alongside early sensory and relational experience. And because the mind is not sufficiently developed to metabolize them, they must first enter the mind of the Other, where they are felt, thought, and reflected. For example, when fear is projected into a receptive parent (the responsive parent, for Bion, performs the containing function), it is made familiar; and through *recognition* is then available to the infant in comprehensible and usable forms. These transformations of raw sensory data (i.e. what he called beta elements, or unprocessed sense data, unassimilated and unsymbolized by the *ego* as 'food for thinking') into alpha elements is necessary for conscious and unconscious life.

In his book, 'Learning from Experience', Bion writes: 'If alpha-function is disturbed and therefore inoperative the sense impressions of which the patient is aware and the emotions which he is experiencing remain unchanged. I shall call them beta-elements. In contrast with the alpha-elements the beta-elements are not felt to be phenomena, but things in themselves' (p. 6). Moreover, because beta elements are not useful for thinking, they must be managed through expulsion. They are also present in the formations of delusion, hallucination and acting out. Unlike alpha elements, beta elements are not subject to change with new information or impression; thus, reality testing is compromised. In sum, beta elements can be transformed only with alpha function.

For Bion, the mind works according to two fundamental principles: first there is the link between the innate (the actual organism) and the experience of perceiving the external world. The infant enters the world with preconceptions (expectations), that is, innate capacities, already wired for action or knowing how to act with a given perception (e.g. the baby knows how to respond, innately, when the nipple is felt against the cheek and responds with suckling). For Bion, this linking was necessary and essential to thinking itself. Here's a simpler statement of the logic: first there is an innate preconception, followed by a realization resulting from the actual perception. The link between the two produces a mental object and a mind with which to hold and think about it. Bion also referred to this process as alpha function: the conversion of raw experience into a mental object. Moreover, the entering of one object into another is not unlike projective identification. Thoughts, thus, exist before there is an apparatus sufficiently developed for thinking. The capacity for thinking (i.e. the apparatus for it) must emerge before one can manage thoughts. For Bion thinking comes into existence to 'cope with thoughts,' and 'thinking is a development forced upon the psyche by the pressure of thoughts and not the other way around' (Bion 1962, p. 179). Bion offers a theory of mind, that is, the capacity to apprehend one's own mental states (i.e. intentions, desires, emotions) and to understand the mental states of others. One of the necessary conditions for these transformations is found in the function of what he called the container (see entry, *container/contained*) and the capacity of the caretaker for *reverie* (see entry, *reverie*).

Some have argued that Bion has two models for understanding 'alpha function'. The earliest, most recognizable and explicit one is based upon a digestive metaphor: the infant empties (i.e. projects) emotion into the caregiver, who then metabolizes it with his or her alpha function. It is then returned to the infant in a useful form. The less explicit one, found in his later writing, is procreative and sees alpha function as internalizations of interactions between the infant and mother; and it is through these interactions that new meaning is created. The two models of alpha function, some argue, the digestive and procreative, work in concert 'to build the capacity for individual and shared narratives' (Lombardozzi, 2010).

Finally, it is to Bion that many in contemporary psychoanalysis turn for thinking about what is called *mentalization* (see entry, *mentalization*) and he's had a very significant influence on our understandings of psychotic phenomena. In the 1950s Bion worked with severely ill patients with thought disorders where he observed how emotions and perceptions fail to become psychic.

point for reflection and practice
- For Bion the fundamental work of therapy is the activity of moving raw emotional experience or perception into the psychic realm.

KEY TEXTS
- Bion, W. R. (1957) 'Differentiation of the Psychotic from Non-psychotic Personalities', *International Journal of Psychoanalysis*, 38(3–4): pp. 266–275
- Mitrani, J. (2008) *A Framework for the Imaginary: Clinical Explorations in Primitive States of Being* (London, UK: Karnac Books)
- Mitrani, J. (2011) 'Excogitating Bion's Cogitations: Further Implications for Technique', *The Psychoanalytic Quarterly*, 80 (3): pp. 671–698
- Sandler, P. C. (2009) *A Clinical Application of Bion's Concepts: Dreaming, Transformation, Containment and Change* (London, UK: Karnac Books)

ambivalence

SEE ALSO **attachment; bad object; depression; developmental stages; object; working alliance/therapeutic alliance**

Ambivalence refers to the coexistence of two opposing feelings, drives, tendencies and impulses, towards the same person, goal or *object*. The term should not be confused with 'ambiguity' (i.e. opposed or unclear meanings). Nor should it be confused with mixed feelings (Rycroft, 1968). For Rycroft, mixed feelings may in fact refer to realistic assessments of the object, social situation or external reality. It may also refer to attitudes or ideas (e.g. positive and negative attitudes towards abortion, exercise, capital punishment). Research (not in psychoanalysis, dynamic psychiatry or *psychodynamic* psychology, where the emphasis is placed on unconscious dimensions of this emotional state) sometimes refers to ambivalence as 'mixed emotions' and shows that the ability to tolerate, use or become aware of these states correlates to resilience, creativity and physical well-being (see Rycroft's early criticism of the confusion between mixed feeling/emotion and ambivalence).

In psychoanalysis, ambivalence was first used by Bleuler (1911) to describe simultaneous contradictory impulses (e.g. love and hate), volitional action (i.e. to engage in action or avoid the same action) or intellect (i.e. holding two contradictory ideas at the same time). The common experience of ambivalence tends to involve the dominance of one or another repressed emotional states. We may commonly hold conscious, loving feelings for a person while at the same time harbouring unconscious and repressed hateful feelings, both expressed at the same time. Freud uses the concept in his paper 'Mourning and Melancholia' (1917), where the occurrence of *depression* following object loss is explained by ambivalence directed at the lost object then redirected at the self. Drug addicts, for example, often feel ambivalence about their drug of choice; they know that the drug has a destructive effect (socially, financially, medically), while simultaneously they seek and use it for the pleasure they derived.

Weisbrode (2012) writes of ambivalence: 'Ambivalence makes us think more of movement than of destination or direction. Whether we go up or down, forward or backward, may not matter as much as how fast or how slow we go, and what we see and do along the way. What we really want seems to be desire itself; or that our desire to want what we cannot have, or more than we can have, is interwoven with fate, much as truth, in Bierce's apropos words, is "an ingenious compound of desirability and appearance. Desire and desirability, once again, are the basis of ambivalence, just as the appearance and reality of desire, the object and the idea of the object"' (pp. 27–28).

For Melanie Klein, ambivalence was fundamental to her understanding of the *depressive position*. The depressive position is achieved and marked in part by the ability to balance love and hate; otherwise, these states alternate, dissociate, or split. The result is ambivalent instability: love and hate abruptly alternate. In the *paranoid–schizoid* position, the infant's world is experienced as either good or bad: it is felt as loving and good when wishes are gratified and good feeling prevails, and bad when left unmet and frustration results. Because early in life a child is unable to distinguish fantasy and reality, the experience of loving and hating is felt to have an actual *affect* on good and *bad objects* in the environment. As these mental states gradually integrate, the ability to tolerate ambivalence increases and with movement into the depressive position, the coexistence of love and hate towards the same object can be tolerated. Klein writes, for the developing child, 'unpleasant disagreeable experiences and a lack of enjoyable ones ... especially lack of happy and close contact with beloved people, increase ambivalence, diminish trust and hope and confirm anxieties about annihilations and external persecution; moreover, they slow down and perhaps predominately check the beneficial process, through which in the long run inner security is achieved' (Klein, 1940, p. 128).

For the sociologist, Zygmut Bauman, ambivalence is an inescapable condition of our modern era. He writes in his very important 1991 book, 'Modernity and Ambivalence', that: 'The ideal that the naming/classifying function strives to achieve is a sort of commodious filing cabinet that contains all the files that contain all the items that the world contains – but confines each file and each item with a separate place of its own (with remaining doubts solved by a cross reference index). It is the non-viability of such a filing cabinet that makes ambivalence unavoidable. And it is the perseverance with which construction of such a cabinet is pursued that brings forth ever new supplies of ambivalence' (p. 2).

points for reflection and practice
- The client may feel ambivalent about the process of therapy: on the one hand recognizing the need for help but also feeling resentful or ashamed that he or she cannot in his or her own ways understand and negotiate his or her emotional lives.
- The client may have ambivalent feeling towards the therapist, as a dynamic of the transference (the importance of which varies among psychotherapeutic models; see entry, *working alliance/ therapeutic alliance*).
- Engle and Arkowitz (2006) offer a very useful integration of psychodynamic, cognitive, and existential approaches to understanding ambivalence.

KEY TEXTS
- Bauman, Z. (1991) *Modernity and Ambivalence* (New York, NY: John Wiley & Sons)
- Benedek, T. (1977) 'Ambivalence, Passion, and Love', *Journal of the American Psychoanalytic Association*, 25 (1): pp. 53–79
- Bleuler, E. (1952) *Dementia praecox* (Joseph Zinkin, Trans.) (New York, NY: International Universities Press; Original work published 1911)
- Eissler, K. (1971) Death drive, ambivalence, and narcissism. *Psychoanalytic Study of the Child*, 26, 25–78
- Engle, D. and Arkowitz, H. (2006) *Ambivalence in Psychotherapy: Facilitating Readiness to Change* (New York, NY: Guilford Press)
- Segal, H. (1964) *Introduction to the Work of Melanie Klein* (London, UK: Heinemann)
- Weisbrode, K. (2012) *On Ambivalence: The Problems and Pleasures of Having It Both Ways* (Cambridge, MA: MIT Press)

anxiety

SEE ALSO **affect; depressive position; good enough mother (holding environment); jouissance; paranoid–schizoid**

Anxiety is foremost an unpleasurable affective state marked by physical sensations signifying the possibility of imminent threat; it is an unconscious, inner state to be avoided. And while this unpleasantness may be difficult to discern and describe, anxiety itself is always sensed. It is not to be confused with fear, which is a state that is accompanied by *real*, recognized external danger. Some make a distinction between 'free-floating' anxiety, where anxiety is generally experienced and more specific or acute anxiety (e.g. panic).

Anxiety is among the most important concepts in the psychoanalytic canon (see also *affect*). Early in his thinking, Freud saw anxiety mechanistically: as a kind of electrical force or transformation of undischarged libido or impedance of affect. And interference with discharge produced anxiety. By 1926 Freud was questioning this understanding and the claim that repression was its source. In one of his most important projects, 'Inhibitions, Symptoms and Anxiety', Freud introduced the notion of 'signal' anxiety and in this reformulation he described two types of anxiety: 'automatic' and 'neurotic'. 'Automatic' anxiety is an affective response to helplessness, overstimulation, overwhelming, annihilation or traumatic experience; here, events unfold too fast for the *ego* to integrate. The result is a feeling of danger, and birth trauma has been seen as its prototype. Laplanche and Pontalis (1988) describe automatic or primary anxiety as 'the subject's reaction each time he finds himself in a traumatic situation – that is each time he is confronted by an inflow of excitations, whether of external or internal origin, which he is unable to master' (p. 48). Neurotic anxiety, mediated by the ego, is defensive and aimed at 'signalling' potential danger rooted in developmental antecedents (i.e. loss of the *object*, of the object's love, annihilation) and the need to ward off the potential of traumatic anxieties. The discomfort found in signal anxiety is aimed at averting more significant danger and its consequences.

Melanie Klein offered another view of anxiety, also rooted in developmental sequelae, and wrote about the primacy of persecutory and depressive anxiety. In the earliest developmental position, *paranoid–schizoid*, the caregiving object is experienced and felt as a separate, part-object, idealized and loved, persecuting and hated. Here the main anxiety is with survival of the object. In the next and *depressive position*, if both love and hate towards the object can be managed, anxiety will shift towards concern for the other as a whole person; this shift in position is accompanied by *guilt* and sadness and a growing sense of love for the object. Emerging depressive anxiety and pain are countered by manic and obsessional defences, and by retreat to the *splitting* and paranoia of the paranoid–schizoid position.

Winnicott described anxieties in relationship to normal development. Thus, for him, there were three principal developmental dynamics, each related to anxieties: integration (and the associated anxiety, disintegration); personalization (and the associated anxiety, depersonalization) and realization (and the associated anxiety, derealization). With integration, the child develops an internal sense of the self as separate with a distinct psychological reality. For integration to occur there must be maternal preoccupation and a good enough mother, not as a container of the child's primitive feelings, but merged and identified with the child, feeling both physical and psychological needs. This has a corresponding anxiety: the loss of separateness or connection between mind and body, or disintegration. Personalization occurs with maternal handling and the facilitation of quiet times, during which the infant comes to feel and experience the indwelling of the psyche in the 'soma'. Realization is the gradual coming to know the temporal and spatial relations; and derealization occurs when one loses one's sense of experiencing and being located in time and space.

Many describe levels of anxiety: annihilation or loss of self or self-cohesion. This is sometimes referred to as psychotic anxiety. Marvin Hurvich (2000, 2003) describes this anxiety as an 'imminent fear of being overwhelmed, of falling apart, dissolving, suffocating, going crazy, losing total control' (p. 579). The second level refers to loss of the object (i.e. fear of losing the loved object or most important person). The third refers to the loss of the love of the object. And the fourth refers to body disintegration.

While the earlier understanding of signal anxiety is backed by recent research (Wong, 1999) some argue that signal anxiety is more accurately described as a subset of unconscious mental processes that function as a signal for danger and that unconscious anticipatory processes are general features of mental life. With traumatic anxiety (and related panic attacks), the ego is overwhelmed by threats from internal dangers. Signal anxiety is used as a kind of early warning system to prepare the ego for meaningful dangers.

Anxiety, for Lacan, is an affect and is to be differentiated from emotion. 'Whereas Freud distinguished between fear (which is focused on a specific object) and anxiety (which is not), Lacan argues that anxiety is not without an object *(n'est pas sans objet);* it simply involves a different kind of object, an object which cannot be symbolized in the same way as all other objects' (Evans, 1996, p. 12). He makes a distinction, moreover, between 'acting out' and the 'passage à l'act.' These affective states are potential transformations of anxiety. This is for Lacan not unlike Freud's early conceptualization of anxiety: an excess of libidinal tension. But for Lacan anxiety results from a surplus of phallic *jouissance*; and where acting out is the result, it is aimed at emptying out the bodies' excess of jouissance, which enables the emergence of desire (Harari, 2013). Lacan also discussed anxiety in relationship to lack: 'All desire arises from lack, and anxiety arises when this lack is itself lacking; anxiety is the lack of a lack. Anxiety is not the absence of the breast, but its enveloping presence; it is the possibility of its absence which is, in fact, that which saves us from anxiety. Acting out and passage to the act are last defences against anxiety' (Evans, 1996, p. 12).

points for reflection and practice
- Assessing the level at which a patient experiences anxiety is an important tool in the assessment of the readiness and ability to tolerate intensive dynamic therapy. Assessing the use and health of signal anxiety is important to diagnosis and treatment. The Hurvich Experience Inventory (HEI) is sometimes used to measure the level or experience of anxiety.
- Assessing the levels of anxiety: annihilation, loss of the object, loss of love of the object, is crucial to understanding readiness and ability to engage and tolerate treatment.
- There are many scales used to assess anxiety: HEI, the Hamilton Scale and many others can be usefully used for screening, especially in conducting group work.

KEY TEXTS
- Freud, S. (1926) *Inhibitions, Symptoms and Anxiety*. Standard Edition, 20
- Hurvich, M. (1989) 'Traumatic Moment, Basic Dangers, and Annihilation Anxiety', *Psychoanalytic Psychology*, 6 (3): pp. 309–323
- Hurvich, M. (2003) 'The Place of Annihilation Anxieties in Psychoanalytic Theory', *Journal of the American Psychoanalytic Association*, 51 (2): pp. 579–616

- Little, M. (1960) 'On Basic Unity', *International Journal of Psychoanalysis*, 41: pp. 377–384
- Roose, S. P. and Glick, R. A. (eds) (2013) *Anxiety as Symptom and Signal* (Hillsdale, NJ: Analytic Press)
- Strongman, K. T. (1995) 'Theories of Anxiety', *New Zealand Journal of Psychology*, 24 (2): pp. 4–10
- Winnicott, D. (1974) 'The Fear of Breakdown', *International Review of Psychoanalysis*, 1: pp. 103–107
- Wong, P. (1999) 'Anxiety, Signal Anxiety, and Unconscious Anticipation: Neuroscientific Evidence for an Unconscious Signal Function in Humans', *Journal of the American Psychoanalytic Association*, 47 (3): pp. 817–841

archetype

SEE ALSO **collective unconscious; conscious (unconscious, preconscious); dream**

For Carl Jung, it is through the integration of what he called the personal 'unconscious' with the *collective unconscious* that one achieves individuation or wholeness. For Jung there are two layers of the unconscious: a personal unconscious, just beneath the conscious mind, incorporating personal psychic content and a deeper level, the collective unconscious (i.e. the accumulated experience of humanity, repeated experience throughout human history). At this deepest level of the psyche are the archetypes (i.e. innate, universal and hereditary, and unlearned modes of thinking and acting in particular ways). These archaic patterns and images, rooted in the collective unconscious, are the psychic equivalents of instincts. The archetypes produce, maintain, and control behaviour and experience. They can also be described as image patterns with quantities of energy charge, innate neuropsychic centres, seeking expression and integration, which are revealed in dreams, myths, mystical practice and belief. And because they are universal, they produce similarity in thought, feeling, images, ideas, across all cultural settings, circumstance, and history. Archetypes function to regulate the human life cycle; over time, we progress through a natural sequence of steps, each driven by archetypes, producing personality and behavioural outcomes. For Jung, 'The archetypes are formal factors responsible for the organization of unconscious psychic processes: they are "patterns of behaviour." At the same time they have a "specific charge" and develop numinous effects which express themselves as affects' (2010, p. 29).

Unlike Freud, Jung argued that the dynamic unconscious was not reducible to an unconscious where sexual and aggressive instincts and repressed wishes were held and expressed. To establish this Jung drew from mythology and fairy tales, the fantasies of psychotic patients, and word association tests. These data were used to explore the images, patterns of behaviour and modes of perception that fill the unconscious mind, accessible to all of humanity (i.e. the archetypes) and has effects principally through the power to organize images and ideas.

The innateness (i.e. *archetype* as a priori structure) of the archetypes has been the subject of contentious and ongoing debate in Jungian psychology. Some argue that archetypes as pre-existing entities do not exist and there is a growing consensus within analytic psychology (i.e. the Jungian scholarly community) that the idea should be abandoned in favour of a developmental and emergentist theory (Goodwyn, 2010; Merchant, 2009). Roesler (2010) claims that Jung had numerous and not always consistent accounts of what he meant by archetype: (1) biological and inborn patterns of perception and behaviour; (2) empirical-statistical (i.e. using the word association test); (3) archetypes as transcendent (i.e. not identified with a time, person or place) and cannot be known (i.e. made conscious); (4) cultural-psychological differentiations between the archetype-as-such and its culturally determined, concrete manifestations (Sotirova-Kohli *et al.*, 2013).

The mother archetype, for the child, is the most important to actualize. Over time, as the *attachment* between mother and child deepens, archetypes are activated in the personal psyches of both mother and child: the mother complex in the child and the child archetype in the mother. It is in this dyadic relationship that the archetypes are mutually activated and sustained and for Jung, unlike many among his contemporaries, the child is not the passive recipient, a tabula rasa, of impressions from the social surround.

Jung, unlike Freud, attended less to the *dream* narrative and more to the *symbolic* content and the relations among symbols. While never fixed or static, Jung identified a fundamental set of archetypes: (1) 'persona' (Latin for 'mask') describes our many modes, masks, or means of self-presentation in different settings and situations. It also serves the purpose of protecting the *ego* from negative images; (2) 'anima' refers to the unconscious or true self, the feminine inner personality, as present in the unconscious of the male; and animus the masculine aspect in men; (3) 'shadow' refers to the sex and life instincts, unconscious repressed ideas, weaknesses, desires, instincts and shortcomings (i.e. some describe this as a darker, wild, or chaotic aspect of the mind). The shadow appears in dreams as snakes, monsters, demons, or other wild and exotic figures; and (4) 'self' (represented by the circle, square, or mandala) refers to integration of the personality, the striving towards wholeness and harmony and individuation, the unification of unconsciousness and consciousness.

Freud and Jung had quite different understandings of the unconscious. For Freud, the unconscious was composed of feelings, thoughts, ideas, images, and experiences which when repressed produce neurotic symptoms. For Jung, each person also possesses a collective unconscious, a group of shared images and common archetypes and these often enter the personal unconscious. Dreams, moreover, are better understood as symbolic reference points of universally shared symbols.

points for reflection and practice
- For Jung, because the unconscious seeks wholeness, the work of therapy is to identify ways of moving clients towards individuation and a sense of wholeness.
- The 'Word Association Experiment' consists of a list of 100 words, to which the client is expected to offer an immediate association. The interviewer measures, using a stop watch, delays in response. This is repeated a second time, noting differences in response. The client then explores words to which there were a longer-than-average response time, a mechanical response, or a different association in the second testing. The results are scored with 'complex indicators' and further explored. The result is a 'map' of the personal complexes, valuable both for self-understanding and in exploring disruptive factors in relationships.
- In therapy, archetypes can be used to evoke powerful images and meanings underlying suffering and healing.
- Unconscious archetypical complexes are in constant flux and are often the *object* of therapeutic work.

KEY TEXTS

- Goodwyn, E. (2010) 'Approaching Archetypes: Reconsidering Innateness', *Journal of Analytical Psychology*, 55 (4): pp. 502–521
- Hopper, E. and Weinberg, H. (eds) (2011) *The Social Unconscious in Persons, Groups and Societies: Mainly Theory* (Vol. 1) (London, UK: Karnac Books)
- Merchant, J. (2009) 'A Reappraisal of Classical Archetype Theory and Its Implications for Theory and Practice', *Journal of Analytical Psychology*, 54 (3): pp. 339–358
- Miller, G. and Baldwin, D. (1987) 'Implications of the Wounded-Healer Paradigm for the Use of the Self in Therapy', *Journal of Psychotherapy & the Family*, 3 (1): pp. 139–151
- Stevens, A. (2013) *Archetype: A Natural History of the Self* (London, UK: Routledge)

attachment

SEE ALSO **affect; affect regulation; alpha and beta elements (and functions); container/contained; developmental stages; mentalization**

Attachment has several referents. First, it may refer to a diverse body of theory, research, infant observation (Jurist *et al.*, 2008), and experiment (i.e. attachment theory). The theory, however, is an amalgam of ideas from ethology, psychoanalysis, neuroscience and cognitive psychology. Second, it is sometimes used to describe discrete behaviours (i.e. gesture and body movement, crying and tears, smiles) aimed at understanding how we form and maintain relationships through proximity. These are sometimes called 'attachment behaviours' or 'attachment-seeking behaviours'. Still others use the term to refer to 'systems of attachment', sometimes called 'working models' (Bretherton, 1999), which produce internalized feelings of security and efficacy. Finally, it may refer to disorders of attachment (i.e. reactive attachment). A sense of security is the aim of attachment and foremost a regulator of emotional experience (Sroufe, 1996).

It could be argued that there are several types of *psychodynamic* babies. There's the baby in Freud's theory: this baby seeks pleasure and is driven to satisfy its states. Freud's infant drives (i.e. libidinal and aggressive) towards the *object* in order to satisfy needs. Then there is the Kleinian, object-seeking baby. For both Klein and Winnicott, the baby is object-seeking and the *drive* is towards relationship with others as primary 'objects' of desire and attention. Finally, there is the attachment-seeking baby. This baby, best described in the works of John Bowlby (1907–1990) and Daniel Stern (1998) exists in the uncertain worlds of *real* relationships and external forces that moment-to-moment alter the course of development. For Bowlby, the Kleinian interest in the child's introjections of fantasies about its parents diverted researchers and clinicians from a more important look into the internalization of the parents' 'real and repeated modes' of relating and character. Attachment, for Bowlby and others, is based on 'actual interactive' experiences not on the fantasies they arouse.

For Bowlby mental health is produced by emotional attachments to familiar, responsive, and sensitive caregivers. While attachment was for Bowlby, and others, biological in origin it also served to maintain a kind of psychological balance whereby the child remains in meaningful relationship, emotionally and spatially, to significant figures. And empirical evidence for attachment is found in a child's behavioural preferences for particular familiar figures and in their seeking proximity, especially when in distress, and in their gradually increasing ability to use familiar caregivers as a secure base to investigate the social and physical environment. Over time, attachment develops into an 'internalized working model' (18–24 months): a world in which the self and others are represented and the future capacities for relating are more or less determined. For Mary Ainsworth, 'securely attached' infants: cry infrequently, find it easy to explore the world when the caregiver is present; in the absence of the caregiver they engage with strangers; they will be visibly upset when the mother departs, and happy upon return. The same child will not engage with strangers in the absence of the mother. 'Insecurely attached' infants engage in little exploratory behaviour and cry frequently, even when held by mothers. 'Not-yet attached' infants show no differential behaviour to the mother.

Researchers have described several 'insecure' styles, strategies, modes, or forms of attachment: (1) In the 'avoidant' mode, the child's strategy is to minimize the need for attachment in order to preempt rejection; 'defensive exclusion' is used to avoid awareness of real neediness and the pain of rejection; (2) In the 'ambivalent' mode, the child clings to the caregiver with excessive submissiveness and role reversal (i.e. child attends to the needs of the caregiver over its own) and as with the avoidant strategy, defensive exclusion is used to avoid anger at the caregiver; (3) In the 'disorganized' mode, often associated with more severe pathology, one often observes contradictory behaviour patterns (i.e. the child simultaneously approaches the caregiver with averted gaze or seeks reunion while exhibiting avoidant or resistant behaviours). Others have shown interest in what has been called the 'transgenerational' transmission of styles of attachment.

Recent attachment theorists (Schore and Schore, 2008) have focused more on *affect* and *affect regulation*. Bowlby's work, which originated during the heyday and ascendance of behaviourism and the strange situation and the description of secure base behaviours, was later superseded by a turn to cognition, attachment narratives, and reflective capacities. Schore and Schore (2008) have argued that there has been a fundamental shift in thinking and research on attachment in a move towards affective 'bodily-based processes, interactive regulation, early experience dependent brain maturation, stress, and nonconscious relational transactions' (p. 10). For them, 'emotion is initially regulated by others, but over the course of infancy it becomes increasingly self-regulated as a result of neurophysiological development. These adaptive capacities are central to self-regulation, i.e. the ability to flexibly regulate psychobiological states of emotions through interactions with other humans, interactive regulation in interconnected contexts, and without other humans, autoregulation in autonomous contexts. Attachment, the outcome of the child's genetically encoded biological (temperamental) predisposition and the particular caregiver environment, thus represents the regulation of biological *synchronicity* between and within organisms' (Schore and Schore, 2008, p. 10; emphasis added).

points for reflection and practice
- The Adult Attachment Interview (AAI) schedule, developed by Mary Main, has been widely used for diagnosis, treatment, and research.
- Recent research shows that the AAI is a useful tool for understanding outcome in psychotherapy for reactive attachment disorder, *depression, borderline* personality disorder and posttraumatic stress disorder (Goldwyn and Hugh-Jones, 2011; Steele *et al.*, 2009; Ravitz *et al.*, 2010).

- Our clinical practice with personality disorders should be informed by recent research on the relationships among personality disorders, attachment and affect regulation (see Sarkar and Adshead, 2006).

KEY TEXTS

- Ainsworth, M. S. and Bowlby, J. (1991) 'An Ethological Approach to Personality Development', *American Psychologist*, 46 (4): pp. 333–341
- Bowlby, J. (1982) 'Attachment and Loss: Retrospect and Prospect', *American Journal of Orthopsychiatry*, 52 (4): pp. 664–678
- Bretherton, I. (1999) 'Updating the "Internal Working Model" Construct: Some Reflections', *Attachment & Human Development*, 1 (3): pp. 343–357
- Jurist, E., Slade, A. and Bergner, S. (2008) *Mind to Mind: Infant Research, Neuroscience, and Psychoanalysis* (New York, NY: Other Press)
- Ravitz, P. *et al.* (2010) 'Adult Attachment Measures: A 25-Year Review', *Journal of Psychosomatic Research*, 69 (4): pp. 419–432
- Schore, J. R. and Schore, A. N. (2008) 'Modern Attachment Theory: The Central Role of Affect Regulation in Development and Treatment', *Clinical Social Work Journal*, 36 (1): pp. 9–20
- Stern, D. N. (1998) *The Interpersonal World of the Infant: A View from Psychoanalysis and Developmental Psychology* (London, UK: Karnac Books)

attacks on linking

SEE ALSO **alpha and beta elements (and functions); mentalization; projective identification**

In his work on *psychosis*, Bion described what he called 'attacks on linking' as the psychotic part of the mind directing destructive (i.e. *ego*-destructive superego) attacks on the links among objects (i.e. emotion, reason). It is when normal *projective identification* breaks down, due to ruptures in mother–infant communication (i.e. the mother/caregiver is unreceptive), that thought itself is compromised. It was in his work with people suffering with schizophrenia that Bion described the psychotic and nonpsychotic parts of the self, common to all people; when these parts are separated, one dominating the other, the gap becomes unbridgeable (Bion, 1967) and the psychotic part of the personality attacks everything enabling awareness of reality; destructive attacks by the psychotic part of the mind are directed at all links among objects. The result is a breakdown in the mental activity necessary for linking: the psychotic part of the self directs attacks against functions necessary for perceiving reality. Bion writes in 'Attacks on Linking' (1959), the 'patient's disposition to attack the link between two objects is simplified because the analyst has to establish a link with the patient ... therefore we should be able to see attacks being made upon it' (p. 308).

Bion also used the concept, 'attacks on linking', to understand *borderline* states. Here, not only is the mind incapable of making links, but mental states are endlessly chaotic. Moreover, because there is a lack of interest in how the mind functions, the therapy is often endlessly chaotic. Finally, attacks on verbal and nonverbal communication are also aimed at the links and mental activity of the therapist and the means by which the therapist establishes contact.

Clinically this reorients the therapist's attention to relations among objects. In practice 'attacks on linking' reorients interventions from the nature of the *object* to the nature of the relations among objects: from structures to functions. Attacks on linking is especially useful when trying to understand how and why a patient attacks the very links made in the work, the attempts to understand, to have knowledge, and to use that knowledge in the unfolding of treatment. With attacks on linking, the inner worlds of the therapist and patient, along with the various forms of communication necessary to their linking, verbal and nonverbal, are often compromised and sometimes destroyed (Lombardi, 2009).

Charles (2011) very nicely combines Bion and Lacan to examine attacks on linking and what Lacan calls 'empty speech' to describe traumatic experience. He uses Bion to think about how attacks on linking leads to difficulty in making meaning of the facts as perceived and experienced. In traumatic experience, we can only know what can be tolerated and over time it becomes increasingly difficult to integrate; therapy is often complicated by the patient sharing only 'bits and pieces of whatever it is that they are having trouble consciously recognizing' (p. 54).

KEY TEXTS
- Aguayo, J. (2009) 'On Understanding Projective Identification in the Treatment of Psychotic States of Mind: The Publishing Cohort of

H. Rosenfeld, H. Segal and W. Bion (1946–1957)', *International Journal of Psychoanalysis*, 90 (1): pp. 69–92

- Bion, W. (1959) 'Attacks on Linking', *International Journal of Psychoanalysis*, 40 (5–6): p. 308
- Charles, M. (2011) *Working with Trauma: Lessons from Bion and Lacan* (New York, NY: Jason Aronson)
- Lombardi, R. (2009) 'Symmetric Frenzy and Catastrophic Change: A Consideration of Primitive Mental States in the Wake of Bion and Matte Blanco', *International Journal of Psychoanalysis*, 90 (3): pp. 529–549
- Martindale, B. and Summers, A. (2013) 'The Psychodynamics of Psychosis', *Advances in Psychiatric Treatment*, 19 (2): pp. 124–131
- Shaw, J. (2014) 'Psychotic and Non-Psychotic Perceptions of Reality', *Journal of Child Psychotherapy*, 40 (1): pp. 73–89

b

bad object

SEE ALSO affect regulation; borderline; defence mechanisms; depressive position; object; splitting

The concept, bad *object*, derives mainly from Melanie Klein's ideas about early development and the experience of unpleasant body sensations (e.g. pain, discomfort, hunger) which are interpreted as coming from an external, hostile environment; persecutory anxieties, first registered in bodily states and from frustration of needs by those in the external world; together these may overwhelm and cause the infant to resort to what Klein and others call primitive defences (see entry, *defence mechanisms*): denial, *projection*, introjection, withdrawal and *splitting*. In an effort to understand and evaluate the psychological, social and physical surround, the child divides experience into categories of 'good' and 'bad'.

For Klein, the early and primitive *ego* is incapable of grasping or conceiving whole objects with their complex and many dimensions; instead the child lives in a unidimensional world of split objects, with either good or bad intentions (Klein, 1932). Projection and introjection, however, are also among the first attempts to differentiate self from other, inside from outside. For Klein, oral incorporation (taking in) and projecting (spitting out) characterize the initial, nurturing and frustrating early object: the mother's breast. Unlike mature whole objects in *Oedipal* development, these early objects are primitive 'part' objects whose existence is determined mostly by their function in the infant's world. Over time and with normal 'development' these splits between 'all-good' or 'all-bad' persons, objects or actions develop into more complex experience, integrations and representations. Thus, the early introjections of good object/breast produce a benign internal world and stimulate healthy ego and personality development. On the other hand, bad objects, when internalized and unassimilated, may become permanent internal threats.

Steven Mitchell (1981), in a brilliant synthesis and integration of thinking on the bad object, argues that Klein fails to show the provenance of the external and internal images, perceptions and phantasies of objects. For Mitchell, Melanie Klein has two quite different moments in the development of her thinking on the 'bad object': before 1934, when theorizing aggression was at the heart of her thinking, and much later when she was thinking about depressive *anxiety* and reparation. When she attended to aggression, she was mostly interested in bad or hateful objects. For Klein, as the infant grows in awareness of their destructive impulses, they may fear they have destroyed the object (i.e. in unconscious phantasy). They may then attempt to inhibit the impulse in order to protect or repair the damage. With *guilt* (i.e. growing awareness of the aggression directed at the object), the infant limits (i.e. reparation) the destructive impulse. There are several important outcomes of this developmental process: growing capacity for toleration of *ambivalence*; increasing capacity for feeling the state between the dominance of the destructive impulse and need to protect the loved object. When the latter is accomplished, the child begins to experience stable object relationships not only with the mother but the others in the social surround. Bad objects, for Klein, emerge from internal states and drives (i.e. projectively) and good objects from the external world (i.e. introjectively). This understanding of the object is closely allied with classical *drive*/instinct theory.

In his conceptualization of the bad object, Fairbairn (1954) shifted the focus from orality and incorporation to motivations driven by defences and actual relating and object relations. He describes an emotionally unpredictable and agonizing world where a child must live with unavailable, unpredictable or chaotic parents. Here, where the child must internalize repress, and split, in order to preserve an *illusion* of the real parents as good, available and predictable, the badness of the parents is internalized. It is now inside the child. The parents are not bad, the child is bad, and the child now feels the burden and necessity of changing in order to elicit love from the parents. With the badness now located inside, where the child feels omnipotent control, it need not face the loss of control that would inevitably follow from the burden of seeing the actual parent as bad.

After the bad aspects of the parent have been internalized, Fairbairn identifies a second process of internalization, which he calls the 'moral defense'. A child, he argues, cannot for long tolerate its unconditional badness, its unlovability. The moral defence enables the child to internalize the good qualities of the parent and, with this defence, the initial *identification* with the bad qualities gives way to a growing sense that its own goodness is available through internalization of the good qualities of the parent (Mitchell, 1981).

In sum, for Klein, the internal object world (and the fantasized relations among internal objects) is an inevitable and essential foundation for human development, for relating and pathology. For Fairbairn, the object world is contingent, not inevitable. Most important, object relations are rooted in real relations, with real parents, along with their inevitable disappointments and unsatisfactory relating. Fairbairn, then, sees object relating as compensatory; he does not identity how relating to good objects offers healthy, ongoing, possibilities for identification and development.

In *borderline* personality organization, there is a tendency for patients to see themselves and others as either 'all-good' or 'all-bad'. These patients also experience identity disturbance, impulsivity, transient impairment in reality testing, poor capacity for mentalization, and tend to use immature defences: splitting and *projective identification* (Gabbard, 1993, pp. 7–18).

points for reflection and practice
- In assessment and treatment, it is important to pay close attention to the capacity to see others more realistically (i.e. possessing good and bad qualities) rather than as fluctuating between all-good and all-bad.
- Some patients remain vigilantly alert, fearful that their objects may betray, reject or damage them.
- It is particularly important to enquire about the history of relationships. These questions can help understand self and object representations and the experience of the object world as predominantly partial or whole. Here are some questions to consider: Are there patterns in the ways relationships begin or end? Do relationships tend to reproduce qualities of relating with early caregivers? Is there a tendency to form relationships radically different or opposed to those in early experience?

- In addition, it is useful to enquire about how patients view the self, how they see others and how they believe others view them.

KEY TEXTS

- Davies, J. M. (2004) 'Whose Bad Objects Are We Anyway? Repetition and Our Elusive Love Affair with Evil', *Psychoanalytic Dialogues*, 14 (6): pp. 711–732
- Frankland, A. (2010). *The Little Psychotherapy Book: Object Relations in Practice* (Oxford, UK: Oxford University Press)
- Kernberg, O. (1995) *Object Relations Theory and Clinical Psychoanalysis* (New York, NY: Jason Aronson)
- Klein, M. (1932) *The Psychoanalysis of Children* (London, UK: Hogarth Press)
- Mitchell, S. (1981) 'The Origin and Nature of the "Object" in the Theories of Klein and Fairbairn', *Contemporary Psychoanalysis*, 17 (3): pp. 374–398
- Mitchell, S. (1984) 'Object Relations Theories and the Developmental Tilt', *Contemporary Psychoanalysis*, 20 (4): pp. 473–499
- Waska, R. (2002) *Primitive Experiences of Loss: Working with the Paranoid-Schizoid Patient* (London, UK: Karnac Books)

body ego

SEE ALSO **container/contained; developmental stages; ego**

Sigmund Freud wrote in the 'Ego and the Id' that, 'The *ego* is first and foremost a bodily ego; it is not merely a surface entity, but is itself the *projection* of a surface' (1923, p. 16; emphases added). For Freud the skin can be both the source and aim of the *drive*. Much has been written about this provocative understanding of mental life. Some have used this idea to suggest that the infant's early experience of the body surface (i.e. sensory-affective stimulation) with the maternal figure sets into motion a major shift in psychic life: from the sensory to the mental. For Esther Bick, a positive experience with skin feeling produces a confident sense of a 'containing *object*' which in turn leads to differentiation of inner and outer: what is inside, what is outside, what is not me.

The skin, the largest human organ, and the cortex are integrally linked in their unique capacities to manage complex stimuli, and it is through ongoing tactile engagements with caregivers that a sense of boundaries is established and maintained. The skin is a physical barrier (i.e. regulating body temperature and the intrusion of potentially dangerous toxins) and a more permeable psychological barrier, both continuously and dynamically engaged with the internal and external worlds, potentially exposed, excited, pleasured, touched and vulnerable (Damasio, 1999). The skin, however, operates involuntarily, through the autonomic nervous system; it is not a source of agency or will except in so far as it can become a means of communication (i.e. blushing, hives). In what Lacan called the lure of spatial *identification*, the skin conveys a sense of visual completeness or seamlessness, perfection and intactness in a world otherwise felt and experienced as complex and chaotic. Isakower's and Lewin's early work looks into how body surface experience (i.e. nursing) enables sensory-affective stimulation and a steady movement of sensory process towards the psyche.

For Didier Anzieu and Turner (1989) the skin ego, also called a psychic envelope, becomes the principal means of communication between mother and infant. Just as the skin as a material organ functions to enclose the soma, the skin ego encloses the psyche; functions of the skin are transferred onto the skin ego and then onto the thinking ego. The skin ego acts to maintain thought. It is a container for ideas and affects. It provides a protective screen and is a register for primary communication with the external environment. It also mediates intersensorial correspondences that support sexual excitation. For Anzieu the concept of skin ego allows for the analysis of fantasies of the container and contained, for more careful consideration of the role of touch between mothers and babies, and *Oedipal* dynamics and prohibitions around touching, and representations of the body in the therapy setting. Skin and touching, moreover, are sources of our first narcissistic feelings of well-being. Finally, Anzieu argued that there is 'no group without a common skin, a containing envelope, which makes it possible for its members to experience the existence of a group self'. Finally, for Anzieu, when the skin ego provides its protective function, it supports a narcissistic envelope and offers the infant a sense of security. When the function is compromised, however, it results in what Anzieu calls the 'envelope of suffering' (e.g. *shame*).

The anthropologist Terence Turner, in his widely known and often-cited 1980 essay, 'The Social Skin', describes how 'at one level, the "social skin" models the social boundary between the individual actor and other actors; but at a deeper level it models the internal, psychic diaphragm between the pre-social, libidinous energies of the individual and "internalized others", or social meanings and values that make up what Freud called the "ego" and "super-ego"' (p. 140). For Turner, skin also functions at the macrosocial level where it along with hair are modified in the interest of various social categories (age groups, adolescents, males, etc.). This he calls the social skin and its various alterations and adornments refer not to individuals but to larger social aggregates and relations and boundaries among them.

In a more recent work on psychoanalysis and the skin, Nicola Diamond (2013) pursues a line of argument not unlike Terence Turner. She argues that the 'skin as a surface always relates to other surfaces from sensory-mirroring surfaces derived from others, to social surfaces such as media surface projections, billboard advertising surfaces; from glossy magazine surfaces to screen surfaces, the skin surface is never fully owned'. She continues, 'this is one way of understanding and developing Freud's reference to the skin ego as not only based in being a surface entity but in fact existing as a surface projection' (pp. 124–125).

points for reflection and practice
- Some argue that many with *borderline* organization benefit from reconstruction of the earliest phases of the skin ego.
- For Anzieu, narcissistic personalities can be seen as having an exceptionally thick skin ego, whereas masochistic and borderline personalities remarkably thin skin ego.
- The functions of the skin offer a rich source of information in diagnosis and treatment.

KEY TEXTS
- Anzieu, D. and Turner, C. (1989) *The Skin Ego* (New Haven: Yale University Press)
- Bick, E. (1986) 'Further Considerations on the Function of the Skin in Early Object Relations', *British Journal of Psychotherapy*, 2 (4): pp. 292–299

- Damasio, A. (1999) *The Feeling of What Happens: Body, Emotion and the Making of Consciousness* (London, UK: Heinemann)
- Freud, S. (1923) 'The Ego and the Id', *Standard Edition*, 19
- Pile, S. (2009) 'Topographies of the Body-and-Mind: Skin Ego, Body Ego, and the Film "Memento"', *Subjectivity*, 27 (1): pp. 134–154
- Pollak, T. (2009) 'The "Body–Container": A New Perspective on the "Body–Ego"', *International Journal of Psychoanalysis*, 90 (3): pp. 487–506
- Turner, T. (1980) 'The Social Skin' in J. Cherfas and R. Levin (eds), *Not Work Alone: A Cross-Cultural View of Activities Superfluous to Survival* (Thousand Oaks, CA: Sage Publications), pp. 112–140

borderline

SEE ALSO **attachment; bad object; defence mechanisms; mentalization; projective identification; splitting**

The term 'borderline' has been used to describe mental states on the border between *neurosis* and *psychosis*: an individual with 'psychotic' symptoms but not psychotic nor becoming psychotic. While the term first appeared in the psychoanalytic literature in the 1930s (Stern, 1938), beginning with Knight (1953), it was more widely used. It most often refers to rapid changes in self-image, lability of mood and behaviour and a life dominated by intense and manipulative relationships. The common defences include *splitting*, primitive dissociation, *projective identification*, omnipotence, denial, disruptive acting out, destructive idealization, devaluation and dramatic and sudden shifts in *affect*.

The concept for much of its history was used exclusively by psychoanalysts, but is now widely used in academic psychology and psychiatry. There is a general consensus in the *psychodynamic* literature and beyond that borderline states must be understood from a developmental perspective and that suffering is rooted in representations of the self and others, in relating and emotional regulation, all of which emerge in healthy and early *attachment* relationships and stable families.

Bateman and Fonagy (2006) argue that borderline personality disorder (BDP) is rooted in disorganized attachment and the failure to develop robust mentalizing (see entry, *mentalization*) capacities. Persons with borderline personality disorder, they argue, have impoverished models of their own and others' mental functions (Bateman and Fonagy, 2004). Fonagy writes,

> their schematic, rigid, sometimes extreme ideas about their own and others' states of mind make them vulnerable to powerful emotional storms and apparently impulsive actions, and create profound problems of behavioral and *affect regulation*. The weaker an individual's sense of their own subjectivity, the harder it is for them to compare the validity of their own perceptions of the way their mind works with that which a 'mind expert' presents. When presented with a coherent view of mental function in the context of psychotherapy, they are not able to compare the picture offered to them with a self-generated model and may all too often accept alternative perspectives uncritically or reject them wholesale. (Fonagy and Bateman, 2006, p. 2; emphasis added)

Histories of borderline patients show hyperactive attachment systems resulting from either personal history or biological disposition, or both. Fonagy and his colleagues argue that this may account for their compromised capacities for mentalization and that 'recovery of the capacity for mentalization in the context of attachment relationships has to be a primary objective', in the treatment of all BPD (Fonagy and Bateman, 2006). Otto Kernberg (1975) describes borderline as a type of 'organization', not as a category of personality or disorder, but as levels of organization or dysfunction rooted in disturbances in perceptions of reality, immature and maladaptive defences, and ways of regulating emotion. For Kernberg, these combine to cause an inability to form complex, integrated representations of others and contributes to interpersonal instability.

Recent research on borderline illness has shown that the marginalization of borderline patients has resulted from a lack of understanding (Fonagy and Bateman, 2006; Shea *et al.*, 2004; Zanarini *et al.*, 2003) and that most with this diagnosis, contrary to common belief, experience substantial 'symptom' reduction. Those with severe symptoms (75%), also requiring hospitalization, achieve significant reduction in symptoms; 50% remission rate after four years. Recurrences are rare, perhaps no more than 10% over six years. These data contrast sharply with outcomes for many Axis I disorders (e.g. affective disorder) where treatment gains are often more rapid but less sustainable.

Fonagy and his colleagues have defined a promising area of treatment called *mentalization*-based treatment. Kernberg's Transference-Focused Psychotherapy (TFP) for borderline organization is aimed at repairing, through transference, 'splits' in affect and thinking along with the integration of split off parts of self and *object* representations. In a recent study, The Cornell Medical College Group compared psychodynamic and dialectical-behavioural therapy (Clarkin *et al.*, 2004): findings show improvement in impulse control, mood fluctuation and quality of relationships; drop-out rates were higher for dialectical behaviour therapy than for other approaches (Fonagy and Bateman, 2006).

Thomas Fuchs (2007), a phenomenological psychiatrist, describes the borderline state as a narrative identity with a continuity of the personal past, present and future. This requires a capacity for integration of contradictory aspects and tendencies into a coherent, overarching sense of self. For Fuchs,

> In 'mature' neurotic disorders, this is only possible at the price of repression of important wishes and possibilities for personal development. Patients with borderline personality disorder lack the capacity to establish a coherent self-concept. Instead, they adopt what could be called a 'post-modernist' stance towards their life, switching from one present to the next and being totally identified with their present state of affect. Instead of repression, their means of defence consists in a temporal splitting of the self that excludes past and future as dimensions of object constancy, bonding, commitment, responsibility and *guilt*. The temporal fragmentation of the self avoids the necessity of tolerating the threatening ambiguity and uncertainty of interpersonal relationships. The price, however, consists in a chronic feeling of inner emptiness caused by the inability to integrate past and future into the present and thus to establish a coherent sense of identity. (p. 397; emphasis added)

points for reflection and practice
- In working with borderline clients, it is important to know how projective identification and splitting are used and how the therapist manages these troubling mental states.
- While the treatment of borderline states often requires confrontation, it is important to be sensitive to the patient's vulnerability: remember that many cannot escape the

feeling that they will yet again be abandoned, this time by their therapist. This includes a fear of utter aloneness and annihilation *anxiety*.

- It is important to be consistent and vigilant about the management of distance and closeness so the patient feels a safe distance, not in any danger of being 'engulfed', yet close enough to form and maintain a 'working alliance'.

KEY TEXTS

- Bateman, A. and Fonagy, P. (2006) *Mentalization-Based Treatment: A Practical Guide* (Oxford, UK: Oxford University Press)
- Bradley, R. and Westen, D. (2005) 'The Psychodynamics of Borderline Personality Disorder: A View from Developmental Psychopathology', *Development and Psychopathology*, 17 (4): pp. 927–957
- Fonagy, P. and Bateman, A. (2006) 'Progress in the Treatment of Borderline Personality Disorder', *The British Journal of Psychiatry*, 188 (1): pp. 1–3
- Fonagy, P., Target, M. and Gergely, G. (2000) 'Attachment and Borderline Personality Disorder', *Psychiatric Clinics of North America*, 23: pp. 103–122
- Fuchs, T. (2007) 'Fragmented Selves: Temporality and Identity in Borderline Personality Disorder', *Psychopathology*, 40 (6): pp. 379–387
- Kernberg, O. (1975) *Borderline Conditions and Pathological Narcissism* (New York, NY: Jason Aronson)

c

collective unconscious

SEE ALSO archetype; synchronicity; wounded healer

Freud and Jung had very different views on the nature and function of the unconscious mind. For Jung, there was both a 'personal' and a 'collective' unconscious. Jung's personal unconscious, like Freud's unconscious, is the site of repressed material, often infantile, and contains traces of a person's past. For Jung, unlike Freud, symptoms are teleological; that is, they serve a purpose, with an unfolding aim: early life experiences create templates for the ways patients solve crises later in life. For Jung, the unconscious is significant not due to individual biography and personal experience, but because we all share a collective history and common experience.

For Jung, reminiscences from early life offer the patient a way of managing symptoms in later life. This is fundamentally different from Freud's view: for Freud, childhood experience is the cause of symptoms. The collective unconscious is the repository of psychic history and future possibility. And because the collective unconscious is universal, and innate, it is inevitable that individuals will share with all others belonging to the same culture and historical moment the archetypes which constitute the central elements of the collective unconscious. The principal aim of Jungian analysis is to promote 'individuation', the means by which the individual achieves differentiation from the collective unconscious.

point for reflection and practice
- In practice, as the content of the personal unconscious is known, the images and motifs of the collective unconscious are also known, which leads to enlarging the personality.

KEY TEXTS

- Hunt, H. (2012) 'A Collective Unconscious Reconsidered: Jung's Archetypal Imagination in the Light of Contemporary Psychology and Social Science', *Journal of Analytical Psychology*, 57 (1): pp. 76–98
- Jacoby, M. (2013) *Individuation and Narcissism: The Psychology of Self in Jung and Kohut* (London, UK: Routledge)
- Jones, R. *et al.* (eds) (2008) *Education and Imagination: Post-Jungian Perspectives* (London, UK: Routledge)
- Stevens, A. (2006) *The Archetypes* (London, UK: Psychology Press)

conflict and compromise formation

SEE ALSO **defence mechanisms**

One way of viewing conflict is to imagine potential struggles among and between agencies (i.e. id, *ego*, and superego) of the human mind, a mind that is in constant conflict with itself. Psychoanalytic theory holds that conflict is the primary cause of *anxiety* and unhappiness. For example, 'the id may be in conflict with the *ego*': one may have to make a choice between an immediate and gratifying *object*/reward or defer and wait for more appropriate or significant ones. The 'id may also be in conflict with the superego'; for example, while hunger and sexual impulses seek gratification (i.e. the id seeks expression, regardless of circumstance), the superego may push back by imposing limits and consequences. Here we are propelled by the force of desire and pulled by the force of conscience. Or there may be 'conflict between the ego and the superego'. Here, everyday, we make choices between acting in realistic ways or by complying with rigidly imposed and unrealistic standards (e.g. always telling the truth). Or the 'id and ego may be in conflict with the superego'. The demands of the id and the demands of the superego often conflict because the ego does its work through unconscious *defence mechanisms*. Here, for example, we may choose to altogether avoid conflict rather than retaliate against a more vulnerable person. Also, the 'id and the superego may be in conflict with the ego': the decision to act realistically but in conflict with both desire and moral conviction (e.g. a Roman Catholic faced with a choice about the use of contraceptives). Finally, the ego may find itself in conflict with the id: for example, perhaps I find myself wanting to hurt or hit someone I intensely dislike but my ego intervenes, increasingly, as I am forced to consider the consequences and penalties.

For most of the history of psychoanalytic thinking, conflict was the 'sine qua non' of theory and practice (Smith, 2005). In 1947, Kris captured the essence of the psychoanalytic project in the phrase: 'human behavior viewed as conflict' (p. 6). While today this broad sweeping claim would not be embraced by most, still most schools will use the term and in very diverse ways. Some are committed to a topographic view of conflict (i.e. the repressing force against expressing agencies). And relational schools focus on conflicting self-organization. The Kleinians focus on conflicts between and among internal objects.

Some describe three kinds of conflicts, all intrinsic to the human condition: internal, internalized and external conflicts. We come to life with internal conflicts, that is, between masculine and feminine, active and passive, and homosexual and heterosexual and most of life is a recursive and continual negotiation among and between them. Internalized conflicts are not there from birth. They come from the social surround in the form of prohibitions (i.e. superego, conscience). The external conflicts refer to the many sources of everyday life and struggle that complicate living and flourishing: racial/ethnic, cultural, family, national, class, neighbourhood. Moreover, it may also refer to 'conscious' and unconscious conflicts, or to conflict as expressed and experienced by the patient. As well, understanding intrapsychic conflict (i.e. unconscious conflict between wishes, defences) requires different methods of understanding from those where it is assumed that it is a mostly subjective state (Stolorow, Brandchaft and Atwood 1987, p. 88).

Brenner (2002) rejected Freud's tripartite division of mind (i.e. id, ego, superego) in favour of compromise formations. For him the superego is both a 'consequence of psychic conflict and a component of it' (p. 120) and there is no structure of mind (i.e. the ego) objectively weighing external reality against the opposing force of other psychic agencies. Here, the 'symptom' can be simultaneously a compromise between a conflicted wish and a defence against it. Panic symptoms, for example, may have several referents: (1) a wish to be taken care of; (2) the denial of anger through the expression of anxiety or body symptoms; or (3) the unconscious expression of anger through coercive help-seeking behaviour. For Brenner, the ego refers to person, the *drive* refers to wish and the superego is a compromise formation.

points for reflection and practice
- For Brenner, in thinking clinically about compromise formations, it is important to consider the role of the symptom in the compromise: between a conflicted wish and a defence against the same wish.
- In conducting evaluations and making judgements about suitability for treatment, it is absolutely essential to consider the nature, intensity and extensive dimensions of conflicts: internal, internalized and external. 'Intensity' refers to the degree of conflict within a given domain (e.g. superego conflicts are mostly external conflicts with a single person or partner but not involving all relationships). 'Extensive conflicts' refer to all relationships, external and internal. If, for example, external conflicts (e.g. family, work, relational, etc.) are significant and sometimes overwhelming, it is important to consider the degree to which the patient can manage the anxiety produced in treatment.

KEY TEXTS

- Brenner, C. (2002) 'Conflict, Compromise Formation, and Structural Theory', *The Psychoanalytic Quarterly*, 71 (3): pp. 397–417
- Dorpat, T. (1976) 'Structural Conflict and Object Relations Conflict', *Journal of the American Psychoanalytic Association*, 24 (4): pp. 855–874
- Kohut, H. (1971) *The Analysis of the Self: A Systematic Approach to the Psychoanalytic Treatment of Narcissistic Personality Disorders* (Chicago, IL: University of Chicago Press)
- Kris, E. (1975) 'The Nature of Psychoanalytic Propositions and Their Validation' in L. M. Newman (ed.), *The Selected Papers of Ernst Kris* (New Haven, CT: Yale University Press), pp. 3–23
- Richards, A. and Willick, M. (eds) (2013) *Psychoanalysis: The Science of Mental Conflict* (New York, NY: Routledge)
- Smith, H. (2005) 'Dialogues on Conflict: Toward an Integration of Methods', *The Psychoanalytic Quarterly*, 74 (1): pp. 327–363
- Stolorow, R., Brandchaft, B. and Atwood, G. (1987) *Psychoanalytic Treatment: An Intersubjective Approach* (Hillsdale, NJ: The Analytic Press)

conscious (unconscious, preconscious)

SEE ALSO collective unconscious; defence mechanisms; ego; primary process and secondary process

Freud described the difference between the conscious and the unconscious in his 1915 metapsychological essay, 'The Unconscious':

> It strikes us all at once that now we know what is the difference between a conscious and an unconscious idea. The conscious idea comprises the concrete idea plus the verbal idea corresponding to it, whilst the unconscious idea is that of the thing alone. ... The idea which is not put into words or the mental act which has not received hyper-cathexis then remains in the unconscious in a state of repression. (pp. 201–202)

The term 'conscious' has many referents: awareness, phenomenal awareness, reflective awareness and phenomenal representation. Awareness can refer to a conscious awareness and a latent awareness. It can also refer to what is immediately given in experience (subjectively).

In psychoanalytic theory the conscious, the preconscious and the unconscious form a dynamic system of mental mechanisms and events. These terms for Freud, however, were not meant to be mere descriptions of events or states of being: each of them operates as mechanisms in the human mind, is potentially causal and through its complex interactions establishes the conditions for human motivation. Freud argued forcefully against conflating or reducing the mental to what is conscious or what is visible in human action (e.g. behaviourism). Within the system Cs, the conscious mind, are perceptions, thoughts, feelings and actions. Moreover, for Freud, consciousness resembles a sensory organ capable of perceiving other mental contents. With a spatial analogy, Freud argued that the preconscious is an especially important site of mediation: it is at this site where impulses are censored or returned to the unconscious (i.e. repressed) or allowed into consciousness. The conscious, moreover, receives information from both the external and internal (i.e. thoughts, feelings, emotions, impulses, bodily sensations) environments. As Freud revised his thinking, this tripartite division of mental functioning gave way to another: the id, the *ego*, and the superego. In this conceptual shift, consciousness became a necessary dimension of the ego: it functioned as a mechanism allowing for awareness of external reality.

Bargh and Morsella (2008), among the most significant academic psychologists (not psychoanalytic) studying the unconscious mind, write that, 'Over the years, empirical tests have not been kind to the specifics of the Freudian model, though in broad-brush terms the cognitive and social psychological evidence does support Freud as to the existence of unconscious mentation and its potential to impact judgments and behavior (see Westen, 1999). Regardless of the fate of his specific model, Freud's historic importance in championing the powers of the unconscious mind is beyond any doubt' (Bargh and Morsella, 2008, p. 1). Indeed, Bargh and his colleagues (1999) argue that quite sophisticated mental processes, perhaps 95%, occur outside of awareness and that our abilities to exercise conscious, intentional control is limited, so 'that most of moment-to-moment psychological life must occur through nonconscious means if it is to occur at all' (p. 462). They have described three forms of automatic self-regulation: automatic effect of perception on action, automatic goal pursuit, and a continual automatic evaluation of experience. It is now common in academic psychology to refer to the unconscious as automatic or as automaticity (Moors and De Houwer, 2006), and many in cognitive science prefer the concept, nonconscious over unconscious, so as to distance the theoretical project from Freud's dynamic unconscious (i.e. his system, ucs, where repression is at work among the three systems, conscious and preconscious). In more recent research on memory, especially on the dynamic relationship between what is called 'explicit' (i.e. conscious) and 'implicit' (i.e. unconscious) memory systems, we've learned much about how memory is stored and accessed. There are two types of explicit memory, generic (e.g. memory related to ideas and facts) and episodic (e.g. memory related to specific autobiographic events or episodes). Implicit memory refers to observable behaviour that lies outside awareness. Procedural memory, a type of implicit memory, includes memory important for skills (e.g. riding a bicycle, swinging a baseball bat, playing the piano).

Turnbull and Solms (2007) argue that research on confabulation, anosognosia, psychiatric disorders and dreams offer compelling evidence for Freud's understanding of the unconscious mind: that 'emotions' and the underlying 'drives' distort our thinking (i.e. executive functions and associated defences) and support irrational and false beliefs (p. 1085).

In group analysis it is common to find the concept, social unconscious (not in the sense used by Jung to refer to *collective unconscious*) when referring to the ways members of society share and transmit certain meanings, especially traumatic ones (Hopper, 2002; Wienberg, 2007, p. 315). For Hopper, one of the key thinkers on the social unconscious, it is best understood as

> the existence and constraints of social, cultural and communicational arrangements of which people are unaware; unaware, in so far as these arrangements are not perceived (not known), and if perceived not acknowledged (denied), and if acknowledged, not taken as problematic ('given'), and if taken as problematic, not considered with an optimal degree of detachment and objectivity. Although social constraints are sometimes understood in terms of myth, ritual and custom, such constraints are in the realm of the 'unknown' to the same extent as the constraints of instincts and fantasies, especially in societies with high status rigidity. However, constraint is not meant to imply only restraining, inhibition, or limitation, but also facilitation, development and even the transformation of sensations into feelings. (p. 126)

Finally, there is a very important literature on what some have called the 'discursive unconscious' (Jones, 2002; Billig, 1997, 1999). In his book, 'Freudian Repression: Conversation Creating the Unconscious', Billig writes that 'the business of everyday conversation provides the skills for repressing, while, at the same time, it demands that we practice those skills. In this respect, language is inherently expressive and repressive' (1999, p. 1).

KEY TEXTS

- Bargh, J. A. and Morsella, E. (2008) 'The Unconscious Mind', *Perspectives on Psychological Science*, 3 (1): pp. 73–79
- Billig, M. (1997) 'The Dialogic Unconscious: Psychoanalysis, Discursive Psychology and the Nature of Repression', *British Journal of Social Psychology*, 36 (2): pp. 139–159
- Billig, M. (1999) *Freudian Repression: Conversation Creating the Unconscious* (Cambridge, UK: Cambridge University Press)

- Busch, F. and Joseph, B. (2004) 'A Missing Link in Psychoanalytic Technique: Psychoanalytic Consciousness', *International Journal of Psychoanalysis*, 85 (3): pp. 567–577
- Colby, K. and Stoller, R. (2013) *Cognitive Science and Psychoanalysis* (London, UK: Routledge)
- Epstein, S. (1994) 'Integration of the Cognitive and the Psychodynamic Unconscious', *American Psychologist*, 49 (8): p. 709
- Hassin, R., Uleman, J. and Bargh, J. (eds) (2005) *The New Unconscious* (New York, NY: Oxford University Press)
- Hopper, E. (2003) *The Social Unconscious: Selected Papers* (London, UK: Jessica Kingsley Publishers)
- Kihlstrom, J. (2013) 'Unconscious Processes', in D. Reisberg (ed.), *Oxford Handbook of Cognitive Psychology* (Oxford, UK: Oxford University Press), pp. 176–186
- Modell, A. (2003) *Imagination and the Meaningful Brain* (Boston, MA: MIT Press)
- Rosenbaum, B. (2003) 'The Unconscious: How Does It Speak to Us Today?', *The Scandinavian Psychoanalytic Review*, 26 (1): pp. 31–40
- Semi, A. (2007) *The Conscious in Psychoanalysis* (London, UK: Karnac Books)
- Turnbull, O. and Solms, M. (2007) 'Awareness, Desire, and False Beliefs: Freud in the Light of Modern Neuropsychology', *Cortex*, 43 (8): pp. 1083–1090
- Weinberg, H. (2007) 'So What Is This Social Unconscious Anyway?', *Group Analysis*, 40 (3): pp. 307–322
- Zepf, S. (2011) 'The Relations between Language, Consciousness, the Preconscious, and the Unconscious', *The Scandinavian Psychoanalytic Review*, 34 (1): pp. 50–61

container/contained

SEE ALSO **affect regulation; alpha and beta elements (and functions); good enough mother (holding environment); projective identification; reverie**

Bion developed the concept 'containing' to describe how through *projective identification* (see entry, *projective identification*) one person contains psychic bits of another (Cartwright, 2013, 2014). Often the concept is used incorrectly to refer to the 'holding environment' (see entry, *good enough mother (holding environment)*). And it is through the dynamic interplay between the container (i.e. parent, caregiver) that the infant's *ego* is built up and in therapy a patient projects unwanted, *anxiety*-ridden, and split off bits of self (i.e. the intolerable parts of affects, self, sensory experience, memory and objects) into the mother/analyst/container to be digested and metabolized. It is then available in a new form before it can be reintrojected (Brown, 2013). Bion (1970) offered three categories of the container–contained relationship: (1) commensal (where two objects share a third to the mutual benefit of all three and where the relationship is inoffensive and promotes coexistence); (2) symbiotic (where one depends on another to mutual benefit and where there is confrontation and growth); (3) parasitic (where one depends on another to produce a third, which is destructive to all three and where envy becomes a function of the relationship) (p. 78). It is with the third category, where reciprocity is lacking between the container and the contained, that difficulties arise. Donald Meltzer (2008) elaborates on Bion's *container/contained* with a new concept, the claustrum. Meltzer describes patients who are both claustrophilic and claustrophobic. They are attracted to the mood states and thoughts of another but soon find themselves struggling to flee, adapt or fight in an effort to ward off the feeling of psychic annihilation. In his book, 'The Claustrum', Meltzer elaborates on the concept of intrusive identification. He identifies three areas of the internal mother's body: head-breast, genital and rectal, where all pathology, perversion, addiction, omnipotence, *narcissism*, and fearfulness, can be understood as a consequence of inhabiting a claustral chamber of the internal mother's body.

These three categories (commensal, symbiotic and parasitic), according to Hinshelwood, describe a caregiver's balance of mind. Some caregivers cannot maintain a balance and all mothers at one time or another will fail at the task. When they fail, according to Hinshelwood, they do so in distinctive ways. He writes that, 'in failing the mother becomes a container that is either too rigid or to fragile ... A rigid mother takes in as Bion describes and utters formal responses, without a *real* understanding of the infant's distress. A fragile mother will, when confronted by her distressed baby, go to pieces and panic. In either case the infant receives back its own *projection* with the implicit message that after all, as it feared, its state of mind is not tolerable. It suffers, in Bion's terms, a "nameless dread" '– i.e. a state of mind that is not thinkable' (Hinshelwood, 1999, p. 1480; emphasis added).

Mothers/parents, teachers, analysts or societies may all serve containing functions. Infants, according to Bion, need more than obligation from their caregivers, however. They need caregivers and therapists able, through *reverie*, to both feel the disturbance/anxiety and in measure become disturbed. Whereas the concept is often used to suggest a somewhat benign function, for Bion it refers more to a processing of experience from the most destructive to affirming life experience. For Thomas Ogden (1992), a contemporary interpreter of Bion, because the relationship between the container and the contained is always nonlinear, it must involve a recursive process of intersubjective dynamics. Grotstein (1978), another recent interpreter of Bion, argues that the container–contained relationship requires fundamental rethinking of 'inner space' as a relation between the mind and its contents. He argues that the container–contained relationship presupposes notions of psychic space or 'inner space' and psychopathology results from states, experiences or a sense of feeling unable to escape a psychic space.

Some have considered at length the relationship between Bion's concept 'container' and Winnicott's 'holding environment' (Caper, 1999; Symington and Ivey, 2009; Symington and Symington, 1996). The Symingtons (1996) have considered the differences between these ideas. For them the container is internal, while holding (i.e. the holding environment) refers to a movement from the internal to the external (Symington and Symington, 1996, p. 58). Moreover, they argue that holding refers to mostly positive, sensuous activity promoting development while containment refers to the nonsensuous and may result in destruction or disintegration (p. 58). For Thomas Ogden (2004),

> Winnicott's holding is seen as an ontological concept that is primarily concerned with being and its relationship to time. Initially the mother safeguards the infant's continuity of being, in part by insulating him from the 'not me' aspect of time. Maturation entails the infants gradually internalizing the mothers holding of the continuity of his being over time and emotional flux. By contrast, Bion's container-contained is centrally concerned with the processing (dreaming) of thoughts derived from lived

emotional experience. The idea of container/contained addresses the dynamic interaction of predominantly unconscious thoughts (the contained) and capacity for dreaming and thinking those thoughts (the container). (p. 1349)

points for reflection and practice
- The therapist must be able to contain the most disturbing aspects of what is projected alongside what is more consciously tolerable.
- Reassurance does not perform a containing function. When used, it tends to suggest that the therapist cannot tolerate disturbing projections and act as a container.
- Caper (1999) views holding as a moment in the process of containment whereby the therapist conveys the capacity to feel and know the patient's reality.

KEY TEXTS

- Bion, W. (1962) *Learning from Experience* (Oxford, UK: Jason Aronson)
- Bion, W. (1963) *Elements of Psychoanalysis* (London, UK: Heinemann)
- Bion, W. (1970) *Attention and Interpretation* (London, UK: Tavistock)
- Brown, L. (2013) 'The Development of Bion's Concept of Container and Contained', in H. B. Levine and L. J. Brown (eds), *Growth and Turbulence in the Container/Contained: Bion's Continuing Legacy–* (London, UK: Routledge), pp. 7–22
- Grinberg, L., Sor, D. and de Bianchedi, E. (1991) *New Introduction to the Work of Bion* (Northvale, NJ: Jason Aronson)
- Hinshelwood, R. D. (1999) 'Countertransference and the Therapeutic Relationship: Recent Kleinian Developments in Technique'. Available at http://dspp.com/papers/hinshelwood.htm
- Hinshelwood, R. D. (2007) 'The Kleinian Theory of Therapeutic Action', *The Psychoanalytic Quarterly*, 76 (S1): pp. 1479–1498
- Meltzer, D. (2008) *The Claustrum: An Investigation of Claustrophobic Phenomena* (London, UK: Karnac Books)
- Meltzer, D. *et al.* (1982) 'The Conceptual Distinction between Projective Identification (Klein) and Container-Contained (Bion)', *Journal of Child Psychotherapy*, 8 (2): pp. 185–202
- Ogden, T. (2004) 'On Holding and Containing, Being and Dreaming', *International Journal of Psychoanalysis*, 85 (6): pp. 1349–1364
- Ogden, T. (1992) 'The Dialectically Constituted/Decentered Subject of Psychoanalysis. I: The Freudian Subject', *International Journal of Psychoanalysis*, 73: pp. 613–626

countertransference

SEE ALSO **projective identification**

'Countertransference', a term first used by Freud in 1910 (pp. 144–145), has a rich, varied and controversial history. Much of the early thinking on the subject was influenced by Freud's view that unconscious reactions by the therapist (these may also include feelings projected by the patient onto the therapist) are to be guarded against, contained or controlled and ultimately overcome. If countertransference is seen as a deficit in the therapist, attention is given to the defensive manoeuvres of the therapist and the need to vigilantly maintain a projective mirror or surface upon which to project. According to this understanding, the therapist is a blank screen onto which fantasies are projected; distortions of the screen are produced by the qualities and conflicts unique to the therapist. Over time this view has changed radically, so much so that today we see countertransference as potentially productive: that is, it may both constrain and enable the work of therapy. In her seminal 1950 essay, 'On Countertransference', Paula Heimann, a student of Melanie Klein's, argued that countertransference could be used as a means of both perceiving and exploring communication. With Klein's idea of *projective identification* (see entry, *projective identification*) subsequent thinking about countertransference has been thoroughly transformed. Attention has turned to how the patient influences the therapist by projecting parts of psychic reality. It is in this way that thinking shifted from a deficit in the analyst (i.e. communication, *affect*, feeling, unrecognized or misrecognized by the therapist) to ways of understanding, perceiving and communicating.

Our more contemporary view of countertransference insists that as the therapist comes to know and feel, most notably his or her emotions, the treatment relationship is aimed at working through the counter-transferential interplay, and effectively using therapist reactions to the client's relational and inner worlds. There is a shared reality, perhaps as a development of the relationship between the therapist and the client. Racker (1968) described two forms of countertransference: 'concordant' and 'complementary'. The first describes an empathic link between the therapist and patient. The second describes the therapist identification with a projectively disavowed *object*-representation; Racker saw this as activation, by the patient, of the therapists' conflicts. Winnicott, in his classic and controversial 1949 article, 'Hate in the Countertransference', describes countertransference in very different terms. For Winnicott, in what he labels 'objective' countertransference, the therapist, is always reacting to the patient in ways that are 'normal' and understandable; they are reactions to the ongoing behaviours and personality of the patient. What was most controversial for Winnicott, however, was the *recognition* that the therapist, like the mother, must be able to tolerate and use hateful feelings. Learning to love, Winnicott argued, requires learning and tolerating hate.

Lacan (2006) understood countertransference in a very general way. For him it referred to 'the sum total of the analyst's biases, passions, and difficulties, or even of his inadequate information, at any given moment in the dialectical process' (p. 225).

There is yet another important debate in our contemporary thinking about countertransference, sometimes called countertransference enactments. Enactments, according to some, occur when the therapist actualizes the transference and joins the patient in acting out intrapsychic conflicts and fantasies.

points for reflection and practice
- There is no doubt that knowing how the therapist feels and responds and how patients use transference, and how their own inner world is impacted, offers the therapy additional means of understanding therapeutic action and process.
- Clients who project often watch for signs of countertransference to indicate that they have affected the therapist and are in control.
- The Kleinians pay close attention to the moment-to-moment interactions between the patient and therapist and the interpretation of transference and countertransference.
- Often, therapists respond in their countertransference with strong negative and sometimes-hateful feelings (see Winnicott's essay, 1949, 'Hate in the Counter-Transference').

KEY TEXTS
- Gabbard, G. (1995) 'Countertransference: The Emerging Common Ground', *International Journal of Psychoanalysis*, 76: pp. 475–486

- Greenberg, J. (1991) 'Countertransference and Reality', *Psychoanalytic Dialogues*, 1 (1): pp. 52–73
- Jacobs, T. (1999) 'Countertransference Past and Present: A Review of the Concept', *International Journal of Psychoanalysis*, 80 (3): pp. 575–594
- Levine, H. (1997) 'The Capacity for Countertransference', *Psychoanalytic Inquiry*, 17 (1): pp. 44–68
- Ogden, T. (1995) 'Aliveness and Deadness of the Transference and Countertransference', *International Journal of Psychoanalysis*, 76: pp. 695–710
- Racker, H. (1957) 'The Meanings and Uses of Countertransference', *The Psychoanalytic Quarterly*, 26 (3): pp. 303–357
- Smith, H. (2000) 'Countertransference, Conflictual Listening, and the Analytic Object Relationship', *Journal of the American Psychoanalytic Association*, 48 (1): pp. 95–128
- Steiner, J. (1994) 'Patient-Centered and Analyst-Centered Interpretations: Some Implications of Containment and Countertransference', *Psychoanalytic Inquiry*, 14 (3): pp. 406–422
- Winnicott, D. W. (1949) 'Hate in the Countertransference', *International Journal of Psychoanalysis*, 30 (2): pp. 69–74

d

defence mechanisms

SEE ALSO conflict and compromise formation; ego

Although Sigmund Freud described defence mechanisms, it was his daughter Anna who offered a more comprehensive account ('The Ego and the Mechanisms of Defence') of their number, kinds and functioning. Foremost, defence mechanisms serve the purpose of reducing *anxiety* produced from psychic conflict (see entry, *conflict and compromise formation*), including external threats to the self. For healthy functioning, impulses cannot without limit seek satisfaction; they must conform to the surrounding world and to the demands of the superego. For example, if the id expresses the desire or impulse for sex with a sibling, there may be conflict with a superego demand (i.e. social conventions against), and anxiety will be produced along with feelings of *shame* and *guilt*. If the anxiety is unbearable, the ego will deploy protective defences. Many describe the operation of defence mechanisms as unconscious blocking, transformations or distortions of unacceptable impulses and their transformation into acceptable forms. Others use these ideas to talk about the myriad ways that painful thoughts and feelings are kept out of awareness. Some argue that the defences are associated with specific *developmental stages*: denial, *projection*, introjection and *splitting* with the oral phase and undoing, reaction formation and isolation with the anal phase.

Anna Freud described ten mechanisms of defence: denial, displacement, intellectualization, projection, rationalization, reaction formation, regression, repression, *sublimation* and suppression. Melanie Klein argued that introjection, projection, and splitting are necessary to healthy development but also have potentially troubling outcomes.

Vaillant described four levels of defence: (1) pathological defences (e.g. psychotic denial, delusional projection); (2) immature defences (e.g. fantasy, projection, passive aggression, acting out); (3) neurotic defences (e.g. intellectualization, reaction formation, *dissociation*, displacement, repression); (4) mature defences (e.g. humour, sublimation, suppression, altruism, anticipation).

In 2000 Phebe Cramer wrote for the 'American Psychologist' a review of the extant research and theory on defence. She observes that,

> Although there were procedural errors in many of the early experimental studies of defense, the *real* sticking point in the refusal to accept the conclusions of these earlier studies was that they implied the existence of unconscious cognition (see Lazarus, 1998). Yet, recently cognitive psychologists have rediscovered the existence of unconscious mental processes. Virtually every leading cognitive psychologist today accepts the premise that mental processes go on outside of awareness. (p. 638; emphasis added)

Cramer argues for the importance of distinguishing between coping and defence (i.e. conscious vs unconscious, intentional vs unintentional).

points for reflection and practice
- It is important to remember that defences can be healthy and protective or quite damaging to self and others. In this way it is important to both recognize and respect the array and uses of defences. Some, for example, need to use the defence of denial when faced with overwhelming stimulation or stress; in these cases, the defence must be respected and in some cases, nurtured.
- Gleser and Ihilevich (1969) developed the Defence Mechanism Inventory and Andrews *et al.* (1993) developed the self-report Defence Style Questionnaire (DSQ). See Hyphantis *et al.* (2011), for recent research on measuring use of defences.
- Recent research (Hyphantis *et al.*, 2011; Perry and Bond 2012) on defences shows evidence of how defensive functioning changes in long-term psychotherapy.
- See Appendix 4 for a list of some defence mechanisms.

KEY TEXTS

- Andrews, G., Singh, M. and Bond, M. (1993) 'The Defense Style Questionnaire', *The Journal of Nervous and Mental Disease*, 181 (4): pp. 246–256
- Cramer, P. (2000) 'Defense Mechanisms in Psychology Today: Further Processes for Adaptation', *American Psychologist*, 55 (6): pp. 637–646
- Cramer, P. (2006) *Protecting the Self: Defense Mechanisms in Action* (New York, NY: The Guilford Press)
- Erdelyi, M. H. and Goldberg, B. (1979) 'Let's Not Sweep Repression Under the Rug: Toward a Cognitive Psychology of Repression' in J. F. Kihlstrom and F. J. Evans (eds), *Functional Disorders of Memory* (Hillsdale NJ: Erlbaum Associates), pp. 355–402
- Fonagy, P. and Target, M. (2003) *Psychoanalytic Theories: Perspectives from Developmental Psychopathology* (London, UK: Routledge)
- Freud, A. (1993) *The Ego and the Mechanisms of Defense* (London, UK: Karnac Books)
- Gray, P. (2005) *The Ego and Analysis of Defense* (Oxford, UK: Rowman and Littlefield)
- Kramer, U. (2010) 'Coping and Defense Mechanisms: What's the Difference?: Second Act', *Psychology and Psychotherapy: Theory, Research and Practice*, 83 (2): pp. 207–221
- Perry, J. C. and Bond, M. (2012). 'Change in Defense Mechanisms during Long-Term Dynamic Psychotherapy and Five-Year Outcome', *American Journal of Psychiatry*, 169 (9): pp. 916–925
- Vaillant, G. (1992) *Ego Mechanisms of Defense: A Guide for Clinicians and Researchers* (New York, NY: American Psychiatric Publishing)

depression

SEE ALSO **ambivalence; diagnosis and the DSM; evidence-based practice**

In *psychodynamic* theory, depression is understood as a complex dynamic between the intrapersonal and interpersonal 'experience of Loss'. Even the *symptom*-based nosology, the DSM, acknowledges the potential connection between loss and depression when depressive symptoms 'are not better accounted for by bereavement'. While first experienced interpersonally, loss is finally felt and repeated intrapersonally. Freud writes that 'An *object*-choice, an *attachment* of the libido to a particular person, had at one time existed; then, owing to a *real* slight or disappointment coming from this loved person, the object-relationship was shattered' (1917, pp. 248–249; emphases added). While Freud argued that many things may contribute to the two possibilities, mourning or melancholia, the loss of a loved object is common to both. And much of *psychodynamic* 'theory' sees depression as self-directed anger.

What leads to mourning and what leads to melancholia is far less clear. No doubt the state of the ego, the maturity and integration of the ego and its functions, and the ego's relationship to the object world, external and internal, have something to do with how loss is experienced. Some argue that immature ego functioning and 'narcissistic' object relations lead to *splitting* and regression (i.e. narcissistic) and to introjection or *identification* with both the frustrating and satisfying qualities of the lost object. While most who experience loss shift libidinal investments to others and replace the love object (i.e. normal mourning), those vulnerable to depression react differently: they withdraw libido from the object into the ego and reinvest it in two ways: (1) 'narcissistic identification' with the love object, or (2) it is invested with 'sadistic' impulses and the superego attacks the ego identifications with the love object by means of harsh self-reproaches. When sadism prevails, libidinal investments in the object are abandoned: the result is depletion of libido in the ego. In Freud's very famous words, 'Thus the shadow of the object fell upon the ego.'

Hanna Segal (1964), from a Kleinian perspective, describes melancholia as a manic-schizoid defence against the *depressive position* (see entry, *depressive position*). For Segal, the melancholic identification with the lost object is projective (i.e. an archaic psychotic defence mechanism). This explains the congruence between the ego and the part-object with which it becomes confused.

For Matthew Ratcliffe (2012), a phenomenologist, depression is best understood as a fundamental change in the experience of temporality. He argues that suffering results from a change in perception of the duration of events or the rate at which time flows.

Most important for Ratcliffe, however, is a change in the structure of temporality: a change in how past, present and future and transitions among them are experienced (p. 115). Ratcliffe writes, of major depression, that loss may be understood as: (1) loss of practical significance; (2) loss of conative *drive* and (3) loss of life projects.

Some argue that depression has both productive and unproductive sides (Gut, 1989). It may protect the self by allowing for withdrawal from the normal routines of everyday life and time for ego to reflect and integrate before entry. And there can be no doubt that some *developmental stages* have as their natural sequelae depressive mood and should not be medicalized or treated as abnormal (i.e. *adolescence*).

Many have argued that depression is a quality of human experience that defies easy description and classification; some argue that contemporary psychiatry and academic psychology tend to reduce the more complex experience of depression to symptom checklists (Horwitz and Wakefield, 2007; Leader, 2008). For most in contemporary psychiatry and psychology depression is seen as a discrete illness, disease or disorder, and sometimes even as a condition reducible to neurochemical events, and if this is true, then depressive states altogether lack meaning and are best understood as epiphenomena of brain disease. The pharmaceutical industry, government agencies and research institutes, psychiatry, advertisers and the entertainment industry all treat depression as if it were a singular, unified thing (Healy, 1997). If only we could quickly identify and name the problem using *evidence-based practice*, like we do for bacterial infections, we'd have a solution at hand. Depression, it seems, defines our era. The World Health Organization (WHO) claims that it will soon be the single most significant public health concern after heart disease and it replaces *anxiety* as the defining symptom of the era.

points for reflection and practice
- We should avoid assuming we know what depression 'is' or claim what depression means for any given person. The meaning and experience of depressive symptoms will be different for each person.
- Many with depressive symptoms often feel trapped in an unending nightmare of self-accusation and *guilt*.
- Emma Gut describes two forms of depression, productive and unproductive. It is useful to think about these forms and how they relate to goals and strategies in working with depressed clients.
- Matthew Ratcliffe makes an important observation regarding the therapeutic value of working with the subtle ways that patients experience changes in the experience of temporality. See, especially, his 2012 article, 'Varieties of Temporal Experience

in Depression'. Below is a summary of how he thinks about temporality in major depression:

1. Loss of the sense of things as practically significant for oneself and perhaps for others too, with or without (2) and/or (4).
2. Partial or complete loss of conative drive/enticing possibilities, with or without (1) or (3) and/or (4).
3. Loss of some or all of one's projects (rather than [1] the sense of significance that such projects presuppose), with or without (2) and/or (4).
4. A sense of passivity before an impending threat, which can accompany any of (1) to (3) above (Ratcliffe, 2012, p. 134).

KEY TEXTS

- Freud, S. (1917) *Mourning and Melancholia*. Standard Edition, 14
- Greenberg, G. (2010) *Manufacturing Depression: The Secret History of a Modern Disease* (New York, NY: Simon & Schuster)
- Gut, E. (1989) *Productive and Unproductive Depression: Success or Failure of a Vital Process* (New York, NY: Basic Books)
- Healy, D. (1997) *The Antidepressant Era* (Cambridge, MA: Harvard University Press)
- Horwitz, A. and Wakefield, J. (2007) *The Loss of Sadness* (New York, NY: Oxford University Press)
- Leader, D. (2008) *The New Black: Mourning, Melancholia and Depression* (London, UK: Penguin)
- Panksepp, J. (2003) 'Feeling the Pain of Social Loss', *Science*, 302 (5643): pp. 237–239
- Ratcliffe, M. (2012) 'Varieties of Temporal Experience in Depression', *Journal of Medicine and Philosophy*, 37 (2): pp. 114–138
- Segal, H. (1964) *Introduction to the Work of Melanie Klein* (London, UK: Heinemann)
- Solms, M. (2012) 'Depression: A Neuropsychoanalytic Perspective', *International Forum of Psychoanalysis*, 21 (3–4): pp. 207–213

depressive position

SEE ALSO **ambivalence; anxiety; depression; depressive position; paranoid–schizoid**

The Kleinians talk about positions as often as they refer to stages. This accomplishes a number of important things. First, it shifts our thinking about early development away from teleology (i.e. inexorable stages unfolding towards a predetermined end) towards recursive and unpredictable open systems. Second, while Klein sees a linear movement from the *paranoid–schizoid* (see entry, *paranoid–schizoid*) to the depressive position, she and her successors acknowledge that this is also an uncertain and recursive movement freighted with *anxiety* and painful *guilt*.

The infant reaches the depressive position once the mother is experienced as a whole *object*, fallible, with good and bad qualities, which can be both loved and hated. This, in turn, leads to the developing capacity to feel and experience separation, but not without feeling responsible for separation and the associated feelings (i.e. hate, aggression). Grotstein (1981) refers to this as the 'primal split'. Seen as the cause of both the separation and irreparable harm done to the love object, the infant experiences mortifying guilt and suffering. And while the infant now feels and recognizes they need and love the whole object mother, jealousy, helplessness, and dependency, amplified by aggressive impulse, continues to cause fear they have damaged or destroyed the mother.

Gradually, depressive anxiety replaces destructive urges with guilt and reparation, and defences found in the paranoid–schizoid position (i.e. *splitting, projection,* denial) give way as the *ego* deepens its capacity to realistically perceive (i.e. the ego is integrated along with the developing capacity to experience and feel the object as both good and bad) and relinquish omnipotent control of the object. And brief separations create conditions for repeated restoration of the missing object 'as an image of representation'. In the depressive position, thus, the capacity for *symbolic* thought emerges. The object is now experienced and felt as both separate and *real*. The result, described by the term, depressive, is a feeling of loss and mourning.

points for reflection and practice
- In practice, it is common to see the term 'depressive position' used in myriad ways. Sometimes it refers to early development and the ego integration resulting from whole object relations and the related capacity to tolerate and manage *ambivalence*.

- Others use the concept to understand the range of state, from normal mourning to severe *depression* (i.e. throughout the life course) and the role hateful aggression plays in the production of guilt, grief and striving for reparation.
- Often the term refers to depressive position functioning: capacity to perceive and feel separateness and to take personal responsibility. It is not uncommon to see this concept used to understand adult depression. Finally, in therapy, painful separations may be relived and reworked.

KEY TEXTS

- Anderson, R. and Segal, H. (eds) (2004) *Clinical Lectures on Klein and Bion.* The New Library of Psychoanalysis (Book 14) (London, UK: Routledge)
- Bronstein, C. (2001) *Kleinian Theory: A Contemporary Perspective* (London, UK: Whurr Publishers)
- Grotstein, J. (1981) *Splitting and Projective Identification* (Northvale NJ: Jason Aronson)
- Ogden, T. (1989) *The Primitive Edge of Experience* (Northvale, NJ: Jason Aronson)
- Spillius, E. B. (1994) 'Developments in Klein's Thinking', *Psychoanalytic Inquiry,* 14 (3): pp. 324–364

developmental stages

SEE ALSO **adolescence; developmental stages; drive; ego; good enough mother (holding environment); imaginary; Oedipal; paranoid–schizoid; real; symbolic; transitional space/transitional phenomena/transitional object**

Freud's psychosexual developmental theory was and remains among the most controversial of his ideas. Like all stage theories, it assumed a logical and necessary progression (i.e. teleology) from simple to complex, from undeveloped to developed and from a potentially regressed (or fixated) state to forward progression. It is especially important to understand the paradigm shift brought about by Freud's linking of the 'psycho' with the 'sexual'. For Freud the human experience is always and necessarily psychosexual. Otherwise, we are left with shallow and one-dimensional reductions of the psychological to empirical sexual behaviours (e.g. Kinsey, 1948, 1953).

Children progress through stages and throughout development libidinal energy shifts in a mostly forward direction towards mastery of stage-specific tasks (i.e. movement from oral and anal dependence towards oral and anal mastery and independence). Libido, thus, has different erogenous zones as a source of energy. Early in development, the infant's libidinal energy is aimed at infantile objects and with progression, the child increasingly cathects to more mature ones. In the 'oral stage' (0–15/18 months) the mouth is the organizing erogenous zone and pleasure is obtained from sucking, eating, biting and spitting. And because the *ego* and superego have not yet fully formed, the id dominates, action is based on the pleasure principle and the infant lacks a developed sense of self. Weaning is crucial to this stage. Here, the infant gradually loses intimate contact with the maternal and feels for the first time profound loss; with weaning, too, the baby gains an awareness of self, that not everything is under its control, and that gratification must be deferred. From eighteen months to three years, 'the anal phase', the pleasure is in the elimination and retention of faeces; it is through social sanction, mostly parental injunctions, that the child learns to control anal stimulation. The pleasure in defecation, moreover, is connected to the child's delight in creating something of its own. From ages three to five or six, the 'phallic phase', the genitals become the dominant *object*-cathexis: urination, its retention and expulsion, is both pleasurable and fascinating, and exploration of anatomical differences is common. It is during this stage, sometimes called the *'Oedipal'* phase (see entry, *Oedipal*), that the child struggles to identify with one or another of the genders, male and female, masculine and feminine, passive and active. Next there is the latency phase, age six to puberty, during which time the urgency of the drives is reduced and libido is transferred from parents to peers and others in the social surround. Finally, there is the genital stage (see entry, *adolescence*), from puberty on, when the sexual urges are reawakened. Those most critical of the stage theory find especially troubling the normative development towards the achievement of heterosexuality (i.e. heteronormativity).

Melanie Klein, Jacque Lacan, and D. W. Winnicott revised in significant and different ways our understandings of developmental stages. While Melanie Klein did not altogether abandon the notion of psychosexual stages, for her, unlike Freud, the superego forms early in life, under the influence of phantasy and conflicting emotions (i.e. love and hate). Every child, according to Klein, introjects objects throughout development, especially the parent, and constructs a superego out of bits of introjected elements. And the very first introjected object, the breast, forms the basis of the superego. Klein proposed two positions: (1) *paranoid–schizoid* position (i.e. in this position, the infant experiences the caregiver as a part, need-fulfilling object; (2) the *depressive position* (in this position, the infant has a growing sense of loss and sadness that is felt in having to relinquish the need-fulfilling object relation to achieve a sense of whole object, ambivalent relations). If love and hate can be tolerated, *anxiety* shifts to a concern for the well-being and survival of the now whole object. This results in *guilt*, sadness and a deepening of love. In normal development the child increasingly occupies the depressive position, but movement between the two are common.

For Winnicott, the infant must first have a sense of connectedness with the mother. With good enough mothering, the mother responds adequately to the child's needs and conveys a sense or *illusion* of omnipotence and control. If all goes well, the child experiences disillusion and gradual disconnection. This, in turn, leads to strengthening of the ego and realization that the feelings and needs of others are significant. Winnicott sometimes called this the 'stage of concern'. Well-timed separations, moreover, produce a growing and healthy sense of independence and a gradual release of omnipotent thinking. The *transitional object* serves an important function in these changes. If the mother throughout these moments fails to take up the child's primitive projections (i.e. frustration, anxiety) the child will eventually lose trust, withdraw or simply adapt to the unreliable environment.

For Lacan, there are three registers in development: *real, imaginary* and *symbolic*. The real, a prelinguistic register, can never be fully known; because it is outside our sensory experience it is never perceived. In the *real* we are dominated by need and satisfaction. And because the real cannot be fully known, we always live with a sense of lack, a motivational force that compels us to seek completion. In the imaginary, we strive to fill the void produced by the real with images of completeness. Here, sometimes called the mirror phase, the child sees images of the self, without language. In the symbolic register, metaphor, sign and symbol dominate; thought and perception is mediated by language. Neurotic symptoms result from a dominance of one register.

point for reflection and practice
- Anna Freud has written an especially strong and practice-relevant essay on early development, 'The Concept of Developmental Lines'. In this very influential essay, she describes the continuous, recursive and cumulative quality of child development and the interactions and interdependencies among and between *drive* and ego-superego development and environmental influence; movement along the lines, forward and backward, is expected; and regression may at times be necessary for managing potential or real stressors. She proposed the use of the 'developmental profile' as an assessment tool.

KEY TEXTS
- Diem-Wille, G. (2011) *The Early Years of Life: Psychoanalytical Development Theory According to Freud, Klein, and Bion* (London, UK: Karnac Books)
- Freud, A. (1963) 'The Concept of Developmental Lines', *The Psychoanalytic Study of the Child*, 18: pp. 245–265
- Ingenhoven, T. and Abraham, R. (2010) 'Making Diagnosis More Meaningful. the Developmental Profile: A Psychodynamic Assessment of Personality', *American Journal of Psychotherapy*, 64 (3): pp. 215–238
- Neubauer, P. (1984) 'Anna Freud's Concept of Developmental Lines', *The Psychoanalytic Study of the Child*, 39: pp. 15–29

diagnosis and the DSM

SEE ALSO **evidence-based practice**

Psychodynamic/psychoanalytic diagnosis has been controversial from its beginnings. And there is a paradox inherent to the process: it is difficult, if not impossible, to diagnose without having considered the case over time and in detail. At the same time, the choice of treatment approach depends on having made a prior commitment to a diagnosis. And the relevance of a diagnosis can only be established after treatment is well underway. Moreover, unlike in clinical medicine, direct empirical observation is impossible. There is simply no realistic way to establish the presence or absence of pathology or illness with a fixed system of meanings and nosology. In clinical medicine, unlike psychodiagnostics, the physician has at his or her disposal a complement to the patient's recollections: direct examination with sophisticated, sensory enhancing technologies (Verhaeghe, 2004).

In psychodiagnostics, the therapist has only one diagnostic instrument: *listening* (Dor, 1998). Joel Dor describes this aptly: 'Because direct examination is out of the question, the only clinical material provided by the patient consists of his or her words, and so from the outset the field of clinical investigation is confined to the act of saying and to what is said' (p. 4). Paul Ricoeur (2012), in a posthumously published work, 'On Psychoanalysis', writes of this dilemma in a chapter, 'The Question of Proof in Freud's Psychoanalytic Writings': 'It is this triangular relation between a procedure of investigation, a method of treatment, and a theory that will hold our attention because it takes the place of the theory-fact relation in the observational sciences. Not only does psychoanalysis deal with "facts" of a special nature ... but what takes the place of the operative procedures at work in the natural sciences is a unique type of relation between the investigatory procedure and the method of treatment. It is this relation that mediates between the theory and the facts' (pp. 22–23).

The latest iteration of the DSM, the DSM-5 (released in 2013), the dominant diagnostic manual/nosology used in the United States and many places around the world, produced a firestorm of controversy from within and outside the established biopsychiatry paradigm. While for decades the US National Institute of Mental Health (NIMH) has used and defended the DSM, just weeks before the release of the most recent version, DSM-5 (spring, 2013), NIMH announced that they would no longer support research using DSM criteria. From outside biopsychiatry, a spate of books, blogs, news and journal articles have documented this most embarrassing moment in the history of Western psychology.

Thomas Insel, Director of the NIMH and a strong advocate of biological reductionism and brain science, commits himself precisely to the reduction of psychiatric phenomena to natural kinds (see Zachar, 2000, for especially important discussion of psychiatric disorders as natural kinds). In Insel's words, below, you clearly see this conceptual move:

> The goal of this new manual, as with all previous editions, is to provide a common language for describing psychopathology.

While the DSM has been described as a 'Bible' for the field, it is, at best, a dictionary, creating a set of labels and defining each. The strength of each of the editions of DSM has been 'reliability' – each edition has ensured that clinicians use the same terms in the same ways. The weakness is its lack of validity. Unlike our definitions of ischemic heart disease, lymphoma, or AIDS, the DSM diagnoses are based on a consensus about clusters of clinical symptoms, not any objective laboratory measure. In the rest of medicine, this would be equivalent to creating diagnostic systems based on the nature of chest pain or the quality of fever. Indeed, symptom-based diagnosis, once common in other areas of medicine, has been largely replaced in the past half century as we have understood that symptoms alone rarely indicate the best choice of treatment. Patients with mental disorders deserve better. NIMH has launched the Research Domain Criteria (RDoC) project to transform diagnosis by incorporating genetics, imaging, cognitive science, and other levels of information to lay the foundation for a new classification system. (Insel, 2013, http://www.nimh.nih.gov/about/director/2013/transforming-diagnosis.shtml)

Ironically, a confederation of psychoanalytic organizations and societies, in offering a rationale for their alternative to the DSM, the PDM (Psychodynamic Diagnostic Manual), concurs with much of what Thomas Insel argues, but from a very different perspective, with very different outcomes. For Insel the solution lies in a kind of radical biological reductionism and pharmaceutical solutions to mental health research and care. For those who collaborated on the creation of the PDM (American Psychoanalytic Association, the International Psychoanalytical Association, the Division of Psychoanalysis of the American Psychological Association, the American Academy of Psychoanalysis and Dynamic Psychiatry, and the National Membership Committee on Psychoanalysis in Clinical Social Work), the aim was to shift attention back to the entire self. The PDM is currently (2014) undergoing a significant revision. The psychodynamic manual and diagnosis is aimed at creating a new conversation and classificatory system based not on narrow, quantitative, observable, descriptive definitions and symptoms but one which recognizes the complexities and inter-relatedness of mental health problems. Moreover, the PDM moves towards an understanding of the self and therapeutic efficacy measured by more than symptom relief. It aims at offering the practitioner a means of assessing, formulating and helping the patient achieve overall mental health, *ego* strength, *affect* tolerance and relational stability.

For most who seek relief from suffering, the DSM diagnostic categories are narrow and limited. First, most do not fit neatly, if at all, into clear-cut diagnostic categories. Second, like Thomas Insel, the DSM sees emotional suffering as a disease, such as cancer or kidney failure or glaucoma. Third, it treats emotional suffering as if it were a discrete (i.e. types of cancer, cells) entity and separable from the person in pain. But most of the problems brought to treatment are woven into the fabric of an individual life. As Jonathan Shedler writes, 'it is less a question of what the patient "has" than who they are – their way of being in the world' (2013).

The Belgian Lacanian psychologist, Paul Verhaeghe (2004), offers the most thorough and theoretically sophisticated critique of the current Western nosology and related practices in his 2004 book, 'On Being Normal and Other Disorders: A Manual for Clinical Psychodiagnostics'. He considers the especially important dynamic between differential diagnosis and treatment choice and the quality and nature of the therapeutic relationship given diagnostic commitments, and how these choices affect treatment, irrespective of the treatment modality. Moreover, for Verhaeghe,

> Whatever approach one takes, a common factor emerges: the diagnosis cannot be limited' only to a given patient under in particular description. The impact of the Other is fundamental. This is the first major difference between medical diagnostics and psychodiagnostics: clinical psychodiagnostics cannot be restricted to the individual. Psychic identity, with its potential psychopathology and aberrant behaviors, must be conceived in such a way that it grants the other a place equally important as the individual's (p. 7).

points for reflection and practice
- It is important to know and understand the difference between symptom-based/descriptive diagnosis and dynamic diagnosis. See, especially, Nancy McWilliams's important

work, 'Psychoanalytic Diagnosis', not only for understanding the difference but for using dynamic diagnosis in everyday practice.

- Symptom-based diagnosis tends to focus clinical attention on behaviours and empirically observable phenomena and altogether overlook the importance of how symptoms, irrespective of their origin and development (i.e. biological, chemical, genetic), always carry and convey meaning.

KEY TEXTS

- Dor, J. (1998) *The Clinical Lacan* (New York, NY: Other Press)
- Gordon, R. M. (2006) 'Psychodynamic Diagnostic Manual', *Corsini Encyclopedia of Psychology*
- Haslam, N. (2000) 'Psychiatric Categories as Natural Kinds: Essentialist Thinking about Mental Disorder' *Social Research*, 67 (4): pp. 1031–1058
- McWilliams, N. (1999) *Psychoanalytic Case Formulation* (New York, NY: Guilford Press)
- McWilliams, N. (2011) *Psychoanalytic Diagnosis: Understanding Personality Structure in the Clinical Process* (New York, NY: Guilford Press)
- Messer, S. and Wolitzky, D. (2007) 'The Psychoanalytic Approach to Case Formulation' in T. D. Eells (ed.), *Handbook of Psychotherapy Case Formulation* (New York, NY: Guilford Press), pp. 67–104
- Ricoeur, P. (2012) *On Psychoanalysis* (Cambridge, UK: Polity Press)
- Shedler, J. (2013). 'Psychodynamic Psychotherapy 101'. Available at http://www.psychologytoday.com /blog/psychologically-minded/201311/psychodynamic-therapy-101
- Verhaeghe, P. (2004) *On Being Normal and Other Disorders: A Manual for Clinical Psychodiagnostics* (New York, NY: Other Press)

dissociation

SEE ALSO **defence mechanisms; self-states**

The relationship between trauma and dissociation has been widely studied and debated recently. As a defence, it is usually thought of as a temporary but significant disconnection aimed at avoiding or postponing a feeling or thought. With dissociation, the disconnection allows one to live outside time and space, to better manage unbearable thoughts, feelings or memories. And with an alternative or dissociated representation of self it is possible to exist in a profound and focused present (e.g. losing track of time): time and self-representation unfold discontinuously.

As a disorder, it refers to a change in consciousness affecting memory and identity. For Spiegel and Cardena, dissociation is seen as structured separations among otherwise integrated mental functions: thought, emotion, memory and identity. This understanding of dissociation suggests a more phenomenological account than what appears in the descriptive DSM (i.e. dissociative amnesia, dissociative fugue, dissociative identity disorder, depersonalization disorder, derealization, dissociative trance disorder). For Fonagy *et al.* (1995), dissociative symptoms are understood as a radical separation of the self from experience. With this separation and with what they call defensive exclusion of experience from the autobiographical narrative, dissociation is linked to trauma. Research shows that many with dissociative disorders have experienced trauma, abuse and neglect. Studies of developmental trauma show two reactions: hyperarousal and dissociation (Schore, 2009). Bromberg (2006) links right brain trauma to autonomic hyperarousal: 'a chaotic and terrifying flooding of *affect* that can threaten to overwhelm sanity and imperil psychological survival' (p. 33; emphasis added). Dissociation is automatically engaged and serves as the defence against arousal dysregulation and overwhelming affective states.

For others, especially those in relational psychoanalysis (see Bromberg, 1998 and Stern, 1999) dissociation refers to an unconscious decision not to interpret experience or in Stern's language, 'keep it unformulated'. In short, according to them, experience cannot be expressed in language.

points for reflection and practice
- Here the purpose of *psychodynamic* therapy is to produce a sense of feeling understood and cared for. Among other things, this reduces the intense annihilation anxieties associated with these mental states and trauma.
- For Philip Bromberg (2006) the therapy must be aimed at a relational dynamic, which allows the patient to reclaim dissociated *self-states*. This is accomplished, for Bromberg,

through what he describes as 'the co-creation of a relational unconscious, via state-sharing, that enables restoration of links between dissociated aspects of self so that the conditions for intra-psychic conflicts and resolution can be present'.

KEY TEXTS

- Bateman, A. and Fonagy, P. (2004) 'Mentalization-Based Treatment of BPD', *Journal of Personality Disorders*, 18 (1): pp. 36–51
- Bromberg, P. (1998) *Standing in the Spaces: Essays on Clinical Process, Trauma, and Dissociation* (Hillsdale, NJ: Analytic Press)
- Bromberg, P. (2006) *Awakening the Dreamer: Clinical Journeys* (New York, NY: Analytic Press)
- Fonagy, P. and Target, M. (1995) 'Dissociation and Trauma', *Current Opinion in Psychiatry*, 8 (3): pp. 161–166
- Guralnik, O. and Simeon, D. (2010) 'Depersonalization: Standing in the Spaces between Recognition and Interpellation', *Psychoanalytic Dialogues*, 20 (4): pp. 400–416
- Howell, E. (2013) *The Dissociative Mind* (New York, NY: Routledge)
- Schore, A. (2009) 'Relational Trauma and the Developing Right Brain', *Annals of the New York Academy of Sciences*, 1159 (1): pp. 189–203
- Spiegel, D. and Cardena, E. (1991) 'Disintegrated Experience: The Dissociative Disorders Revisited', *Journal of Abnormal Psychology*, 100 (3): pp. 366–378
- Stern, D. (1997) *Unformulated Experience: From Dissociation to Imagination in Psychoanalysis* (Hillsdale, NJ: Analytic Press)Stern, D. (2004) 'The Eye Sees Itself: Dissociation, Enactment, and the Achievement of Conflict', *Contemporary Psychoanalysis*, 40 (2): pp. 197–238

dream

SEE ALSO **archetype; collective unconscious; mentalization; unconscious (see conscious)**

Two towering figures dominate much of our current understanding of dreams, Sigmund Freud and Carl Jung. For Freud, the dream serves two principal functions: psychological and physiological. Physiologically they serve to protect sleep by controlling disturbing stimuli. Psychologically, they function as wish fulfilment. Because repression, the mechanism through which we restrain unbearable, threatening fears, wishes, thoughts, is never fully effective, it returns (i.e. return of the repressed) to us through jokes, slips, symptoms and dreams. There are several key ideas in Freud's theory of dreams: 'latent content', 'manifest content', 'dream-work', 'repressed wishes', 'condensation', 'displacement', 'dramatization' and 'elaboration'. Through dream-work, by disguising repressed desires and wishes, the raw material of the dream (e.g. wishes and fears, thoughts, day residue) is transformed into manifest content.

The manifest content refers to that which the dreamer can relate to or recall upon waking. Behind this lies the latent content or disguised and distorted version of the manifest. Because the superego is at work protecting the conscious mind from disturbing desires, wishes, images and thoughts, the effort to remember the dream is often difficult. Here, with work, the true significance and meaning can be discovered as the dream is interpreted with the translation of manifest into latent content. With displacement, desire or feeling intended for one *object* or person is shifted onto an unrelated person or object in the manifest content. Condensation is the combined effect of two or more latent thoughts into a single manifest dream state or image.

Today, most psychoanalysts reject the notion that dreams are simple transformations of latent into manifest content (Blechner, 2001) and that the dream must finally be reconverted into latent content for adequate understanding. Nor does understanding the dream require associations to the dream. Nor are all dreams simple expressions of a disconcerting wish. Blechner (2013) writes: 'The censorship occurs not when we create the dream, but when we try to understand our own dream' (p. 167). In Freud's time as well it was not known that dreams occur throughout the night. Finally, surely there is no single explanatory account or cause of dreaming, in neuroscience or psychoanalysis.

For Carl Jung, unlike Freud, the dream was not the disguised hidden wish but evidence of a sort of natural truth whose central purpose was compensation for narrow views of the self. Jung, unlike Freud, did not think dreams should be interpreted using the method of *free association*. For Jung, the dream is to be understood through close examination of specific images. Some, for example, dream of snakes or rockets. Jung would not look for evidence of the sexual in these symbols, but for why the one dream contained a snake and the other a rocket. In understanding this difference, the interpretation becomes significant.

In contemporary psychoanalysis, Fonagy *et al.* (2012) have argued that the dream: (1) functions as a means to metabolize emotional life; (2) results from *mentalization* (see entry, *mentalization*); (3) is essential to the formation of an internal world and subjectivity (Fonagy, 2007); (4) is a crucial source of information on affects; and (5) reactivates and symbolizes emotions related to traumatic experience stored in implicit memory.

Filip Kovacevic (2013) describes Lacan's approach to understanding the dream. For him there are two aspects. First there is

'imagining the symbol', that is, analyzing the transformation of the *symbolic* idea into the image, which is the work of actual dreaming with the dream as the final product. And, second, 'symbolizing the image', transforming the given image into the symbol, which is the work of actual dream interpretation. Here Lacan introduced one of the ideas that marked his entire psychoanalytic opus, which is that 'the unconscious is structured like a language.' This means that what is done in dream interpretation is actually the kind of translation of the material which was already translated once before. And, as in every other translation, certain shades of meaning (sense) will inevitably be lost. This is why Lacan emphasized Freud's correctness in claiming that no dream could be completely analyzed – there is always something that cannot be recalled on awakening. (p. 80; emphasis added)

Finally, Blass (2002) approaches dream theory from what she calls, 'experiential quality of meaningfulness'.

point for reflection and practice
• Fonagy (2012) and colleagues have shown that 'dreams are a pre-symbolic transitional stage in thought fulfilling a key function in the patient's processing of emotional material, particularly of an overwhelming or traumatic kind; dreams are key to a comprehensive understanding of the patient's unconscious attitudes and preconscious thoughts, particularly in relation to the clinical situation; dreams on the couch are part of a complex pattern of communication established between patient and analyst over a considerable period charged with the burden of carrying content concerning all aspects of transference and *countertransference* communication' (2012, p. xxiv; emphasis added).

KEY TEXTS

- Blass, R. (2002) *The Meaning of the Dream in Psychoanalysis* (Albany, NY: SUNY Press)
- Blechner, M. J. (1995) 'The Patient's Dreams and the Countertransference', *Psychoanalytic Dialogues*, 5 (1): pp. 1–25
- Blechner, M. J. (2001) *The Dream Frontier* (New York, NY: Routledge)
- Fonagy, P. *et al.* (eds) (2012) *The Significance of Dreams: Bridging Clinical and Extraclinical Research in Psychoanalysis* (London, UK: Karnac Books)
- Fosshage, J. L. (2013) 'The Dream Narrative: Unconscious Organizing Activity in Context', *Contemporary Psychoanalysis*, 49 (2): pp. 253–258
- Freud, S. (1900) *The Interpretation of Dreams*. Standard Edition, 4–5
- Kovacevic, F. (2013) 'A Lacanian Approach to Dream Interpretation', *Dreaming*, 23 (1): pp. 78–89
- Loden, S. (2003) 'The Fate of the Dream in Contemporary Psychoanalysis', *Journal of the American Psychoanalytic Association*, 51 (1): pp. 43–70

drive

SEE ALSO **attachment; conflict and compromise formation; ego; sublimation**

For Freud, the energy necessary for psychic life is produced by both libido and aggression and expressed, released or made available for use through the body: the drives. Psychic energy, moreover, is continuously generated but present in uneven amounts. Most importantly, while the source of the drive is biological, the drive itself is always a psychic representation; drives, thus, can be known only through their effects, just as gravitational fields are known only through their effects. Freud, in using the German word, 'Anlehnung' (to lean on) avoids the problem of reductionism: the drive is formed when the psyche leans on the soma (i.e. the drives are rooted in the body but not reducible to the body and thus should not be equated with the more limited notion of fixed instinct).

Many in *object* relations theory hold that the human infant is not driven towards pleasure but towards seeking object connection. Ronald Fairbairn and Harry S. Sullivan assert this position most radically and argue that primary motivations for action are to be found in the object relation. Others (e.g. Loewald, Winnicott and

Sandler) hold that drive states are the outcome of particular affective frames of the mother–infant relations. Here, the drives emerge not from bodily states but from the actual relationship (see entry, *attachment*). Kernberg (2001), in one among the many attempts to rethink the drive theory, argues that affects are among the central motivators for behaviour. Not only do they perform a communicative function in the infant–caregiver relationship; they also structure and organize the drive states.

In France, the dual drive theory and the relationship between drive and object have been reimagined, especially in the works of Jean Laplanche (2004) and André Green. Both consider the importance of unconscious destructive and self-destructive drives and how they manifest in attacks on object relations. They are especially interested in the role unconscious erotization plays in the mother–infant relation. Green (2012), in his revision of drive theory, writes:

> But what I am proposing which is new is that we consider the drive as matrix of the subject. In point of fact it is absolutely impossible to attempt to conceive of the foundations of the subject without seeing the work of the drive in operation. An 'I', or a subject with its instinctual dimension amputated, is an inanimate, mechanical, operative and, if you wish, cognitive entity. What defines the drive is, on the one hand, as Freud indicated, that it is a limit or border concept between the psychic and the somatic which grafts the psyche definitively on to the body. And, on the other hand, that it is the demand of the body made on the mind – 'the demand for work' – so that the mind finds solutions that make it possible to overcome the situation of lack. It demands an end to the tensions that inhabit it and cries out for satisfaction. In other words, the development of the psyche is less dependent on its relation with reality than on the necessity of dealing with internal constraints, pushing the mind to search for solutions in order to obtain the satisfactions that it is lacking. (p. 114)

Drive theory aligns with contemporary debates on emergentism (Elder-Vass, 2010): Because the psyche 'leans' on the soma, the drives will be highly variable and specific to both person and developmental history. The drive has a source (the body/biology), an aim (expression and cessation of excitation by discharge) and an object (person, self, mouth, breast, genitals, anus) and can be differentiated into what Freud called partial or component drives (oral, anal). The term 'cathexis' is used to describe the amount of libido or energy transferred or invested in an object, idea or person for need satisfaction. With anticathexis, the *ego* recognizes the need to inhibit unrealistic, immoral or unacceptable demands of the id.

Paul Verhaeghe (2011), a contemporary Lacanian, writes of the important distinction Lacanians make between desire and drive:

> In contrast with a drive, desire does not wish to be satisfied in so far as this satisfaction implies an end. On the contrary, assuming that desire has a goal, it is for it to remain intact, to continue. The goal of desire is to go on desiring. A desire for inconsolability. The pleasure that is gained from this has a different nature from the pleasure of the fulfillment of this desire. It seems that these are two entirely different pleasures. It is by no means rare for the last form to be experienced as a disappointment, showing that the first type of pleasure was experienced as being more important. A toddler leafing through advertising brochures in the weeks leading up to Christmas is always looking for 'it', trying to make a choice. He/she is actually very little different from the adolescent leafing through forbidden magazines also dreaming of 'it', also hesitating, searching. In each case 'it' can never fulfill the expectation. In the transition from desire to gratification, something is lost that could neither be expressed in the desire nor achieved in its fulfillment. (p. 151)

points for reflection and practice
- In our everyday practice, we often talk about patients with 'impulse control' problems or difficulties with *affect regulation*; yet seldom do we seek the connections that these ideas have to the literature and thinking on drive states.
- Many ego psychologists refer to drive fusion: the joining of the libidinal and aggressive drives to produce a kind of neutral energy for effective action, learning and appropriate levels of feeling. Many refer to this as sublimated (see entry, *sublimation*) energy, made available for creative thinking.

KEY TEXTS
- Elder-Vass, D. (2010) *The Causal Power of Social Structures: Emergence, Structure and Agency* (Cambridge, UK: Cambridge University Press)

- Fairbairn, W. (1954) *An Object-Relations Theory of the Personality* (New York, NY: Basic Books)
- Freud, S. (1915) *Instincts and Their Vicissitudes.* Standard Edition, 14
- Freud, S. (1920) *Beyond the Pleasure Principle.* Standard Edition, 18
- Freud, S. (1923) *The Ego and the Id.* Standard Edition, 19
- Green, A. (2005) *Key Ideas for a Contemporary Psychoanalysis: Misrecognition and Recognition of the Unconscious* (London, UK: Routledge)
- Greenberg, S. and Mitchell, J. (1983) *Object Relations in Psychoanalytic Theory* (Cambridge, MA: Harvard University Press)
- Kernberg, O. (2001) 'Object Relations, Affects, and Drives: Toward a New Synthesis', *Psychoanalytic Inquiry,* 21 (5): pp. 604–619
- Laplanche, J. (2004) 'The So-Called "Death Drive": A Sexual Drive', *British Journal of Psychotherapy,* 20 (4): pp. 455–471
- Sandler, J. and Sandler, A. (1998) *Internal Objects Revisited* (London, UK: Karnac Books)
- Sullivan, H. S. (1953) *Interpersonal Theory of Psychiatry* (New York, NY: W. W. Norton & Company)

e

ego

SEE ALSO defence mechanisms; imaginary; symbolic

With the introduction of the structural theory (1923), Freud postulated a tripartite division of the mind: the id, the ego and the superego. Freud never uses these terms and preferred the German, 'Das Ich', 'Das Es' and 'Das Über-Ich', to the Latinized versions (Bettelheim 1983). Obviously, these were not meant to refer to *real* things, nor do they have neurological correlates; this was a 'model' of the mind, not to be confused with the actual brain or with a specific mind. Moreover, these were not discrete and separate but overlapping agencies or functions of the mind. With this fundamental shift in thinking, Freud assigned to the ego the role of mediator between the id and reality, acting as a kind of regulator of the id's urge towards expression of desire. The ego, governed by the reality principle, functions as a conductor, directing the id towards more appropriate expressions. And to achieve the repression of inappropriate desire and urge, the ego deploys 'mechanisms of defence' (see entry, *defence mechanisms*). The ego, in short, converts, diverts and transforms the id's urgings into more pragmatic and realistic satisfactions. It moves to control and regulate the id's influence, to achieve satisfaction despite the limitations imposed by reality. While the id forms an image of the desire or pushes towards its expression, the ego strategizes to realize desire and through time, borrowing psychic energy from the id, builds capacity and function: memory, perception, self-awareness. Finally, the inchoate urges and needs of the id give way to a formed ego and a unique self emerges.

Heinz Hartman, in his controversial modification of Freud's structural theory, postulated that a healthy ego requires a sphere of conflict-free and 'autonomous ego functions': memory, perception, motility and reality testing among them. In this sphere, ego functions emerge not only free of conflict but also innately, and on a predictable, maturational timetable. A healthy ego, in short, functions free of psychic conflict and treatment aims at the expansion of the conflict-free sphere; the role of therapy is to form an alliance with healthy parts of the ego in its battle to subordinate the drives. For Melanie Klein, the ego, in its early development, protects itself from its own destructive impulse through its *projection* into an external *object* (Klein, 1932).

In one of the most important and lasting critiques of ego psychology, Jacque Lacan distinguishes between the 'ideal ego' and the 'ego ideal'. The 'ideal ego', for Lacan, exists in what he calls the *'imaginary* order' and the 'ego ideal' in the *'symbolic* order' (see entries, *mirror stage, imaginary* and *symbolic* orders). The ideal ego refers to the ego's striving for perfection in what Lacan called the mirror stage, when the infant first sees itself in the mirror (6–18 months) and in seeing the image of the self, the child experiences a discordance between the idealizing image in the mirror and the actual and more chaotic reality of real bodies. In the mirror the child imagines a whole, complete and bounded object. It refers to the idealized self-image in the imaginary order (Lacan sometimes called this the small Other): the way we would like to be, or like others to see us. The 'ego ideal', by contrast, refers to the self as seen from the ideal point: the point of perfection, the agency whose gaze we impress with our ego image. Lacan referred to this as the big Other who watches over me and propels me to give my best, the Ideal-I to be followed and actualized.

points for reflection and practice
- Ego Function assessment (EFA) is used as a quantitative technique for assessing ego functions.
- The Psychosocial Inventory of Ego Strengths (PIES) (Markstrom and Marshall, 2007; Markstrom *et al.*, 1997) is used as a self-report measure for Erikson's ego strengths.
- The assessment of ego strength is aimed at understanding the patient's ability to maintain a sense of identity when confronted with conflict or distress.

KEY TEXTS
- Busch, F. (1995) *The Ego at the Center of Clinical Technique* (Lanham, MD: Jason Aronson)

- Goldstein, E. (1995) *Ego Psychology and Social Work Practice* (New York, NY: Simon and Schuster)
- Gray, P. (2005) *The Ego and Analysis of Defense* (Oxford, UK: Rowman & Littlefield)
- Hartmann, H. (1964) *Essays on Ego Psychology: Selected Problems in Psychoanalytic Theory* (Madison, CT: International Universities Press)
- Lacan, J. (1977) *The Mirror Stage as Formative in the Function of the I as Revealed in Psychoanalytic Experience* in *Écrits: A Selection* (A. Sheridan Trans.) (London, UK: Tavistock), pp. 1–7
- Markstrom, C. and Marshall, S. (2007) 'The Psychosocial Inventory of Ego Strengths: Examination of Theory and Psychometric Properties', *Journal of Adolescence*, 30 (1): pp. 63–79
- Wallerstein, R. (2002) 'The Growth and Transformation of American Ego Psychology', *Journal of the American Psychoanalytic Association*, 50 (1): pp. 135–168
- Žižek, S. (2006) *How to Read Lacan* (London, UK: Granta)

emerging adulthood

SEE ALSO **adolescence; developmental stages; gender**

In 1995, Jeffrey Jensen Arnett introduced the idea of emerging adulthood to capture what he and growing numbers of psychologists and sociologists describe as a new stage in human development: emerging adulthood. Today, his research has evolved into a transdisciplinary professional society, journals and hundreds of research projects and monographs. What was once described in the developmental literature as late *adolescence* or early adulthood has now been reimagined as emerging adulthood. Across social, class, race and educational background, Arnett finds a pattern: a shared sense of feeling in-between, a liminal space. This new phenomenon, Arnett and others describe as a product of recent changes in economic life. On the one hand, these young people feel and experience a growing distance from adolescent struggles, conflicts and dependencies. While Arnett (2007) has aligned himself with a mostly anti-psychoanalytic understanding of youth development, it's almost impossible to imagine the relevance of his work without the concept of psychic conflicts. Indeed, his entire oeuvre is premised on notions of psychic conflict, though unstated. On the other, they share a perception of feeling intractable dependence on family ties. What most surprised Arnett in his early research, however, were their accounts of struggles with personal identity. More recently, arguments have been made that during this new period, substance abuse, addiction and risky behaviours may be tolerated or even promoted (Sussman and Arnett, 2014). Quite reminiscent of Erikson's language, the features of emerging adulthood include:

> 1) Age of identity exploration. Young people are deciding who they are and what they want out of work, school and love; 2) Age of instability. The post-high school years are marked by repeated residence changes, as young people either go to college or live with friends or a romantic partner. For most, frequent moves end as families and careers are established in the 30s; 3) Age of self-focus. Freed of the parent- and society-directed routine of school, young people try to decide what they want to do, where they want to go and who they want to be with – before those choices get limited by the constraints of marriage, children and a career; 4) Age of feeling in between. Many emerging adults say they are taking responsibility for themselves, but still do not completely feel like adults; 5) Age of possibilities. Optimism reigns. Most emerging adults believe they have good chances of living 'better than their parents did,' and even if their parents divorced, they believe they'll find a lifelong soul mate. (Tanner and Arnett, 2009, pp. 39–45)

point for reflection and practice
- Many, if not most, of the theorists of emerging adulthood have altogether elided the *psychodynamic* implications of the theory. This leaves the theory ontologically flat and clinically limited. In short, how are changes in the timing of transitions internalized and experienced as conflicts?

KEY TEXTS
- Arnett, J. J. (2004) *Emerging Adulthood: The Winding Road from the Late Teens through the Twenties* (Oxford, UK: Oxford University Press)
- Arnett, J. J. (2007) 'Suffering, Selfish, Slackers? Myths and Reality about Emerging Adults', *Journal of Youth and Adolescence*, 36 (1): pp. 23–29
- Sussman, S. and Arnett, J. J. (2014) 'Emerging Adulthood: Developmental Period Facilitative of the Addictions', *Evaluation & the Health Professions*. Published Online. DOI: 10.1177/0163278714521812

empathy

SEE ALSO developmental stages; good enough mother (holding environment)

The role of empathy in the development of self has not figured prominently in classical psychoanalytic theory; however, for interpersonal psychoanalysts, *object* relations theorists, and self psychologists, empathy has emerged as a central idea, especially in understanding the emotional link between a child and caregiver, and the efficacy of the therapist–client relationship. For Heinz Kohut, empathy refers to the 'capacity to think and feel oneself into the inner life of another person' (1974, p. 82) and is central to the method of psychoanalysis (i.e. empathy is the instrument used by psychoanalysts to collect and use data). For Kohut, while empathy accomplishes a kind of affective merger, *identification* or attunement, it is not clear how his understanding accounts for why one may also 'laugh or cry with someone and yet have little understanding about why the other is laughing or crying' (Hollan, 2008, p. 476). Ralph Greenson, in the 1960s, considered the role of empathy in *countertransference*. After Greenson an increasing emphasis was given to the role of empathy in therapeutic communication. Others (Buie, 1981) have looked at the specific psychological mechanisms at work in this dynamic form of intuitive communication, specifically empathy. 'From the metapsychological perspective, the debate continues between those who assign empathy a decisive role in the discovery of the unconscious and the therapeutic activity of the psychoanalyst (Heinz Kohut) and those who deny that empathy can play a role in identifying the unconscious' (Buie, 1981, p. 287).

Halpern (2001) describes empathy as a combined cognitive and emotional capacity to understand 'how and why a person is angry, not only that he or she is angry'. There is also an intersubjective dynamic to empathy: 'one cannot empathize with another until one's imaginings about the other's emotional states and perspectives can be confirmed or disconfirmed in ongoing interaction' (Hollan, 2008, p. 476).

In phenomenological psychology and philosophy, an important distinction is made between two approaches to understanding empathy, both of direct relevance to *psychodynamic* thinking and practice: 'theory' and 'simulation' (Zahavi, 2008). While both aim at conceptualizing interpersonal understanding, the 'theory' approach (Ratcliffe, 2012) maintains 'that our ability to understand other people's mental states depends upon deployment of a systematically organized body of conceptual knowledge, which is domain-specific and largely tacit. Simulation theorists, in contrast, emphasise the ability to use our own cognitive resources to model the mental states of other people (see e.g. Davies and Stone, 1995)'.

Recent work in social psychology (Banissy and Ward, 2007; De Wall, 2010; Gazolla *et al.*, 2006) aims to examine the neuronal foundation of empathy. They argue that empathy operates automatically, has an adaptive significance in human evolution and operates through imitation and mimicry. They look in particular at mirroring and at the single-cell and neural-system levels to develop an argument for cognitive and social psychological constructs. Ironically, it's hard to find the social in the social psychological, given that they argue that an essential 'neural mirroring solves the "problem of other minds" (how we can access and understand the minds of others) and makes intersubjectivity possible, thus facilitating social behavior' (Iacoboni, 2009, p. 653).

points for reflection and practice
- Empathy is one experiential mode of grasping emotional states as well as a 'perceptual' activity that may operate in conjunction with logical inquiry (Halperin, 2001, 2003).
- It is important to examine the barriers to empathy: *anxiety,* countertransference, time limitations.
- Phenomenologists have much to contribute to our understanding of empathy and how we practice. See, in particular, the work of Matthew Ratcliffe (2012) and Douglas Hollan (2008).

KEY TEXTS
- Buie, D. (1981) 'Empathy: Its Nature and Limitation', *Journal of the American Psychoanalytic Association,* 29 (2): pp. 281–307
- Charon, R. (2001) 'Narrative Medicine', *The Journal of the American Medical Association,* 286 (15): pp. 1897–1902
- Gibbons, S. (2011) 'Understanding Empathy as a Complex Construct: A Review of the Literature', *Clinical Social Work Journal,* 39 (3): pp. 243–252
- Grant, D., and Harari, E. (2011) 'Empathy in Psychoanalytic Theory and Practice', *Psychoanalytic Inquiry,* 31 (1): pp. 3–16

- Greenson, R. (1960) 'Empathy and Its Vicissitudes', *International Journal of Psychoanalysis*, 41: pp. 418–424
- Hollan, D. (2008) 'Being There: On the Imaginative Aspects of Understanding Others and Being Understood', *Ethos*, 36 (4): pp. 475–489
- Halpern, J. (2001) *From Detached Concern to Empathy: Humanizing Medical Practice* (New York, NY: Oxford University Press)
- Halpern, J. (2003) 'What Is Clinical Empathy?' *Journal of General Internal Medicine*, 18 (8): pp. 670–674
- Kohut, H. (1959) 'Introspection, Empathy, and Psychoanalysis', *Journal of the American Psychoanalytic Association*, 7 (3): pp. 459–483
- Orange, D. (2002) 'There Is No Outside: Empathy and Authenticity in Psychoanalytic Process', *Psychoanalytical Psychology*, 19 (4): pp. 686–700
- Ornstein, P. (2011) 'The Centrality of Empathy in Psychoanalysis', *Psychoanalytic Inquiry*, 31 (5): pp. 437–447
- Pigman, G. (1995) 'Freud and the History of Empathy', *International Journal of Psychoanalysis*, 76: pp. 237–256
- Ratcliffe, M. (2012) 'Phenomenology as a Form of Empathy', *Inquiry*, 55 (5): pp. 473–495
- Schwaber, E. (1981) 'Empathy: A Mode of Analytic Listening', *Psychoanalytical Inquiry*, 1 (3): pp. 357–392

envy, greed, jealousy, gratitude

SEE ALSO **ambivalence; depressive position; developmental stages**

For Melanie Klein, envy, greed, jealousy and gratitude form a cluster of mental states and developmental possibilities. Envy is foremost experienced as an angry feeling or sadistic (oral and anal) expression of destructive impulse directed at the mother's breasts (i.e. the crucial source of nourishment over which the infant exercises no power). Klein referred to the impulse as 'primary destructiveness' (i.e. innately present but elaborated by the environment and adverse experience). Envy, however, is not just a destructive feeling aimed at someone possessing or enjoying something desirable; its power is realized in the impulse to spoil it or take it. Hanna Segal writes that often underlying envy is a 'wish to exhaust the object entirely, not only in order to possess all its goodness but also to deplete the *object* purposefully so that it no longer contains anything enviable' (1974, p. 41 emphasis added). Marcus West (2010) argues that the experience of envy is indexed to personality. He writes 'that envy is a secondary phenomenon related to the psyche's early functioning which has an implicit aversion to separation and difference and a preference for sameness. This is not an explicit behavioural principle, such as Freud's understanding of the pleasure principle; instead it represents the psyche's means of recognizing, classifying, making sense of, and thereby processing the infant's experience' (p. 460).

Priscilla Roth (2008) writes that 'Any study of envy is at the same time a study of the defences constructed against envy, and these defences are constructed not only because envy is an inherently painful emotion, nor because it is felt to be so reprehensible and *guilt*-inducing. The experience of envy is defended against because it is an acknowledgement of the otherness of the other, with all the terrifying consequences that arise from such an acknowledgement: foremost, dependence on an object who is not under one's control' (p. 8).

While envy involves dyads, jealousy is experienced in triangles. Jealousy, for Klein, 'is based on envy, but involves a relation to at least two people; it is mainly concerned with love that the subject feels is his due and has been taken away, or is in danger of being taken away, from him by his rival' (1957, p. 181). Rooted in *Oedipal* dynamics, jealousy expresses a wish for an exclusive relationship to the primary object. Some have argued for a quantum of 'good enough' jealous feeling for coping with *ambivalence* and what Minsky (1998) calls the normal precariousness of gendered identity. Freud writes of jealousy: 'Jealousy is one of those affective states, like grief, that may be described as normal. If anyone appears to be without it, the inference is justified that it has undergone severe repression and consequently plays all the greater part in his unconscious mental life' (1922, p. 197). For Yates, on the other hand, jealousy takes a particular and unique form with contemporary constructions of masculinity: 'because male jealousy has histori-cally occupied a key psychosocial role in helping to define and guard the social and emotional boundaries of male subjectivities. It is thus not surprising that if men are finding it hard to cope with the uncer-tainty and losses of modernity, then jealousy is one of the main places where such anxieties might emerge' (Yates, 2000).

While 'greed' shares with envy a powerful aggressive impulse it lacks the spoiling quality; in short, one may intensely desire what another possesses but the desiring does not produce or lead to the destruction of the person possessing that quality.

'Gratitude' for Klein is the opposite of envy and, like this entire cluster of mental states, has its origin in early development, environmental possibilities and *ego* integration of early conflicts. With a reduction in greed and envy, there is an increase in the wish to preserve and spare the good object. Gratitude not only modifies envy but it also brings repeated experience of pleasure in gratifying exchanges, thus enabling gratitude at deeper levels and increasing capacity for making 'reparation'. Klein emphasizes that gratitude is the goal of the psychoanalytic process (Polledri, 2003).

In her work on jealousy, Marcianne Blévi (2009) presents a series of very useful and rich case studies focused on the intractability of jealousy. She argues that jealousy is especially complicated by the fact that the jealous person cannot let go of the feeling and that the jealous state is maintained because it substitutes for feeling nothing and is rooted in a psychic history of damaged trust in self and others.

points for reflection and practice
- It is important in practice to distinguish between envy and jealousy as they each entail very different relational and intrapsychic dynamics.
- Unresolved jealousy can lead to difficulty in forming and maintaining meaningful relationships.
- Envy and jealousy may also lead to difficulty in sharing, ownership, possessiveness. For therapeutic purposes it is essential to discover and pinpoint the roots of destructive envy or jealousy. Unbalanced and troubled family relationships are often sources of these ways of feeling and relating.

KEY TEXTS
- Blévis, M. (2009) *Jealousy: True Stories of Love's Favorite Decoy* (New York, NY: Other Press)
- Clarke, S. (2003) 'Psychoanalytic Sociology and the Interpretation of Emotion', *Journal for the Theory of Social Behavior*, 33 (2): pp. 145–163
- Klein, M. (1957) *Envy and Gratitude: A Study of Unconscious Forces* (London, UK: Hogarth Press)
- Richards, B. (2000) 'The Anatomy of Envy', *Psychoanalytic Studies*, 2 (1): pp. 65–76

- Sayers, J. (2000) *Kleinians: Psychoanalysis Inside Out* (London, UK: Polity Press)
- Winnicott, D. W. (1965) 'The Development of the Capacity for Concern' in D. W. Winnicott (ed.), *The Maturational Process and the Facilitating Environment: Studies in the Theory of Emotional Development* (London, UK: Hogarth Press and the Institute of Psycho-Analysis), pp. 73–82
- Wurmser, L. and Jarass, H. (eds) (2011) *Jealousy and Envy: New Views about Two Powerful Feelings* (New York, NY: Taylor & Francis)
- Yates, C. (2000) 'Masculinity and Good Enough Jealousy', *Psychoanalytic Studies*, 2 (1): pp. 77–88

evidence-based practice

SEE ALSO **diagnosis and the DSM; positivism and critical realism; social constructivism (or anti-essentialism)**

The term 'evidence-based practice' (EBP), sometimes called empirically supported treatment (EST), refers to interventions, in health and mental health care, backed by research which shows statistically significant effectiveness of treatment. The movement began in the 1990s, mostly in physical medicine, and then spread rapidly throughout the helping professions. The criteria used to establish research norms, however, tend to altogether elide theoretical, qualitative and case study research; quantitative methods (e.g. random control trials, systematic reviews) are used to narrowly define what counts as evidence. In her recent criticism of RCT, British philosopher of science Nancy Cartwright argues that the RCT is not the 'gold standard' it is often assumed to be. She argues that the RCT does not provide evidence or results exportable to other policy or practice environments and 'that something works "somewhere" is no warranty for it to work "for us" or even that it works "generally"' (Cartwright, 2007).

Clinical social work, along with clinical psychology, has increasingly faced challenges to the case-study method of producing and conveying knowledge in the moment-to-moment and over the lifetime of long clinical encounters. Best described as a social movement, now called evidence-based practice, or promising practices, or best practices, EBP pervades the entire universe of human services and helping practices (e.g. business, medicine, nursing, education) and has been led in mental health mostly by researchers in the academy, in alliance with the insurance and pharmaceutical industries, managed care companies and NIMH. EBP calls for special and singular kinds of evidence and manualized (i.e. standardized, one-size fits all) approaches to practice (Cartwright, 2007, 2011). And the expectation is to provide a kind of supporting evidence and guidelines for 'appropriate' or 'best' or even 'ethical' practice that we would not imagine from many in the natural and physical sciences (e.g. we know the existence of gravity, for example, not because we see it but because it has effects which can be explained by abstract theory).

Much of the research, moreover, supporting the evidence-base movement derives from a longer history of pragmatism, behaviourism, and positivist research methods in the United States. The influence from each, especially in the United States, is important. The pragmatist claim is: that which is, is that which works (e.g. medication works, therefore it must have something to do with what causes the illness) focuses attention on outcomes and instrumental logics (i.e. you make this intervention and you get this result, despite context and the enormous variability of human experience, social and mental life). The behaviourist claim, not unrelated to pragmatism is: mental life and human suffering fundamentally lack meaning and can be addressed through empirical, measurable and instrumental interventions. The positivist claim, which dominates most contemporary clinical science (especially in medicine and psychiatry and much of academic psychology) is: explanation and understanding are conflated with or reduced to prediction (i.e. if C and D follow with regularity from A and B, they must somehow be causally related). All of the above undervalue or altogether elide the nature and quality of the human relationship in the helping encounter (e.g. education, medicine, psychotherapy).

What constitutes a psychoanalytic fact, moreover, has always been in dispute and will no doubt always remain contentious. Ricoeur identified four criteria according to which a 'psychoanalytic fact' is delimited and distinguished from observable facts: (1) the intimate relation between psychoanalytic facts and language and meaning (i.e. the semantic dimension of desire); (2) the significance of transference and the intersubjective field dominant in the psychoanalytic situation; (3) the coherence and resistance of psychical reality opposed to material reality; and (4) the narrative character of psychoanalytic experience.

While recent research on the effectiveness of *psychodynamic* therapy (see Shedler, 2010; Hinshelwood, 2013) 'uses methods from the EBP movement to argue for the effectiveness of treatment, for the most part psychodynamic approaches are under assault in academe, from insurance companies, and funding agencies, even as empirical research has begun to corroborate many of the most significant analytic ideas: the role and importance of understanding unconscious processes, including implicit affective and motivational processes; the importance of early *attachment* in later development and psychopathology; the role of personality as a diathesis for many disorders and the source of much of their comorbidity; and the role of the therapeutic relationship in effecting change in psychotherapy'(Bradley and Weston, 2005, p. 927; emphasis added).

Webb (2001, p.76) similarly argues, 'rather than conceiving of social workers and clients as social billiard balls, passively bounding through a world of causal and objective relations, they should be conceived as dynamic, interconnected agents who make decisions according to heuristic devices which are bound up with specific cultural formulations'. In his discussion of evidence-based interventions and social work, Webb identifies four (p. 75) related dimensions for consideration:

- Evidence-based interventions as 'mediated' by changes in information and communication technologies as they combine with other developments, such as new organizational and policy structures.
- Evidence-based interventions as 'situated' in highly varied and complex practitioner and client decision-making environments.
- Evidence-based intervention knowledge as 'provisional' and developing.
- Evidence-based intervention implementation as 'pragmatically' driven.

Webb further asserts that evidence-based interventions do not slide 'smoothly and naturally between the external world of "facts" and subjective world of "mental processes"' (p. 75).

Irwin Hoffman (2009) has offered for psychoanalysis an especially important critique of the EBP and his 2009 paper sparked contentious debate and many rejoinders. He argued that psychoanalysis is best understood as a nonobjectivist, hermeneutic paradigm where existential uncertainty dominates the analytic encounter. Therapists, he argued, make decisions, moment by moment, 'influenced by culture, by sociopolitical mind-set, by personal values, by *countertransference*, and by other factors in ways that are never fully known'. And due to what he called the 'consequential uniqueness' of each interaction and the indeterminacy associated with the free will of the participants', he defended the individual case study as the best means of advancing knowledge in psychodynamic theory and practice (p. 1043).

points for reflection and practice

- Practitioners are challenged in the era of managed care and evidence-based practice to think about what counts as evidence, how evidence is understood and how evidence is represented in the mental health record.
- One must always ask questions about what they take to be true or knowable (i.e. the ontological questions) because not everything we take to be true is empirically observable (i.e. gravity, dreams, drives).

KEY TEXTS

- Bradley, R. and Westen, D. (2005) 'The Psychodynamics of Borderline Personality Disorder: A View from Developmental Psychopathology', *Development and Psychopathology*, 17 (4): pp. 927–957
- Cartwright, N. (2007) 'Are RCTs the Gold Standard?' *BioSocieties*, 2 (1): pp. 11–20
- Drisko, J. W. and Grady, M. D. (2012) *Evidence-Based Practice in Clinical Social Work* (New York, NY: Springer)
- Gray, M., Plath, D. and Webb, S. A. (2009) *Evidence-Based Social Work: A Critical Stance* (London: Routledge)
- Hoffman, I. Z. (2009) 'Doublethinking Our Way to "Scientific" Legitimacy: The Desiccation of Human Experience', *Journal of the American Psychoanalytic Association*, 57 (5): pp. 1043–1069
- Hofmann, S. G. and Weinberger, J. (eds) (2007) *The Art and Science of Psychotherapy* (New York, NY: Routledge)
- Rustin, M. (2010) 'Varieties of Psychoanalytic Research', *Psychoanalytic Psychotherapy*, 24 (4): pp. 380–397

extimacy

SEE ALSO conscious (unconscious, preconscious)

This neologism, coined first by Jacque Lacan, has been used especially by critical psychologists (Pavón-Cuéllar, 2014) to challenge conventional distinctions between exteriority and interiority, surface and depth, outside and inside. The concept refers to the equal ontological status of inside and outside. The unconscious, for example, is not an expression of interiority. It is fundamentally intersubjective. Pavón-Cuéllar (2014) writes that 'expressions of the duality exteriority-intimacy would be hypothetically replaceable by the notion of "extimacy," which precisely joins exteriority with intimacy, and states explicitly the interpenetration and mutual transformation of both spheres. These spheres are no longer what they were in conventional psychology. They actually fade away. Exteriority is rather intimacy, but intimacy, as exteriority, is rather an "extimacy" that is no longer either intimacy or exteriority' (pp. 661–664).

KEY TEXTS

- Pavón-Cuéllar, D. (2010) *From the Conscious Interior to an Exterior Unconscious: Lacan, Discourse Analysis, and Social Psychology* (London: Karnac Books)
- Pavón-Cuéllar, D. (2014) 'Extimacy' in Thomas Teo (ed.), *Encyclopedia of Critical Psychology* (New York: Springer)

f

fantasy (vs phantasy)

SEE ALSO object; projection

Some make a distinction between phantasy and fantasy and, while not without controversy (Laplanche and Pontalis, 2012), the former generally refers in Kleinian language to unconscious, prelinguistic, early stages of development, where reality is not yet differentiated from imagination. According to the Kleinians, it is through phantasy that the infant comprehends the world: imagines it, relates feelings to objects, makes distinctions between inside and outside, comes to have thoughts about the world and relates to it (i.e. through *projection* and introjection). 'Infantile feelings and phantasies leave, as it were, their imprints on the mind, imprints that do not fade away but get stored up, remain active, and exert a continuous and powerful influence on the emotional and intellectual life of the individual' (Klein, 1975, p. 290). For Kleinians, phantasies are essential to our understanding not only of development but also more generally of thought, behaviour and the internal *object* world. Phantasy may also function in the formation and maintenance of object relations: good and *bad objects* are produced through projection and introjection. Phantasy enables the construction of identity and, through projection, social relations with others. Phantasies, thus, modify experience and the surrounding world by infusing it with meaning and significance.

Phantasies, according to some, are necessary to the transformation of instinct into thoughts and images; hunger, for example, may produce the phantasy of a satisfying object. Moreover, because phantasies derive from instincts at the border of the physical and psychical, they are experienced as both physical and mental events; the child sucking a thumb experiences a phantasy of feeding. And for Klein, because phantasy is developed in play, it is with play therapy that early development can be best understood, not through the method of *free association*.

Paul Verhaeghe writes of fantasy,

Why do we have fantasies anyway? Fantasy – the representation, staging or detailed spinning out of a story – is undoubtedly one of the most essential components of eroticism. Without it, the erotic element is reduced to the animal level and is not even erotic anymore. With fantasies, it becomes human. Moreover, these fantasies cannot be limited to individual daydreams. They also form the basis of every kind of art. As Freud wrote in his article on 'Creative Writers and Day-Dreaming', the artist successfully expresses his own fantasies in such a way that others can also enjoy them, with the ultimate intention of acquiring power and erotic allure. (p. 10)

For some the shift in spelling, from phantasy to fantasy, signifies a fundamental difference in the quality of mental events. Fantasy, here, may refer to conscious daydreaming, *reverie* and imaginings about the future, wish or desire.

point for reflection and practice
- Unconscious phantasies, based on enquiry into the nature and quality of object relations, may be used to think about past and present experiences.

KEY TEXTS
- Bott Spillius, E. (2001) 'Freud and Klein on the Concept of Phantasy', *International Journal of Psychoanalysis*, 82 (2): pp. 361–373
- Forrester, M. (2006) 'Projective Identification and Intersubjectivity', *Theory & Psychology*, 16 (6): pp. 783–802
- Grotstein, J. (2008) 'The Overarching Role of Unconscious Phantasy', *Psychoanalytic Inquiry*, 28 (2): pp. 190–205
- Isaacs, S. (1943) 'The Nature and Function of Phantasy', *International Journal of Psychoanalysis*, 29 (1948): pp. 73–97
- Klein, M. (1975) *Love, Guilt and Reparation and Other Works 1921–1945* (London, UK: Karnac Books)
- Kris, A. (1996) *Free Association: Methods and Process* (Revised and Updated Revision of the Yale University Press, 1982) (Hillsdale, NJ: The Analytic Press)

- Laplanche, J. and Pontalis, J. (2012) *The Language of Psychoanalysis* (London, UK: Karnac Books)
- Riccardo, S. (2003) *Unconscious Phantasy* (London, UK: Karnac Books)

free association

SEE ALSO **dream**

Free association, the method introduced by Freud to replace hypnosis, is aimed at producing uncensored thoughts and feelings, thereby allowing greater access to unconscious motivation. The technique asks the patient to altogether abandon socially acceptable or prescribed conventions of communication by freely associating or saying whatever comes to mind. The method assumes that memories are ordered in associative networks and that over time the crucial ones will surface. The therapist, by assigning no special attention or importance to particular elements in the unfolding narrative, must remain in a state of equally open receptivity, or 'evenly suspended attention' in order grasp the flow of associations. For Freud, in the free-flowing expression of thought and feeling one finds evidence of conflicts/tension between unconscious impulse and a censorial repressive system aimed at the concealment of meaning and the preservation of safety. This is not unlike his understanding of how the *dream* is constructed: unconscious impulse (i.e. fantasy and wish) seek discharge but face resistance and censorship. It is only through various forms of substitution that the discharge is accomplished. With free association, such as dreaming, substitution is more easily accomplished than in normal waking life. In Freud's later thinking, his attention shifted to the relationship between resistance and its principal manifestation: transference. Others, especially Melanie Klein and Bion, understood this to mean that the content of speech in an analytic encounter refers reciprocally to both the phantasy of the patient and the therapist.

Recent research (Gabbard and Westen, 2003) shows that the method of free association may contribute to neurological rewiring of the brain.

KEY TEXTS

- Bollas, C. (2002) *Free Association* (Cambridge, UK: Icon Books)
- Gabbard, G. and Westen, D. (2003) 'Rethinking Therapeutic Action', *International Journal of Psychoanalysis*, 84: pp. 823–841

- Hoffer, A. and Youngren, V. (2004) 'Is Free Association Still at the Core of Psychoanalysis?' *International Journal of Psychoanalysis*, 85 (6): pp. 1489–1492
- Kris, A. (1992) 'Interpretation and the Method of Free Association', *Psychoanalytic Inquiry*, 12 (2): pp. 208–224
- Kris, A. (1996) *Free Association: Methods and Process* (Revised and Updated Revision of the Yale University Press, 1982) (Hillsdale, NJ: The Analytic Press)
- McDermott, V. (2003) 'Is Free Association Still Fundamental?' *Journal of the American Psychoanalytic Association*, 51 (4): pp. 1349–1356

g

gender

SEE ALSO adolescence; developmental stages

The understanding of gender in psychoanalysis shares with most of modern social and psychological theory a long, complex and troubled history. It should be noted at the outset that Freud never used the terms 'gender' or 'gender identity'. Today, for many, it is taken for granted that gender and sex refer to fundamentally different realities. Over time *psychodynamic* ideas have been challenged and revised by feminist, queer and race theorists. Foremost among the critics has been a loosely associated group of scholars and practitioners using *social constructivism* (sometimes also called anti-essentialism) to explain gender, gender identity, sexuality and early development. For some among the more radical of these critics, gender is both rooted in and reducible to the social and *symbolic* world and altogether lack connection to the body or materiality (Coole and Frost, 2010; Elder-Vass, 2013, p. 121); gender expressions, accordingly, change moment-to-moment in relation to certain performative possibilities (Butler, 1993). In sum, we perform our genders, pick and choose them, and through performance, lines of development result in enormous complexity and diversity. What gets left out of these varied social constructionist accounts, however, are the ways that once an aspect of being human in the world has been socially constructed (and no doubt gender, like race, is among those realities), it comes to be felt, experienced and expressed as immutable and embodied (i.e. gendered bodies). Surely not all aspects of human being and suffering are constructed with equal measures of potential or in their performative doing and undoing. And it is in clinical practice where the actual experience of gender (i.e. its felt, experienced aspect) is especially salient.

John Money (1965) first used the term 'gender identity' to describe the relative sense of feeling and being masculine or feminine and to differentiate the subjective experience of gender from socially prescribed roles. Soon after, Robert Stoller (1968), a psycho-analyst, joined with the anthropologist Gilbert Herdt, to conduct ethnographic work in the Pacific and to write series of essays and books aimed at differentiation of the biological from the psycho-logical: masculinity and femininity, social constructs, were not to be confused with the biological realities of male and female. Stoller called the fixed sense of maleness and femaleness the 'core gender identity', determined in the second year of life, just before the *Oedipal* phase. For Stoller, as well, there were three factors contributing to the formation of core identity: biology and hormonal factors; sex assignment at birth; and social/environmental influences. Stoller, moreover, unlike Freud, did not imagine that the early and primary *identification* was masculine. The boy and the girl, Stoller argued, start with a core female identity rooted in maternal symbiosis. Thus, core identity is nonconflictual and occurs through identifica-tion. Stoller has been widely criticized for retaining an essentialized conception of identity formation and for failing to understand the diversity and multiplicity of gender.

Fast (1978) proposed that gender identity results from a more complex and dynamic process of differentiation. Gender in her view was unbounded and undifferentiated from the very beginning; through socialization children come to have a sense of their male-ness or femaleness. Moreover, for Fast, narcissistic disappoint-ments result from a growing sense of difference and differentia-tion and the child's growing awareness that gender choices must be made. Fast has since been criticized for the emphasis given to differentiation, and in some ways this was not a significant depar-ture from Stoller.

Others convincingly argue that male dominance and gendered subjects are produced by dominant ideologies related to moth-ering and traditional families, where it is primarily women who assume responsibility for care-taking (see Chodorow, 1994) and in infancy boys and girls traverse very different developmental pathways. For boys, separation from the maternal is motivated by a cultural imperative to form identifications with the social power of the father, whereas for girls, their continuing and close relation-ships with mothers yield a very different sense of self: symbiotic and continuous. Because girls, unlike boys, develop with different

and closer relations with mothers, they have fluid psychic boundaries and greater capacity for intimacy. They are left, however, with a
diminished access to public culture.

For boys, according to Jessica Benjamin (1995, 1998), masculinity is inscribed through denial of original identifications with
mothers; the father is experienced as the central figure for individuation and the boy sees mother's goodness as a seductive threat to
independence. The Oedipal logic, for Benjamin, traps us in binary
ways of thinking: identification with same-sexed parent alongside
the sexual object choice of the other.

Harris refers to gender as soft assembly: gender is an assembly
with widely diverse content and patterns, with multiple pathways,
lacking a telos. Moreover, it serves equally diverse psychological
and social purposes. Ken Corbett (1997, 2001) argues that our
thinking about development and gender has been dominated by a
normative logic of what he calls centrality. For Corbett the dominant developmental paradigm altogether elides the necessity for
the marginal experience. At the margins, he argues, one finds the
homosexual or 'invert' and for Corbett the object of therapy is to
restore a 'queer ethic' and expand mental freedom, which results
from steady social and psychological opposition to the norm: health
is mental freedom (2001a, p. 320). Gender, moreover, for Corbett,
has regulatory effects, constraining a person by its embedded social
stereotypes and rules.

For feminists working from a Lacanian perspective, gender
constructions must be addressed through discourse and language.
It is through language that privileged discourses of gender are
enabled and power is exercised. And it is through the child's entry
into culture and language, through 'The Law of the Father', that
oppressive constructions of gender and sexuality are encoded.
Some French Lacanian feminists (Luce Irigaray, Helene Cixous
and Catherine Clement) have engaged in a political project, 'écri-
ture féminine', where they argue that women must challenge and
abandon the neutral, objective, scientific discourse of masculinity
for a creative and rebellious and subjective experience of the feminine body. It is only in this way that women can live outside patriar-
chal structures and oppositions: female/feminine; sex/subject. For
Irigaray and Cixous, this entails celebration of a more diffuse and
autoerotic sensuality.

points for reflection and practice

- Corbett (2001a) cautions clinicians not to mistake gender normality for health. He and many others argue that gender is not an entity; but functions in multiple and over determined ways as surface and performance.
- Chodorow (1994) and some object relations practitioners advocate for dual *parenting* as a way of addressing gender imbalances: 'balances generated by gendered extremes, as children would be able to view both parents as individuals-in-relation, experience men and women as both self- and other-oriented, and view both sexes as inhabiting private and public domains.'

KEY TEXTS

- Benjamin, J. (1998) *The Bonds of Love: Psychoanalysis, Feminism, & the Problem of Domination* (New York, NY: Pantheon)
- Chodorow, N. (1994) *Femininities, Masculinities, Sexualities* (Lexington, KY: University Press of Kentucky)
- Cohler, B. J. and Galatzer-Levy, R. M. (2000) *The Course of Gay and Lesbian Lives: Social and Psychoanalytic Perspectives* (Chicago, IL: University of Chicago Press)
- Corbett, K. (1997) 'It Is Time to Distinguish Gender from Health: Reflections on Lothsteins's "Pantyhose Fetishism and Self Cohesion: A Paraphilic Solution?"' *Gender & Psychoanalysis*, 2: pp. 259–271
- Corbett, K. (2001) 'Faggot = Loser', *Studies in Gender & Sexuality*, 2 (1): pp. 3–28
- Corbett, K. (2001a) 'More Life: Centrality and Marginality in Human Development', *Psychoanalytic Dialogues*, 11 (3): pp. 313–335
- Fast, I. (1984) *Gender Identity* (Hillsdale, NJ: Analytic Press)
- Harris, A. (2005) *Gender as Soft Assembly* (Hillsdale, NJ: Analytic Press)
- Herdt, G. and Stoller, R. (1992) *Intimate Communications: Erotics and the Study of Culture* (New York, NY: Columbia University Press)
- Kulish, N. (2010) 'Clinical Implications of Contemporary Gender Theory', *Journal of the American Psychoanalytic Association*, 58 (2): pp. 231–258
- Layton, L. (2013) *Who's That Girl? Who's That Boy? Clinical Practice Meets Postmoderngender Theory* (Vol. 2) (London, UK: Routledge)
- Magee, M. and Miller, D. (2013) *Lesbian Lives: Psychoanalytic Narratives Old and New* (London, UK: Routledge)

- Salamon, G. (2010) *Assuming a Body: Transgender Theory and Rhetorics of Materiality* (New York, NY: Columbia University Press)

good enough mother (holding environment)

SEE ALSO   alpha and beta elements (and functions); container/contained; reverie; transitional space/transitional phenomena/transitional object

D. W. Winnicott (1896–1971), an English paediatrician and psychoanalyst, offered especially useful and innovative ways of thinking about the social and psychological dynamic between mothers (caregivers) and infants. He shared with Melanie Klein, one of his major influences, an understanding of how children come to feel and know the mother as separate and independent, with both good and bad qualities. The 'good enough' caregiver produces a facilitating environment (i.e. holding), adapts to the infant's needs and demands and feels the child's need to transition towards autonomy on his or her own terms. It is only gradually based upon the child's increasing capacity to tolerate maternal failure that the good enough parent reduces the nearly total adaptation to the infant's needs. These moments of failure, in turn, enable adaptation to the external environment and contribute to the developing internal world and healthy sense of autonomy. These well-timed and steady moves towards autonomy, both maternal and infant, moreover, enable the infant to gradually predict subtle environmental changes and develop a sense of control. Autonomy, because it is never fully achieved, means that throughout life we seek moments of comfort, dependence and belonging.

While Winnicott offered a way of understanding the essential role of the empathic and attuned caregiver, mothers, in much of *psychodynamic* theorizing, are less well defined. They are most often viewed as having a singular purpose and developmental line: understanding and satisfying needs. In their recent edited volume on mothering, Mendel and Turrini (2003) argue that in psychoanalytic theory and practice too much emphasis is attributed to the role of the mother as an *object* necessary to meeting the needs of the child. The mother and her needs, however, are not seen in relation to the sustaining environment. They write,

> We know that to respond in an empathic, accurate, and satisfying way to the child while preserving one's differentiated identity, and

indeed growing with the legendary task of motherhood, requires a well-developed adult who can negotiate the multitude of conflictual forks in the process of helping the child's development. (p. 299)

They argue that much of the literature treats the maternal figure as 'undefined entity, singularly placed in the world with one goal only, the understanding and satisfaction of the needs of the child' (pp. 299–300). Good enough mothering, however, requires a 'good enough environment', where the complexity of mothering is understood as a dynamic not only between caregiver and child but also between the mother and her holding environment. In short, not all environments (i.e. economic, healthcare, educational, religious, racial, ethnic, and national) produce good enough opportunities for mothers to engage in healthy relationships with their children.

points for reflection and practice
- Peter Blos offers a very useful way of understanding mothering with a three generational model: the mother, the mother's mother and the new child. He states, 'the maternal tasks are to integrate the new and the old, the *real* and the imagined, the interior and the social in such a way that a new, stable aspect of the personality is formed – the mother' (from Mendell and Turrini, 2003, p. 5).
- In working with parents and mothers, it is important to avoid taking a pathologizing stance towards *parenting*, which may lead to withdrawal or *depression* and prevent useful self-exploration.

KEY TEXTS
- Alizade, A. M. (ed.) (2006) *Motherhood in the Twenty-First Century* (London, UK: Karnac Books)
- Mendell, D. and Turrini, P. (eds) (2003) *The Inner World of the Mother* (Madison, CT: Psychosocial Press)
- Winnicott, D. W. (1953) 'Transitional Objects and Transitional Phenomena', *International Journal of Psychoanalysis*, 34: pp. 89–97

guilt

SEE ALSO **ego; shame**

Guilt, *shame*, embarrassment and pride are often described as 'self-conscious' emotions rooted in self-reflection and self-evaluation

(Tangney, 2007). Some argue that shame and guilt are different expressions of the same *affect* and that guilt is a species of moral shame (Tomkins 1963; Izard 1977). Guilt has two sides. Its destructive aspect exacts self-evaluation and punishment for misdoings and may produce symptoms (e.g. *depression*). While guilt results from the *recognition* of negative attributes or behaviours, it has another side, sometimes called 'prosocial', which may motivate positive, normative action (i.e. norm-governed, compliant behaviour). While a sense of guilt is without doubt necessary for orderly social life, guilty feelings cannot all be explained by reference to their social function. Research shows that guilt often involves not only prosocial behaviour but also reparative action: *empathy,* altruism and caregiving (Batson, 1987; Baumeister *et al.,* 1994; Tangney and Dearing, 2002). Others, especially Tangney and Dearing, argue that this grouping of self-conscious emotions provide essential feedback on the status of one's social and moral acceptance.

Psychodynamic theory distinguishes between conscious and unconscious guilt. Conscious and healthy guilt leads to repair of a damaged relationship, whereas unhealthy guilt leads to self-punishment where damage may be done to the self. Healthy guilt also has a quantity: it tends to correspond to the magnitude of the act. One form of guilt, sometimes called neurotic, forms in childhood around ambivalent unconscious feelings directed at internal representations of the parents. While normal guilt tends towards resolution through repair of damage caused to the relationship, neurotic guilt continues unabated through self-punishment. Some psychodynamic theorists use the idea of signal guilt to explore how the mind mobilizes the affect of guilt to avoid future misdeeds (i.e. one recalls the affect from the earlier action in order to prevent current or future action). Kleinians differentiate persecutory guilt (i.e. self-torment) from depressive guilt. With depressive guilt, the concern is with reparation and caring. Grinberg (1965), a Kleinian, makes a distinction between 'persecutory guilt' and 'depressive guilt'. With this differentiation, one may more clearly see the dynamics in the nature of the *object* relations.

While Freud saw the conscience as one function of the superego, Carveth (2013) argues that the superego and conscience have distinct functions. Carveth postulates the need for a fourth mental structure, the conscience:

Whereas Freud himself viewed conscience as one of the functions of the superego ... I argue that superego and conscience are distinct mental functions and that, therefore, a fourth mental structure, the conscience, needs to be added to the psychoanalytic structural theory of the mind. I claim that while both conscience and superego originate in the so-called pre-*Oedipal* phase of infant and child development they are comprised of contrasting and often conflicting identifications. The primary object, still most often the mother, is inevitably experienced as, on the one hand, nurturing and soothing and, on the other, frustrating and persecuting. Conscience is formed in *identification* with the nurturer; the superego in identification with the aggressor. There is a principle of reciprocity at work in the human psyche: for love received one seeks to return love; for hate, hate (the talion law). (p. 287; emphases added)

For Lacan, guilt (Seminar 7) in the clinical setting should be not ignored nor should the analysand be persuaded not to address guilty feeling. For Lacan, if there is guilt present in the work it is because the analysand 'is guilty'. The goal of the work is to determine the source of the guilt. Guilt, moreover, is not irrational. It exists as ethically *real*. For Lacan 'the only thing one can be guilty of is having given ground relative to one's desire' (Seminar 7, p. 319).

points for reflection and practice
- It is important in practice to distinguish guilt from self-punishment, recalling that genuine guilt mobilizes and self-punishment paralyses; genuine guilt leads to repair. Self-punishment produces withdrawal from relatedness.
- There is a significant literature exploring the differences among shame and guilt and the clinical implications. See especially significant work by Tangney and Dearing (2003), 'Shame and Guilt'.

KEY TEXTS
- Carnì, S. *et al.* (2013) 'Intrapsychic and Interpersonal Guilt: A Critical Review of the Recent Literature', *Cognitive Processing*, 14 (4): pp. 333–346
- Carveth, D. L. (2010) 'Superego, Conscience, and the Nature and Types of Guilt', *Modern Psychoanalysis*, 35 (1): pp. 106–130

- Carveth, D. L. (2013) *The Still Small Voice: Psychoanalytic Reflections on Guilt and Conscience* (London, UK: Karnac Books)
- Gilligan, J. (2003) 'Shame, Guilt, and Violence', *Social Research: An International Quarterly*, 70 (4): pp. 1149–1180
- Hughes, J. M. (2007) *Guilt and Its Vicissitudes: Psychoanalytic Reflections on Morality* (London, UK: Routledge)
- Reiner, A. (2009) *The Quest for Conscience and the Birth of the Mind* (London, UK: Karnac Books)
- Singh, K. (1996) *Guilt (Ideas in Psychoanalysis)* (London. UK: Icon Books)
- Stolorow, R. (2011) 'Toward Greater Authenticity: From Shame to Existential Guilt, Anxiety, and Grief', *International Journal of Psychoanalytic Self Psychology*, 6 (2): pp. 285–287
- Tangney, J. P. and Dearing, R. L. (2003) *Shame and Guilt* (New York, NY: Guilford Press)
- Tracy, J., Robins, R. and Tangney, J. (eds) (2007) *The Self-Conscious Emotions: Theory and Research* (New York, NY: Guilford Press)

i

identification

SEE ALSO developmental stages; mirror stage (and mirroring)

Identification, for Freud, describes a process by which one seeks to assimilate an aspect or attribute into the self such that one appears more like others, and it through a series of such identifications that subjectivity is constituted. There are two ways in which the term is often used: where the subject identifies the self with the other and where the subject identifies the other with the self. The term, however, does not refer to *object* choice: for example, if a child identifies with a parent, it wants to be like the parent. If the child makes the parent the object choice, it is to have or possess the parent, not to identify with him or her. The term should not be confused with incorporation and introjection: both these refer to drawing the object towards the self, and it is also different from imitation, which is voluntary and conscious. Ultimately, for Freud, the concept of identification has a central place in his understanding of how the human subject is constituted.

Meissner (1970) offers a useful typology of Freud's different understandings of identification: (1) *Dream* identification: a form of condensation in dreaming by which the subject's *ego* represents itself as other figures in the dream's manifest content; (2) Hysterical identification: the assimilation of a property or symptom of an object by the subject as an expression of a resemblance derived from a common element which remains unconscious; (3) Primary identification: the original and primitive form of emotional *attachment* to an object prior to any object which regressively replaces the abandoned object relation by introjection of the object; (4) Oral incorporation is again appealed to as a model but in a different sense, as dictated by the precedence of an object-cathexis; (5) Partial (secondary) identification: a form of identification based on the perception of a common quality which does not depend on an object relation (p. 563).

We often talk about a primary and two forms of secondary identification. Primary refers to the earliest identification with our primary attachment figures. Narcissistic (secondary) identification refers to identifications following loss or abandonment and partial (secondary) identification is based on identifications with a special characteristic or quality of another (i.e. their looks or dress).

For Lacan, identification describes a process whereby one becomes so captivated with an object in the external world (i.e. a person) that it becomes an aspect of the subject's self-image (Lacan used the term 'captation' to describe this). Also for Lacan, in the development of the psyche during the mirror stage, infants are captated by the image of their own bodies, and this becomes the foundation for subsequent identifications.

Finally, some have argued that identification is rooted in fundamental biological and neurological processes. Olds (2006), for example, argues, using evolutionary biology, that identification has phylogenetic precursors and that genetics and infant observation offer useful insights into individual processes of identification. Neuroscience, he argues, especially recent work on mirror neurons, offers unique insight into the biological mechanisms of imitation and its relationship to identification.

point for reflection and practice
- It is crucial to make clear the distinctions among the concepts, identification, internalization and introjection.

KEY TEXTS
- Braddock, L. (2011) 'Psychological Identification, Imagination and Psychoanalysis', *Philosophical Psychology*, 24 (5): pp. 639–657
- Etchegoyen, R. H. (1985) 'Identification and Its Vicissitudes', *International Journal of Psychoanalysis*, 66 (1): pp. 3–18
- Meissner, W. W. (1970) 'Notes on Identification: Origins in Freud', *The Psychoanalytic Quarterly*, 39 (4): pp. 563–589
- Moncayo, R. (2012) *The Emptiness of Oedipus: Identification and Non-Identification in Lacanian Psychoanalysis* (London, UK: Routledge)
- Olds, D. D. (2006) 'Identification: Psychoanalytic and Biological Perspectives', *Journal of the American Psychoanalytic Association*, 54 (1): pp. 17–46

- Sandler, J. (ed.) (2012) *Projection, Identification, Projective Identification* (London, UK: Karnac Books)

illusion

SEE ALSO developmental stages; narcissism; transitional space/ transitional phenomena/transitional object

Most often we tend to use the term 'illusion' to refer to deception or ideas or beliefs we hold in order to protect ourselves from threatening or unacceptable realities. Winnicott used the term in a very different way. For him, illusion was a necessary condition for the infant to reach or connect with reality. The infant, when hungry, fantasizes the mother's breast coincident with the appearance of the actual satisfying breast. It is at the moment of illusion that the infant imagines that it has conjured up the mother's breast. For Winnicott it is the infant's desire for the mother's breast that creates it (Phillips 2007, p. 83; Ogden, 2001), and it is in this way that for Winnicott (1958), 'fantasy is more primary than reality, and the enrichment of fantasy with the world's riches depends on the experience of illusion' (p. 153), and is the principal source of the illusion. Most importantly, it is through her reliable and predictable presence that the infant makes contact with reality (Caldwell and Joyce, 2011) and the illusion gradually is replaced by a more realistic picture of the caregiver, her smells, affects and so on. Unlike Freud, Winnicott argues that the infant's earliest experience of the external world is not through primary *narcissism* but through what he calls 'primary creativity'. Here the infant imagines its own independently created experience of the outside world. And when the caregiver is absent, a threat to the self is experienced and deeply felt.

KEY TEXTS

- Caldwell, L., and Joyce, A. (eds) (2011) *Reading Winnicott* (London, UK: Routledge)
- Ogden, T. (2001) 'Reading Winnicott', *The Psychoanalytic Quarterly*, 70 (2): pp. 299–323
- Phillips, A. (2007) *Winnicott* (London, UK: Penguin)
- Winnicott, D. W. (1958) *Collected Papers: Through Paediatrics to Psycho-Analysis* (London, UK: Tavistock)

imaginary

SEE ALSO **ego; real; symbolic**

For Jacques Lacan the psyche is divided among three orders, domains or registers: the *Real*, the Imaginary and the *Symbolic*. The Imaginary, though rooted in the prelinguistic/presymbolic, refers not to our imagination in the conventional understanding of the term but to the *object* world, the images of objects, the outlines and separations among objects (missing in the Real). In the imaginary (the mirror phase), the child sees an image of the self, recognizes the self and makes demands. The infant in this stage is without speech, without bodily coordination or motor control. With the *recognition* of separateness from the mother and the world, and the resulting sense of a lost world (i.e. the real), the child feels *anxiety*. In this register demand replaces need; demand, unlike need (which in the *Real* is satisfied), however, is aimed at making the Other part of the self (as experienced in the now lost state of nature). And because demand (i.e. while needs can be realized, demands are necessarily and always unsatisfiable) cannot be realized it is a continual reminder of loss and lack. In the mirror stage, the child misrecognizes or mistakes the image for a complete, whole, stable, coherent self, which cannot correspond to the actual child. The image, impossible to realize, is a fantasy functioning to compensate for the sense of lack or loss. Lacan calls this the 'Ideal-I' or 'ideal *ego*'.

point for reflection and practice
- Bruce Fink writes that 'the more the analyst operates in the imaginary mode, the less she can hear. Our usual way of *listening* – both as "ordinary citizens" and as analysts – primarily involves the imaginary register and makes us rather hard' (Fink, 2011).

KEY TEXTS
- Bowie, M. (1993) *Lacan* (Cambridge, MA: Harvard University Press)
- Fink, B. (2007) *Fundamentals of Psychoanalytic Technique: A Lacanian Approach for Practitioners* (New York, NY: W. W. Norton & Company)
- Jean-Michel, R. (ed.) (2003) *The Cambridge Companion to Lacan* (Cambridge, UK: Cambridge University Press)

j

jouissance

SEE ALSO   extimacy; imaginary; Oedipal; real; symbolic

Lacan used this term to describe the paradoxical qualities of sexual pleasure or enjoyment, that is, how pleasurable qualities turn into painful experience. This 'too muchness' of jouissance is an uncontrollable satisfaction, an excess and intolerable degree of excitement or pleasure, beyond the pleasure principle (i.e. the pleasure principle places limits on pleasure). It is simultaneously tempting and disruptive, impossible and alluring. Lacan writes: 'It starts with a tickle and ends up bursting into flames' (1991, p. 83). Bruce Fink (2011) describes jouissance 'as the kind of enjoyment or satisfaction people derive from their symptoms ... It is not a "simple pleasure," so to speak, but involves a kind of pain-pleasure or "pleasure in pain" ... or satisfaction in dissatisfaction. It qualifies the kind of "kick" someone may get out of punishment, self-punishment, doing something that is so pleasurable that it hurts (sexual climax, for example), or doing something that is so painful that it becomes pleasurable' (p. 69).

Feminists – Irigaray (1985), Kristeva (1980), Cixous, Mitchell (2001), Rose (2005) – have used jouissance in many ways. For Irigaray, because 'hysterical jouissance' lies outside the paternal, it is unrepresentable (1985, pp. 357–360). For Cixous, feminine jouissance is without phallic limit, unrestrained and wild. For Kristeva, feminine jouissance refers to a quality that escapes the *symbolic*, *Oedipal* limits, and language.

points for reflection and practice
- In practice Bruce Fink has referred to 'jouissance crisis' (1997, pp. 8–9) as a 'satisfaction crisis': 'in which the analysand's former ways of enjoying himself (whether in an explicitly

sexual manner or otherwise) have broken down and he comes to analysis asking the analyst to help him restore them to their former efficacy (2011, p. 91).

- The psychoanalysis is aimed at understanding the myriad means by which one uses and produces *jouissance*.

KEY TEXTS

- Declercq, F. (2004) 'Lacan's Concept of the Real of Jouissance: Clinical Illustrations and Implications', *Psychoanalysis, Culture & Society*, 9 (2): pp. 237–251
- Fink, B. (1997) *A Clinical Introduction to Lacanian Psychoanalysis: Theory and Technique* (Cambridge, MA: Harvard University Press)
- Fink, B. (2007) *Fundamentals of Psychoanalytic Technique: A Lacanian Approach for Practitioners* (New York, NY: W. W. Norton & Company)
- Irigaray, L. (1985) *This Sex Which Is Not One* (Ithaca, NY: Cornell University Press)
- Kristeva, J. (1980) *Desire in Language: A Semiotic Approach to Literature and Art* (New York, NY: Columbia University Press)
- Lacan, J. (1992) *The Seminar of Jacques Lacan. Book 7: The Ethics of Psychoanalysis 1959–1960* (Dennis Porter, Trans.) (New York, NY: W. W. Norton & Company)
- Mitchell, J. and Rose, J. (eds) (1983) *Feminine Sexuality: Jacques Lacan and the École Freudienne* (London, UK: Palgrave)
- Rose, J. (2005) *Sexuality in the Field of Vision* (London, UK: Verso)

1

listening

SEE ALSO **empathy; wounded healer**

Many have argued that psychoanalytic method, irrespective of theoretical commitments (i.e. *ego, drive,* self, *object,* relational, Lacanian),
is defined by a special kind of *listening* or attention through listening.
And a few have considered the influence of phenomenology on
the psychoanalytic discussion of listening and on the connection
between Freud and phenomenology, including Freud's own philosophical debt to his teacher, Brentano (Tauber, 2010; Wertz, 1993):
the importance of direct observation over theory and construction;
bracketing theory and preconception (i.e. the natural attitude); self-
reflection and *empathy.* Donna Orange (2010) speaks quite directly
to the phenomenological approach to listening:

> Likewise, a listening hermeneut may try energetically to
> convince the interlocutor (Gadamer, 2003). But implicit and
> explicit forms of participation in the patient's suffering create a
> world of compassion that brings new experiential possibilities.
> This hermeneutic participation, however, is a way of being-
> with, not a formula or technique (Orange *et al.,* 1997) for doing
> clinical work. Where there was indifference, humiliation, rejec-
> tion, shattering loss, and the like, compassionate therapeutic
> understanding does not simply replace or heal by intentionally
> providing new experience. Instead, treating a person as end-
> lessly worth understanding, deeming his or her suffering as
> worth feeling together, and having an attitude of compassion
> implicitly affirms the human worth of the patient. The psycho-
> analytic or psychotherapeutic relationship can accord to the
> patient, often for the first time, the dignity of being treated as
> the subject of one's own experience. (p. 115)

For Freud, a uniquely psychoanalytic listening is characterized by what is often translated as 'evenly hovering attention'. This is, however, more than a mere tuning of the ear, or steady training of the hearing instrument. This refers to the phenomenology of listening (Horowitz, 2012; Ihde, 1976; Stocker, 2013). Freud offered his most well-known description of the state of mind necessary for this kind of attention in 1912:

> To put it in a formula: he must turn his own unconscious like a receptive organ towards the transmitting unconscious of the patient. He must adjust himself to the patient as a telephone receiver is adjusted to the transmitting microphone. Just as the receiver converts back into sound waves the electric oscillations in the telephone lines which were set up by sound waves, so the doctor's unconscious is able, from the derivatives of the unconscious which are communicated to him, to reconstruct the unconscious, which has determined the patient's *free associations*. (pp. 115–116; emphasis added)

For Theodor Reik, 'The psychologist has to learn how one mind speaks to another beyond words and in silence. He must learn to listen with what Reik calls "the third ear"' (1948, p. 144). For Reik, psychoanalytic listening is sequenced. It starts with unconscious conjectures about the patient's mental life and concludes with conscious formulation. Conjectures emerge from the intersubjective field and reciprocal understanding of therapist's and patient's unconscious dynamics.

For the ego psychologist Jacob Arlow (1995), analytic listening involves foremost a special way of showing how the patient's mind works. The aim for Arlow is a kind of listening that has a specific outcome: adaptive compromise formations. This is a kind of listening that places the analyst in the privileged position of knowing the truth. Arlow writes: 'Analysts must respond in the same way but inwardly to themselves. Analysts intervene not to enter the conversation but to elucidate for the patient the nature of the conversation' (p. 215).

Bruce Fink, a Lacanian, argues that listening is not a well-developed skill among psychotherapists. He offers several reasons: personal, structural and the tendency to listen to in relation to the self. Of the latter, he argues, we will often listen to a narrative with a similar story in mind, or even a more extreme one. We imagine how we have experienced something similar to what we're hearing. We do this, he argues, because we want to identify with the experience of the patient, or to somehow know that experience, or imagine what the experience might have been like for us. This means, of course, that our habitual ways of listening tend to focus on the listener, our own perspective, the listener's experience and similar life circumstances, feelings and so on. In this mode of listening, we imagine that we can finally 'relate' to the other. In the therapeutic encounter, we hear ourselves saying: Fink writes: 'I know what you mean', 'Yeah', 'I hear you', 'I feel for you' or 'I feel your pain' (perhaps less often 'I feel your joy'). At such moments, we feel sympathy, empathy or pity for this other who seems like us; 'That must have been painful (or wonderful) for you', we say, imagining the pain (or joy) we ourselves would have experienced in such a situation. When we are unable to locate experiences, feelings or perspectives that resemble the other person's, we have the sense that we do not understand that person – indeed, we may find the person strange, if not obtuse or irrational. When someone does not operate in the same way that we do or does not react to situations as we do, we are often baffled, incredulous or even dumbfounded. We are inclined, in the latter situation, to try to correct the other's perspectives, to persuade him or her to see things the way we see them and to feel what we ourselves would feel were we in such a predicament. In more extreme cases, we simply become judgemental: How could anyone, we ask ourselves, believe such a thing or act or feel that way? Most simply stated, our usual way of listening overlooks or rejects the otherness of the other (Fink, 2007, pp. 1–2).

KEY TEXTS

- Akhtar, S. (2012) *Psychoanalytic Listening: Methods, Limits, and Innovations* (London, UK: Karnac Books)
- Arlow, J. (1995) 'Stilted Listening: Psychoanalysis as Discourse', *The Psychoanalytic Quarterly*, 64 (2): pp. 215–233
- Arnold, K. (2006) 'Reik's Theory of Psychoanalytic Listening', *Psychoanalytic Psychology*, 23 (4): pp. 754–765
- Bromberg, P. (1994). '"Speak! That I May See You": Some Reflections on Dissociation, Reality, and Psychoanalytic Listening', *Psychoanalytic Dialogues*, 4 (4): pp. 517–547

- Chodorow, N. (2012) 'Analytic Listening and the Five Senses', *Journal of the American Psychoanalytic Association*, 60 (4): pp. 747–758
- Fink, B. (2007) Fundamentals of Psychoanalytic Technique: A Lacanian Approach for Practitioners (New York, NY: W. W. Norton & Company)
- Hamer, F. (2012) 'Evocative Space Where Listening Begins', *Journal of the American Psychoanalytic Association*, 60 (4): pp. 781–789
- Ihde, D. (2007) *Listening and Voice: Phenomenologies of Sound* (Albany, NY: SUNY Press)
- Meissner, W. (2000) 'On Analytic Listening', *The Psychoanalytic Quarterly*, 69 (2): pp. 317–367
- Reik, T. (1948) *Listening with the Third Ear: The Inner Experience of a Psychoanalyst* (New York, NY: Grove Press)
- Rubin, J. (1985) 'Meditation and Psychoanalytic Listening', *Psychoanalytic Review* 72 (4): pp. 599–613
- Wertz, F. (1993) 'The Phenomenology of Sigmund Freud', *Journal of Phenomenological Psychology*, 24 (2): pp. 101–129

m

mentalization

SEE ALSO affect regulation; alpha and beta elements (and functions); container/contained

Just as human beings use their minds to interpret their own behaviours, desires, feelings and thoughts, they must also use their minds to interpret the mental worlds of others. Mentalization is a concept used to describe the mutual *recognition* of complex mental states, of self and other, along with the capacity to see mental states as independent from action and behaviour. When we mentalize we are sometimes aware of what's happening in our minds and in the minds of others. This has been called 'explicit or conscious mentalization'. We know it is explicit when we puzzle over the reasons, intentions or causes of thoughts, feelings and actions, of our own and others. This explicit aspect of mentalization enables our sense-making and our capacity for the expression of feeling in language, in our own words. In this explicit mode of mentalizing we keep mental states in mind; we are using our attention to be mindful of what others are thinking and feeling as we simultaneously observe our own states. We ask ourselves, for example, 'why did I feel that way after she said that, or did I cause her to feel *shame* when I observed her slumping?' Here, you notice, through your own personal stories and narratives, how communication unfolds and how it is affected by thought and feeling.

Yet there is another and implicit dimension to the process. Think of implicit or unconscious mentalization as a kind of habit. It is a natural, seamless, moment-to-moment aspect of human communication and interaction. In the psychology of memory, it could be said that this occurs in implicit, nondeclarative memory. For example, we are seldom aware of the many, and complex, ways in which our relating with others unfold. In our usual conversation, for example, we do not consciously attend to the gestures, the stops and starts, and the subtle and unspoken ways in which we recognize and acknowledge divergent perspectives and understandings. And we generally respond to the emotional states of others without the more active kinds of attention found in explicit mentalization. There is yet another important and temporal dimension to mentalizing. With the ability to mentalize about present, past and future, we differently envision the contexts and possibilities for communicating and relating. For example, mentalizing solely in the present, 'I see you are crying; did I cause you to worry', may limit understanding and *empathy*. You can also be aware of the historical context for the worry: 'The news about your father's cancer must be very disturbing, especially since it has reoccurred, and you've had to hear this news many times before.' The broader context might also take into account the history of losses in life. In each case, the scope of mentalization changes.

While it comes naturally, mentalization is not something that everyone does with equal measure of success and the failure to mentalize can result in serious problems. For many, when mentalization founders, the spontaneous sense of being in control of behaviour is lost. We lose our sense of identity, our coherence and our capacity to navigate our relational world with emotional understanding as a compass. With successful mentalization, moreover, comes our ability to self-regulate, to understand and use humour and engage in play, to imagine, learn new things, create, and to take the perspective of others with a certain degree of surprise and novelty, and to empathize. In its absence, relationships can be compromised, responsibility for action gets collapsed, friends are alienated and family communication becomes chaotic. And other things, such as addiction and *depression*, can easily interfere with our capacity to mentalize (Allen and Fonagy, 2002).

Peter Fonagy and colleagues maintain that symptoms of *borderline* personality disorder (BPD) result from deficits in the capacity for mentalization. This capacity, they argue, is the outcome of healthy engagements with caregivers in early childhood; when child–caregiver relationship is troubled or chaotic, the capacity for mentalization is affected. Mentalization-based therapy, therefore, is aimed at increasing this ability. Research shows the importance of mentalizing and that mentalization – for clinicians, patients, and family members – is a crucial component to all treatment methods.

Wilfred Bion proposed a theory of mind that involved the transformation of what he called beta elements (raw emotional experience) into alpha elements (higher mental functioning) in the caregiver relationship. His ideas are influential; see entry, *alpha and beta elements (and functions)*; and *container/contained* – for discussion of these important ideas; their relationship to mentalization is interesting and unmistakable. Likewise, there are many who talk about *mindfulness* and mindful therapies, which – while less fully developed – also use ideas related to the concept mentalization.

points for reflection and practice
- Research shows that personality disorder may result from specific deficits in mentalizing and that treatment should be focused on development of mentalizing capacity (see Bateman and Fonagy, 2004).
- Mentalizing may be crucial to the process of establishing and maintaining an effective treatment relationship and therapeutic alliance.
- Failure of mentalizing in *attachment* relationships lies at the core of abuse and neglect, as well as more insidious forms of trauma, leading to difficulty with emotional regulation.

KEY TEXTS
- Allen, J. G. and Fonagy, P. (2002) *The Development of Mentalizing and Its Role in Psychopathology and Psychotherapy* (Technical Report No. 02–0048) Topeka, KS: Menninger Clinic, Research Department. Available at https://docs.google.com/document/edit?id=1dgf064aakcao8v–pleas2pmyk4uiwyaax_otbzdbb8
- Bateman, A. and Fonagy, P. (2004) 'Mentalization-Based Treatment of BPD', *Journal of Personality Disorders*, 18 (1): pp. 36–51
- Fonagy, P. *et al.* (2002) *Affect Regulation, Mentalization, and the Development of the Self* (New York, NY: Other Press)
- Target, M. and Fonagy, P. (1996) 'Playing with Reality: II. The Development of Psychic Reality from a Theoretical Perspective', *International Journal of Psychoanalysis*, 77 (3): pp. 459–479

mindfulness

SEE ALSO **affect regulation; empathy; selfobject**

The concept of mindfulness has taken Western psychology by storm and has crossed over into neuroscience, management, education and politics. While mindfulness originates in Buddhist meditation practice (Kabat-Zinn, 2003), it has evolved into much more than meditation. It is described as a state of consciousness or a concentration of attention (or focused awareness) in a particular way, with purpose and intention, and without making judgements. It requires a conscious awareness of experience as it unfolds, moment-to-moment (Brown and Ryan, 2003). For Daniel Siegel, one of the key proponents of mindfulness therapy and research, mindfulness is best described as the integration of, and development of, what he calls 'executive forms of attention'. These forms of attention, he argues, lead to a developing capacity for self-regulation, what he calls the balancing of emotion: more effective and healthy responses to stress and improved social skills.

Mindfulness approaches to therapy have in common a nonjudgemental shift of attention to present experience. The approach is now commonly used in mindfulness-based cognitive therapy (MBCT) mindfulness-based stress reductions (MBSR), acceptance and commitment therapy (ACT) and dialectical behaviour therapy (DBT). The intentional redirection of focus away from disturbing or preoccupying mental states, frightening or troubling thoughts, must be accompanied by observation and acceptance of current reality and what it offers, regardless of whether it is good or bad.

points for reflection and practice
- Mindfulness is generally delivered through various meditation practices. The client is asked to redirect focus to the present.
- Much of the therapy is aimed at helping the client recognize the emotions and feelings implicated in meandering thoughts and the associated physical sensations or urges.
- Most of our lives we are engaged in doing, being active. Mindfulness therapy is aimed at observing, not doing.

KEY TEXTS

- Brown, K. W. and Ryan, R. M. (2003) 'The Benefits of Being Present: Mindfulness and Its Role in Psychological Well-Being', *Journal of Personality and Social Psychology*, 84 (4): pp. 822–848
- Kabat-Zinn, J. (2003) 'Mindfulness-Based Interventions in Context: Past, Present, and Future', *Clinical Psychology: Science and Practice*, 10 (2): pp. 144–156
- Kabat-Zinn, J. (2005) *Coming to Our Senses* (New York, NY: Hyperion)

mirror stage (and mirroring)

SEE ALSO **imaginary; real; selfobject; symbolic**

The mirror stage is among Lacan's most important concepts. Human infants (6–18 months), Lacan proposed, see and experience their image reflected in a mirror or represented through the mother or caregiver. While Lacan initially proposed specifically timed *developmental stages* or moments, he later argued that the mirror is essential to the production of human subjectivity and becomes the organizing experience in the *Imaginary* register. From the very beginning the imagistic nucleus of the *ego* is suffused with caregiver narratives (i.e. 'discourse of the Other') and encouragements to recognize themselves in the mirror (e.g. 'such a cute little nose, such cute blue eyes'). The ego is in this way not an organized, integrated or unitary accomplishment, nor the source of autonomous agency, an imagined place of the autonomous 'I'; it is instead a site for projected desire and fantasy of Others. Here, according to Lacan, the ego is an *object*, not a subject, even though the senses suggest otherwise; it is not the site for autonomous agency, a free, true 'I', in control of its own destiny.

The psychic consequence of self-*recognition* is the formation of a mental representation, the 'Ideal-I'. While the infant's *identification* with its image becomes the template for the emerging self, the image of a unified and whole body fails to correspond with the infant's actual material and physical experience and vulnerabilities. This misrecognition (or méconnaissance) is magnified as the infant assumes the subject position of the image and reflects back on its actual, limited and imperfect self, producing the trauma of imperfection and the perpetual desire to realize an unattainable ideal. The misrecognition, moreover, grounds the agency of the ego, before its social determination, in a fictional direction.

It has been quite common (Malin, 2011) to juxtapose Kohut's thinking on mirroring with Lacan's, and the consensus is that they have radically opposed understandings. For Kohut the infant must experience 'positive' mirroring from caregivers and in the social surround for healthy development. It is through what Kohut and others call 'mirror reactions' that differentiation of the self from the not self is enabled. Mirror reactions are, moreover, essential to the resolution of primary *narcissism*. Kohut uses the term 'mirror transference' in 'The Psychoanalytic Treatment of Narcissistic Personality

Disorders' (1968), and later in, 'Analysis of the Self' (1971). In the mirror transference, the grandiose self is mobilized and expressed as: 'I am perfect and I need you in order to confirm it.' When it is very archaic, it can easily result in feelings of boredom, tension and impatience in the analyst, whose otherness is not recognized. *Countertransference* is thus a sign of it. For Kohut, the mirror transference takes three forms: (1) fusion, the most archaic, involves a merger of self with other; (2) with twinship or alter-ego transference, the other is experienced as being like the self; (3) in mirror transference, the therapist serves client needs.

For Lacan (1949) the mirror phase, 'although normal, institutes the ego as a fundamentally narcissistic defense against "motor impotence and nursling dependence" (p. 76),' whereas with Kohut, mirror processes promote unity and cohesion required in the normal formation and development of the self (Malin, 2011, p. 62).

points for reflection and practice

- What is important in practice is understanding that we are not merely ignorant of the gap separating unreality of the mirrored image from the true self. This gap is already what creates a sense of self from the beginning and without it we remain in a continual state of dependency.
- 'In the mirror stage, Lacan compressed the two phases into one. At the very moment when the ego is formed by the image of the other, narcissism and aggressivity are correlatives. Narcissism, in which the image of one's own body is sustained by the image

of the other, in fact introduces a tension: the other in his image both attracts and rejects me' (Julien, 1996, p. 34).

- With Kohut's mirror transference, fusion, the therapist/analyst is seen as omnipotent and tyrannical and is experienced as an extension of the self.

KEY TEXTS

- Julien, P. (1996) *Jacques Lacan's Return to Freud: The Real, the Symbolic and the Imaginary* (New York, NY: New York University Press)
- Kirshner, L. A. (2004) *Having a Life: Self-Pathology after Lacan* (New York, NY: Analytic Press)
- Kirshner, L. A. (ed.) (2011) *Between Winnicott and Lacan: A Clinical Engagement* (New York, NY: Taylor & Francis)
- Kohut, H. (1968) 'The Psychoanalytic Treatment of Narcissistic Personality Disorders: Outline of a Systematic Approach', *The Psychoanalytic Study of the Child*, 23: pp. 86–113
- Kohut, H. (1971) *The Analysis of the Self: A Systematic Approach to the Psychoanalytic Treatment of Narcissistic Personality Disorders* (Chicago, IL: University of Chicago Press)
- Lacan, J. (1977) 'The Mirror Stage as Formative in the Function of the I as Revealed in Psychoanalytic Experience' in *Écrits: A Selection* (A. Sheridan, Trans.) (London, UK: Tavistock), pp. 1–7
- Malin, B. D. (2011) 'Kohut and Lacan: Mirror Opposites', *Psychoanalytic Inquiry*, 31 (1): pp. 58–74
- Muller, J. (1985) 'Lacan's Mirror Stage', *Psychoanalytic Inquiry*, 5 (2): pp. 233–252
- Pines, M. (1984) 'Reflections on Mirroring', *International Review of Psychoanalysis*, 11 (1): pp. 27–42
- Shengold, L. (1974) 'The Metaphor of the Mirror', *Journal of the American Psychoanalytic Association*, 22: pp. 97–115

n

narcissism

SEE ALSO developmental stages; selfobject

Narcissus, the handsome son of the river god Cephissus and the nymph Liriope, in Ovid's tale, rejects the love of Echo, who after withdrawing into a lonely place leaves behind only a trace or echo of her voice. The goddess Nemesis, however, hears her pleas for vengeance and Narcissus is forced to fall in love with his own reflection, a fate he cannot endure. He is condemned to sit by a pool of water, watching his reflection until he dies and is transformed into the narcissus flower. The term 'narcissism', thus, refers to self-love. For Freud the *ego* has an original cathexis, a primary narcissism; as the infant gradually redirects a portion of libido to the *object* world, according to Freud there is a developing tension between ego-libido and object-libido. Moreover, Freud described (1914) primary and secondary stages and forms of narcissism. The infant's own ego, in primary narcissism, becomes the first object of libidinal love; Freud saw this primary, basic, sexually charged desire directed at the self as normal. Primary narcissism is objectless and precedes the *recognition* by the infant of a separate object (Freud, 1914). Primary narcissism describes the condition of all infants: an exclusive focus on their own bodies and needs.

Secondary narcissism, found in pathological states, occurs when libido is withdrawn from objects in the world. Beginning with his 1914 essay 'On Narcissism: An Introduction', Freud talks about narcissism in four ways: (1) as sexual perversion, (2) as a stage in development, (3) as libidinal cathexis of the ego and (4) as object choice. With narcissistic object choice, Freud argued, one libidinally invests in: (a) what he himself is (i.e. himself); (b) what he himself was; (c) what he himself would like to be and (d) someone who was once part of himself (1914, p. 90).

Because Klein imagined the drives as essentially entangled with objects, both internal and external, she abandoned the concept of 'primary narcissism'. The infant, for Klein, is more profoundly and deeply in relation with others and the object world (1932, p. 33). Dismissal of the concept, however, was not a trifling adjustment to the theory. The concept had been used as an explanatory concept with a wide range of purposes: tics (Ferenczi, 1921), schizophrenia (Freud, 1914), and as a tool for understanding rigid resistances within the psychoanalytic situation (Abraham 1919). Klein and her collaborators took issue with these accounts. For them, these seemingly narcissistic manifestations – e.g. tics (Klein 1925), schizophrenia (Klein, 1960) and extreme resistances in analysis (Reviere, 1936) – are not mental states lacking objects (i.e. only the ego as an object). For Klein, the content and nature of relations with objects (i.e. *real* people in the outside world and phantasized images of others) are the most important determinants of our mental lives, normal and pathological.

There have been many and sometimes confusing attempts to rethink Freud's conceptualization of narcissism. Among the most well known of these is Heinz Kohut's reformulation. For Kohut, while a degree of narcissism is common, it may become pathological when normal *empathy* is absent and others are used ruthlessly to their own ends. Narcissistic pathology results from a lack of parental empathy throughout early development. The result is a deficit in capacity to regulate self-esteem. In adult life, there is a tendency to move between irrational overestimation of the self and equally troubling irrational feelings of inferiority. And the solution is in turning to others for regulation of self-esteem. For Kohut the object of narcissistic demand is the *selfobject*: an object or person undifferentiated from the self and serving the needs of the self.

Finally, it is important to note that historians (Lunbeck, 2014) and social theorists (Lasch, 1991) have used the concept to explore broader social and cultural dynamics. For Christopher Lasch, after World War II, the United States suffered from what he called 'organized kindness'. What emerged within the culture (e.g. sexual liberation, radical political movements, spiritual cults), he argued, was not unlike what some call 'pathological narcissism'. Lasch argued that cultural narcissism produced for the self a need for continual external validation. Elizabeth Lunbeck (2014) disagrees. For her Lasch and others failed to see a crucial development in the history of psychoanalytic thought: the positive function of narcissism. Lunbeck shows how the analytic world clashed over understandings of the concept (i.e. how much self-love, self-esteem and self-indulgence was normal and desirable?). Some, she shows, supported the ascetic side of narcissism and dissenters saw in narcissism gratification. She turns to Kohut to support her argument for 'normal narcissism'. Lasch and the cultural critics tended to see only the pathological side of narcissism.

points for reflection and practice
- The diagnosis and treatment of narcissism require understanding its protective function for the maintenance of internal control and self-esteem.
- In adult life, there is a tendency to move between irrational overestimation of the self and equally troubling irrational feelings of inferiority. And the solution is turning to others for regulation of self-esteem.

KEY TEXTS
- Kohut, H. (1971) *The Analysis of the Self: A Systematic Approach to the Psychoanalytic Treatment of Narcissistic Personality Disorders* (Chicago, IL: University of Chicago Press)
- Lasch, C. (1991) *The Culture of Narcissism: American Life in an Age of Diminishing Expectations* (New York, NY: W. W. Norton & Company)
- Lunbeck, E. (2014) *The Americanization of Narcissism* (Cambridge, MA: Harvard University Press)
- Mitchell, S. A. (1986) 'The Wings of Icarus: Illusion and the Problem of Narcissism', *Contemporary Psychoanalysis*, 22 (1): pp. 107–132
- Sandler, J., Fonagy, P. and Person, E. S. (eds) (2012) *Freud's on Narcissism: An Introduction* (London, UK: Karnac Books)

neurosis

SEE ALSO **mirror stage (and mirroring)**

For Freud, unlike *psychosis*, 'in neurosis the *ego* suppresses part of the id out of allegiance to reality, whereas in psychosis it lets itself be carried away by the id and detached from a part of reality'

(1997, p. 207; emphasis added). Neuroses result from inadequately repressed internal impulses seeking expression, or from external traumatic events (e.g. sexual overwhelming or abuse, trauma); while most people live with neurotic conflicts, some have serious and debilitating symptoms that *affect* working, loving and leisure. Freud argued that the ego often seeks advantage through illness: the symptom, thus, enables the ego to avoid conflict between the ego and the id. The symptom, a substitute for the unacceptable impulse, reduces, displaces or distorts.

Neurosis is a concept often used in a very general way to describe psychological distress. In psychoanalysis it refers to an aspect or quality of psychosexual development. The neuroses (e.g. *anxiety*, obsessions, phobias and hysteria) do not lead to a break with reality. American psychologists and psychiatrists stopped using it as a diagnostic category with the third addition (1980) of the DSM.

For Freud there is an important distinction to be made between 'actual' and 'psychoneuroses'. The actual neuroses result from *real* difficulties with sexual functioning; the psychoneuroses were rooted in early and unconscious psychic conflicts. While actual neurosis and psychoneurosis have similar origins (i.e. in the inability to physically represent or elaborate internal pressure), with actual neurosis the somatic dominates. With psychoneurosis, the psyche constructs meaningful symptoms that can be mentally represented (i.e. hysterical, obsessional), which yield interpretative possibilities. Understanding how the mind moves towards psychic elaboration is a major challenge and may indeed be the central most important issue in an era dominated by body symptoms and body modifications (Verhaeghe and Vanheule, 2005).

For Lacan, neurotic phenomena are intrinsic to being human. We are, according to his logic, always and inevitably seeking and identifying with illusory and unattainable fantasies of wholeness and unattainable desires. These aims, however, are always beyond our reach and what many would consider to be the hallmarks of mental health are in fact illusory: integration, ego integration, equilibrium, self-awareness.

KEY TEXTS

- Freud, S. (1953–74) *The Standard Edition of the Complete Psychological Works of Sigmund Freud* (James Strachey Trans.) 24 Vols (London, UK: Hogarth Press)

- Green, A. (2005) *Key Ideas for a Contemporary Psychoanalysis: Misrecognition and Recognition of the Unconscious* (London, UK: Routledge)
- Kirshner, L. (2013) 'Trauma and Psychosis: A Review and Framework for Psychoanalytic Understanding', *International Forum of Psychoanalysis*. Published Online 4 June. DOI: 10.1080/0803706X.2013.778422
- Verhaeghe, P. and Vanheule, S. (2005) 'Actual Neurosis and PTSD: The Impact of the Other', *Psychoanalytic Psychology*, 22 (4): pp. 493–507

O

object

SEE ALSO **bad object; objet a (objet petit a)**

The concept, *object*, has several and sometimes confusing refer-ents. In philosophy, it is generally contrasted with the conscious 'subject' or observing agent; the object, then, is the passive thing to be observed; in short, the 'object relates to a subject'. In psychoanal-ysis, the subject–object relationship is made problematic: objects are invested (i.e. cathected) with energy. Objects, thus, are all organ-ized around desire and may be people or even abstract ideas. Apart from the external object (the *real* person, the body or part of body), the 'object' must always be understood as a 'theoretical construct' or term, not an 'observational' one; thus, it refers to the empirical thing, or events, or a person or a bodily zone, only through its effects. Psychoanalysts will often refer to *transitional objects* (see entry, *tran-sitional objects*), part-objects, total objects, narcissistic, internal and external objects, selfobjects, object relationships and object choices. Just as we know and feel the presence of gravity (not by seeing it), we know and feel the presence of our object world – through the effects produced by it, within us and in our intersubjective lives. The concept, object, thus is used by psychoanalysts (and others) from different schools of thought as a tool for understanding the complexities of our psychic and relational worlds.

It is often used to refer to the object of one's sexual desire. It is commonplace, in psychoanalytic theory and beyond, to refer to 'object choice' (e.g. 'he has a same-sex object choice' or 'her object choice is heterosexual'). Freud used object choice to refer to the earliest rela-tionships with caregivers – the objects of need and desire. Object was also used by Freud to describe the focus of the drives.

The significant psychological events, for Freud, are produced by excess or deficiency of gratification. The object is the principal means through which gratification is achieved or disallowed. Primary *narcissism*, for Freud, occurs when libido is directed towards the *ego* and is the earliest developmental stage. For Freud, the 'anaclitic object choice' refers to the child's libidinal (i.e. sexual instincts) investment in the mother, whereas the 'narcissistic object choice' (see also *narcissism*) refers to libidinal investments in the self. The former, in adult life, is found among those seeking partners who promise to fulfil dependency needs once met (in fantasy or reality) by parental figures, mother or father. With the anaclitic object choice, a man will seek a nurturing woman and a woman a protective man. The latter, for Freud, is found in homosexuality (i.e. where libidinal energy flows towards the self or among parents who invest in their children without regard to the child's need for autonomy or for respecting their bodily independence). Freud also explored the relationship between the *drive* (see also, *drive*) and the object (see, 'Instincts and Their Vicissitudes', 1915). Here, borrowing heavily from Newtonian physics (i.e. with forces, drives and impacts, his metaphorically rich language conjures up electrical charges, their oppositions or polarities) he described drive excitations emanating from inside the organism (what he called, using a metaphor from hydraulics, 'pressure') and to their satisfaction (what he called the 'aim' of the drive). In short, the *object* is the means by which the drive attains its 'aim'. The object is produced by fluctuating impulses – unconscious, preconscious and conscious – or cathexes (i.e. exchange of energy), which are reciprocally exchanged.

'Internal object' has several uses and referents. It is often used in referring to body sensations or to parts of the self. It is also used in referring to imagined or internal representations of external objects. Internal objects may be seen and experienced as qualities or aspects of the self: identified or assimilated or felt as separate from but at the same time alien forces within the self. For Klein, experiences and relations with others may be internalized to preserve and protect them. These various internalized object relations, thus, become the basis for mood, behaviour and the sense of self. For Fairbairn, internal objects are rooted in real external objects (i.e. the actual parents), fragmented and recombined. Ogden (2010) writes of Fairbairn's thinking:

> [T]he most important (life-sustaining) task faced by the infant is not simply that of establishing and maintaining a loving tie

with the mother who is capable of giving and receiving love. At least as important to the psychical survival of the infant is his capacity to extricate himself from his futile efforts to wring love from the external object mother who is experienced as unloving. The infant achieves this life-saving psychological manoeuvre by developing an internal object world (an aspect of mind) in which the relationship with the external unloving mother is transformed into an internal object relationship. (p. 102)

Grotstein (1997) describes internal objects as 'orphans' or 'renegade subjects' or 'split off aspects of conscious subjectivity', which appear in dreams, symptoms, delusions and so on, and dramaturgically encode unmentalizable psychic pain, which can then be thought or mentalized.

'Part object', a concept introduced by Melanie Klein, can be found in Freud's early writing on the 'partial drive'. Part-objects refer to fragments of things or persons: a mouth, hand, genital. Part-objects can be extrapolated to represent the whole object.

Lacan referred to the object as the objet (a). For him, the (a) is related to the small other (i.e. 'l'autre'), and the 'l'autre' has a character or quality that makes it the object of desire. (a) is then seen as the cause of desire. It is both the cause of desire and lack itself.

KEY TEXTS

- Clarke, G. and Scharff, D. (eds) (2014) *Fairbairn and the Object-Relations Tradition* (London, UK: Karnac Books)
- Grotstein, J. (1997) '"Internal Objects" or "Chimerical Monsters"? The Demonic "Third Forms" of the Internal World', *Journal of Analytical Psychology*, 42 (1): pp. 47–80
- Ogden, T. (2010) 'Why Read Fairbairn?' *International Journal of Psychoanalysis*, 91 (1): pp. 101–118
- Mitchell, S. (1981) 'The Origin and Nature of the "Object" in the Theories of Klein and Fairbairn', *Contemporary Psychoanalysis*, 17 (3): pp. 374–398
- Sweet, A. (2012) 'Internal Objects and Self-Destructive Behaviours: A Clinical Case Highlighting Dissociation, Splitting and the Role of the Primitive Super-Ego in the Addictions', *The Scandinavian Psychoanalytic Review*, 35 (2): pp. 116–126

objet a (objet petit a)

SEE ALSO **ego; imaginary; mirror stage (and mirroring); symbolic; transitional space/transitional phenomena/transitional object**

Jacques Lacan uses *objet petit a* while referring to the infant's gaze into the mirror, where it sees the image of its *ego* ideal. Most importantly, however, it is the first of the unfolding moments of desire for the Other; here it is a desire for the idealized self. The 'objet petit a' refers to a desire that lacks in form and language and for Lacan, because desire is always the desire 'of' the Other, there is inevitable frustration and disappointment resulting from the impossibility of adequately symbolizing or knowing the desire of the Other: we never know what the Other truly wants from us. But it is also this very property of the object, its unreachable nature, that compels our seeking, longing and reaching for it, and makes it compelling and desirable. Lacan (1958) once described desire as a remainder once satisfaction of physiological needs is subtracted from demand for maternal attention.

Kirshner (2008) writes of objet petit a,

> Unlike the *transitional object*, which I believe Lacan considered a sign of the child's entry into the *symbolic* order as a separate subject, the objet petit a cannot be concretized as an actual thing. In this sense, it has been compared to the part object fantasy of Kleinian theory in that it represents an *imaginary* link between the infantile body and the mother – the breast, for example. However, it is neither a concrete feature of her anatomy nor a specific memory, but the fantasy of a loss established retrospectively, after the child has been 'subjectified'. The step of becoming a subject (through entry into the symbolic order) leaves a gap between human reality and the *real* of nature that, like *transitional space*, affects all subsequent experience. (p. 88; emphases added)

point for reflection and practice
- The work of psychotherapy is to help the patient/subject recognize that desire is not just the desire of the Other; therapy should also endeavour to understand desire and the important role of specific unconscious fantasies in the construction of desire and in investing objects with particular significance.

KEY TEXTS

- Kirshner, L. (2005) 'Rethinking Desire: The Objet Petit A in Lacanian Theory', *Journal of the American Psychoanalytic Association*, 53 (1): pp. 83–102
- Lacan, J. (1977) 'The Subversion of the Subject and the Dialectic of Desire in the Freudian Unconscious' in *Ecrits: A Selection* (A. Sheridan, Trans.) (London, UK: Tavistock), pp. 292–325

oedipal

SEE ALSO **attachment; developmental stages; gender; mirror stage (and mirroring)**

The Oedipal complex is foremost among Freud's most controversial and widely contested ideas. During the Oedipal phase, Freud argued, children develop powerful libidinal strivings for only one parent (the opposite sex), and powerfully rivalrous and jealous feelings towards the other. While boys and girls, in Freud's view, are innately masculine, femininity for girls is a secondary construction. To successfully enter what Freud called the triangular Oedipal phase, girls must relinquish their innate masculinity by transforming the aim (i.e. active, phallic), the *object* (i.e. mother) and the erotogenic zone (i.e. clitoris) of the originating masculine sexual *drive*. Thus, the boy and girl share pre-Oedipal emotional worlds, both attached to the maternal figure and sexually undifferentiated. Here Freud made one of his most controversial claims: the little girl is but a little man waiting to be transformed.

For a young male child, *anxiety* results from the fear that the father will one day violently intervene (i.e. castration) in his loving relationship with his mother. As a young boy becomes aware of differences between male and female anatomy, he concludes that the female has been emasculated and that his genitals may be removed as the rival father seeks retribution from the child for desiring the

maternal figure. For the young boy, the Oedipal *attachment* to the mother follows the pre-Oedipal attachment and is only interrupted with the paternal threat of castration. And while boys and girls begin in a shared, emotional and sexually undifferentiated pre-Oedipal world (i.e. attached to the mother), the girl in Freud's theory eventually becomes a little man. It is also here where Freud postulates an especially controversial notion: a single, masculine libido and the original desire (i.e. for the mother) is associated with the masculinity and activity. 'Penis envy', moreover, emerges when the girl sees herself as lacking, and her attraction for her father results in a desire to (re)possess the missing organ. Also, at some point, the young girl must relinquish her first object choice, her mother, for the appropriate one: her father. Castration for girls, moreover, does not lead to resolution of the Oedipal and because of this, according to Freud, the Oedipal conflict persists and accounts for their weaker superegos and capacities for *sublimation*. The girl's attraction to the father and rivalry with mother has been called the Electra complex.

For Jacque Lacan, sexual difference (see entry, *mirror stage (and mirroring)*) does not exist prior to representation and is enabled by movement around the Oedipal Complex, and by submitting to castration (i.e. the phallic function) the child enters into significa-tion. In short, it is the phallus that enables the movement from immersion in immediacy to a meaningful representational world.

Freud's critics observe that: (1) the Oedipus complex and the masculine have been generalized to encompass the psychic life of girls; (2) this generalization fails to account for the unique-ness of Oedipal dynamics for girls and the particularity of femi-nine characteristic (i.e. object relationships, defences and social dynamics). Many of Freud's critics turn attention to the importance of separation in the triangular situation of females. For Kulish and Holtzman, 'misunderstanding how these separation conflicts tie into triangular "Oedipal" relationships can lead to a "preoedipaliza-tion" of the dynamics of girls and women' (Kulish and Holtzman, 2000, p. 1413).

Luce Irigaray, a French feminist psychoanalyst and social theo-rist, argues that because Freud saw the little girl as a little man, the dynamic between the mother and daughter is misrecognized, resulting in suppression of maternal lines of descent, whereby, priv-ileging the name of the father (i.e. the order of patrimony enabling the sons to inherit the father's name) subsumes birth to the father. For Irigaray, thus, the pre-Oedipal relation between the mother and daughter does not enter the signifying order. In Lacanian language, this means that the mother and daughter relation does not enter the *symbolic* (see entry, *symbolic*). The outcome of this exclusion is far-reaching. Alongside the loss and repression of the maternal connection is the capacity for naming and identifying that loss. And because it is not in memory, the loss cannot be mourned. It is in this way, for Irigaray, through what she calls genealogical asymmetry, that the father's name is memorialized and the mother's body is sacrificed. It is also here that she identifies the foundation for the legitimacy of patriarchy (Irigaray, 1985, 1993).

KEY TEXTS

- Hall, J. (2008) 'Relinquishing Orthodoxy: One Freudian Analyst's Personal Journey', *The Psychoanalytic Review*, 95 (5): pp. 845–871
- Irigaray, L. (1985) *Speculum of the Other Woman* (Ithaca, NY: Cornell University Press)
- Kulish, N. and Holtzman, D. (2008) *A Story of Her Own: The Female Oedipus Complex Reexamined and Renamed* (New York, NY: Jason Aronson)

p

paranoid-schizoid

SEE ALSO ambivalence; bad object; depressive position; developmental stages; ego

Melaine Klein used this term to describe internal and external *object* relations, anxieties and defences. Often the concept was used to refer to a specific developmental moment in early life but also continuing into childhood and throughout adult life. The paranoid position, in development, precedes the *depression* position. Note the importance of the use of the term 'position'; it is used quite deliberately to connote, not a fixed and inexorable 'stage', but a recursive movement between mental states and organizations. The most significant mental states described by this concept are *splitting* of the object and the self into good and bad qualities and *projection*. Lacking the capacity for integration in early life, the infant uses splitting along with introjection and projection to manage anxieties related to the death instinct, birth, hunger and frustration. In splitting (both the *ego* and the object), the infant projects, at different times and in different ways, feelings of love and hate. These are then projected into different parts of the mother (e.g. the breast) where the mother is experienced as both bad (i.e. depriving, frustrating, not always available) and good (i.e. gratifying, fulfilling, available). Then the projected parts, good and bad, are introjected. There is a recursive movement of projection and introjection (sometimes called re-introjection) along with the additional defences of omnipotence and idealization. The *bad object*/experience is managed with omnipotent control and denial and the good experience is idealized as a defence against the persecuting object. When all goes well, splitting serves the crucial function of helping the infant internalize and retain the feelings and mental states associated with the good object/experience and to secure a psychic organization sufficient for integration of the bits and pieces of the self; most importantly, this integration and working through leads to the *depressive position*; with the achievement of the depressive position, the infant (and adult) develops an increasing capacity to manage ambivalent mental states and treats the object as a whole person over which concern, *guilt* and reparation dominate. If this is not achieved, the result is a quality of splitting that leads to fragmentation, disintegration of the ego, schizoid defences and the potential for the development of severe illness.

Sociologists have used the concepts, *paranoid–schizoid*, depressive position, and their associated defences, projection and splitting, to think about the intractability of racism, homophobia and other social processes (Rasmussen and Salhani, 2010).

KEY TEXTS

- Clarke, S. (2000) 'Psychoanalysis, Psychoexistentialism and Racism', *Psychoanalytic Studies*, 2 (4): pp. 343–355
- Clarke, S. (2002) 'On Strangers: Phantasy, Terror and the Human Imagination', *Journal of Human Rights*, 1 (3): pp. 345–355
- Rasmussen, B. and Salhani, D. (2010) 'A Contemporary Kleinian Contribution to Understanding Racism', *Social Service Review*, 84 (3): pp. 491–513
- Steiner, J. (1979) 'The Border between the Paranoid-Schizoid and the Depressive Positions in the Borderline Patient', *British Journal of Medical Psychology*, 52 (4): pp. 385–391
- Sullivan, R. E. (2005) 'Social Theory, Psychoanalysis, and Racism', *Contemporary Sociology: A Journal of Reviews*, 34 (2): 139–140
- Tan, R. (2006) 'Racism and Similarity: Paranoid-Schizoid Structures Revisited' in R. Moodley and S. Palmer (eds), *Race, Culture and Psychotherapy: Critical Perspectives in Multicultural Practice* (New York, NY: Routledge), pp. 119–129

parapraxis

SEE ALSO **conflict and compromise formation**

Parapraxis (Greek), a word never used by Freud, means alongside normal practice. Freud used the German, Fehlleistung, or 'faulty achievement', to describe a mental error in speech or memory, writing, reading or action. In popular language, these errors are called Freudian slips. It was in his book, 'Psychopathology of Everyday Life', where Freud sought to demonstrate how parapraxes function. These errors result from repressed material, slips that occur when we intend one thing in speech or action but say or do another. And, like the symptom, parapraxes are seen as compromise formations or conflicts between conscious intent and repressed thought or feeling. While mental errors may appear unintentional or as simple mistakes, in psychoanalysis they are understood to be motivated and unconsciously determined (i.e. with a cause). The parapraxes, because they occur frequently in everyday life, demonstrate the presence and action of the unconscious.

KEY TEXTS
- Freud, S. (1901) *The Psychopathology of Everyday Life*. Standard Edition, 6
- Freud, S. (1915–17) *Introductory Lectures on Psychoanalysis*. Standard Edition, 15–16

parenting

SEE ALSO **adolescence; developmental stages; evidence-based practice**

We live in an era of no-fault parenting. We put our children in childcare and entrust them to caregivers as if they were like all other fungible commodities. We assume that they can be passed off daily to substitute caregivers without the knowledge of their inner worlds, daily struggles and worries. And we do this knowing that the nature and quality of early relationships matter (Phillip and Shonkoff, 2000). We then blame parents and schools, especially working-class parents (Rubin, 1976), for the pressures and consequences of living and working and attempting to love in a world where two incomes aren't enough, neighbourhoods and schools are deteriorating and safety nets have contracted. It is a world where economic disparities (Piketty, 2014) have eliminated the middle class and the burden of caring for children presents unprecedented challenges. And after more than a century of liberal economic policies and social and behavioural science research and related policy interventions, our social problems are getting worse (Cartwright, 2012). How can we expect parenting practices to change or improve when the world around most parents is collapsing?

Evidence-based parenting interventions have been tested and tried. In 1966, psychologist Diana Baumrind published an article

'Effects of Authoritative Parental Control on Child Behavior' in 'Child Development'. In this and subsequent decades of work she and her colleagues have identified and studied four styles or categories of parenting: (1) authoritative (democratic style): where parents are attentive, forgiving, teach proper behaviour, use clear rules and use appropriate punishment and reward when rules are violated; (2) authoritarian (strict parenting style): imposes high expectations, uses minimal communication, parents offer minimal reasoning for rules and limits and exact harsh penalties; (3) permissive (parent acts as friend): limited expectations and child encouraged to make independent decisions; (4) uninvolved (parent neglects child): puts own life before the child, provides basic needs with little interaction.

In a very interesting intellectual move, Baumrind manages to elide the entire psychoanalytic canon on parenting, mother–infant dynamics (Fraiberg *et al.*, 1975; Fraiberg, 1959; Freud, 1965; Mahler, 1974) and understanding parenthood as a developmental process (Benedek, 1959; Furman, 1994; Parens, 1975). There were two rather odd exceptions, Theodor Adorno and Eric Fromm: both were immersed in psychoanalytic thinking and practice, and both were interested in human development and personality. Baumrind, however, used them only to think about authoritarianism and even then with a very superficial and perfunctory understanding of their work (Darling and Steinberg, 1993). What she did not grasp was the importance of understanding parenthood as a developmental process and the unconscious dynamics of parental choices (Cohen, 1998; Demick, 2002; Furman, 2001; Novick, 2010 Watson *et al.*, 1992). And that choice has left the now vast literature on the subject mostly descriptive and without a developmental theory sufficient to explain how and why parental styles vary, within and among social classes and ethnic groups.

In her important essay on developmental lines, Anna Freud (1963), along with many others in the 1950s and 1960s, began to think about parenting as a developmental process or stage. The Hanna Perkins Center and therapeutic school in Cleveland, Ohio, has integrated psychoanalytic thinking on parenting and parenting stages (from Winnicott, Fraiberg, Mahler, Benedek) in an especially useful way. They see children and parents recursively negotiating four developmental phases and conflicts: (1) doing for; (2) doing with; (3) standing by to admire; and (4) letting go. This is a version of Vygotsky's (1978) 'zone of proximal development' but with a clear articulation of the psychic conflicts and unconscious dynamics at play. While childhood and parenthood necessarily begins with 'doing for' and moves towards independence and mastery (bowel, mobility, eating, etc.) it is not a neat linear or always conscious process. When sick, even as an adult, one easily needs 'doing for'. Yet there are times when parents and children remain stuck in a phase of 'doing for', where dependency conflicts and struggles dominate and separation is difficult. And I would argue that this is a potential conflict and phase in every culture; again at the end of life, 'doing for' presents new challenges and potential conflicts. For some parents, 'doing with' is a particularly difficult struggle. Vygotsky (1962, p. 108) described this phase very nicely in his work on the zone of proximal development: a space between the level of independent performance (i.e. what the child can accomplish independently) and the level of assistance needed (i.e. what the child can manage with support). And in our culture, where working parents are strapped for time and resources, 'doing with' presents significant challenges; it is impossible to imagine that substitute care can perform the tasks necessary for scaffolding at this early stage of mastery. It may be the case that in our digital age (Lanier, 2010; Rushkoff, 2013; Turkle, 2012), where devices substitute for relationships, 'doing with' and mastery in early life may be seriously compromised and even never achieved. 'Standing by' is an equally complicated moment in parental and child development. It is difficult for some parents to admire: some parents feel envy and others are narcissistically invested in their children. Some parents promote independence before children are prepared and some children (i.e. parentified) seek independence before they are developmentally prepared for it. Likewise, in later life, some desire and seek independence when it is just beyond their reach or sometimes easily achievable with family and caregiving environments to promote it. Many parents have and care for children to meet their own narcissistic needs and children then do not have an existence in their own right. Finally, 'letting go' is often difficult. Some parents and mothers prefer infants and strive in their caregiving to keep a child from developing. And some parents cannot let go of their latency-age child as they reach into puberty and *adolescence*. And 'letting go' at the end of life presents its own difficult challenges.

KEY TEXTS

- Baldwin, E. N. (2014) 'Recognizing Guilt and Shame: Therapeutic Ruptures with Parents of Children in Psychotherapy', *Psychoanalytic Social Work*, 21 (1–2): pp. 2–18
- Demick, J. (2002) 'Stages of Parental Development', *Handbook of Parenting*, 3, pp. 389–413
- Freud, A. (1963) 'The Concept of Developmental Lines', *The Psychoanalytic Study of the Child*, 18: pp. 245–265
- Furman, E. (1994) 'Early Aspects of Mothering: What Makes It So Hard to Be There to Be Left', *Journal of Child Psychotherapy*, 20 (2): pp. 149–164
- Furman, E. (2001) *On Being and Having a Mother* (Madison: CT: International Universities Press)
- Hoffman, L. (2003) 'Mothers' Ambivalence with Their Babies and Toddlers: Manifestations of Conflicts with Aggression', *Journal of the American Psychoanalytic Association*, 51 (4): pp. 1219–1240
- Nilsson, M. (2006) 'To Be the Sole Therapist: Children and Parents in Simultaneous Psychotherapy', *Journal of Infant, Child, and Adolescent Psychotherapy*, 5 (2): pp. 206–225
- Novick, K. K. and Novick, J. (2010) *Emotional Muscle: Strong Parents, Strong Children* (USA: Xlibris Corporation)
- Oram, K. (2000) 'A Transitional Space: Involving Parents in the Play Therapy of Their Children', *Journal of Infant, Child, and Adolescent Psychotherapy*, 1 (4): pp. 79–98
- Reynolds, D. (2003) 'Mindful Parenting: A Group Approach to Enhancing Reflective Capacity in Parents and Infants', *Journal of Child Psychotherapy*, 29 (3): 357–374
- Siskind, D. (1997) *Working with Parents: Establishing the Essential Alliance in Child Psychotherapy and Consultation* (New York, NY: Jason Aronson)
- Torsti, M. (1998) 'On Motherhood', *The Scandinavian Psychoanalytic Review*, 21 (1): pp. 53–76
- Tsiantis, J. (ed.) (2000) *Work with Parents: Psychoanalytic Psychotherapy with Children and Adolescents* (London, UK: Karnac Books)
- Vygotsky, L. (1962) *Thought and Language* (Cambridge, MA: MIT Press)
- Watson, P. J., Little, T. and Biderman, M. D. (1992) 'Narcissism and Parenting Styles', *Psychoanalytic Psychology*, 9 (2): pp. 231–244
- Woods, M. Z., and Pretorius, I. M. (eds) (2011) *Parents and Toddlers in Groups: A Psychoanalytic Developmental Approach* (London, UK: Routledge)

positivism and critical realism

SEE ALSO **social constructivism (or anti-essentialism)**

For positivists, explanation results when regularities have been identified, ordinarily in closed systems: event (x), then event (y). Antecedent conditions in the chain of events, such as x, may be added to and measured with increasing degrees of sophistication – what we call statistical methods – and may tell us, at most, that an event did occur or, sometimes, will occur; however, there is no requirement to show 'why' two or more events in constant conjunction produce a subsequent event. Grounds for expecting an event to occur, thus, are confused with the causal explanation for why an event occurred; in short, explanation is reduced to prediction.

Positivist epistemology, in its conflation of prediction with explanation, presents a problem for how we account for human agency in our explanation of events or subjectivity: human agents change the antecedent conditions, often not consciously or rationally. This is, of course, one of the factors complicating, enormously, the data produced by *psychodynamic* theory and psychoanalysis; that is, antecedent conditions are never contained within closed systems, but are always under the influence of dynamic forces, acting recursively in open systems as the work of therapy or analysis proceeds (see Ricoeur's criterion for facts in psychoanalysis, 2012, pp. 12–22). Moreover, positivism claims that knowledge necessarily derives from atomistic sense experience.

Roy Bhaskar, a critical realist, examines the nature of experimental activity within the human sciences by drawing our attention to the problems positivism produces by creating closure in necessarily open systems. It is with this issue that psychodynamic practice and psychoanalytic theory ultimately confronts its positivist critics (e.g. Popper *et al.*). It is in the act of closure that the scientist triggers, for instance, a biological mechanism to observe its powers and internal structure in the absence of intervening forces. Closure is, first, only achieved through activity, scientific work explicitly directed at isolating a single mechanism. Closure in psychodynamic theory and practice is possible only a posteriori or as historical explanation; we have closure only after an event has unfolded and, thus, no longer under the direct influence of variables in open systems. It was in this way that Freud, like Marx and Darwin, was more an archaeologist or natural historian. Yet even in the natural sciences closure can be said to properly exist only when the mechanism is isolated by virtue of a carefully constructed experimental situation, or when other intervening mechanisms, their powers and liabilities, are well known, accounted for and theorized (Collier, 1994, p. 33).

Still, when an approximation to closure is achieved, the knowledge claims generated have certain, definite limit: outside the laboratory mechanisms operate with open systems, alongside multiple others (p. 34). Thus, genetics may be able to discover the function of a particular gene in isolation – perhaps one day even map a static vision of the human genome, but the random variation in the development and growth of any organism at the level of the cell, what is commonly referred to as 'developmental noise', constitutes an open system at work – the organism – thus introducing variation that cannot be predicted from the genetic structure (Lewontin, 1991, p. 27). '[I]n open systems mechanisms operate and have effects other than those they would have in experimental situations, due to the co-determination of these systems by other mechanisms' (Collier, 1994, p. 36). Thus, when we move beyond the organism to consider the world external to it, even further complexity is introduced. Changing environments constitute the conditions of possibility for genes, behaviours, thought or feeling, while the organisms simultaneously create their own environment.

KEY TEXTS
- Kline, P. (2013) *Fact and Fantasy in Freudian Theory* (London, UK: Routledge)
- Ricoeur, P. (2013) *On Psychoanalysis* (Cambridge, UK: Polity Press)

primary process and secondary process

SEE ALSO **developmental stages; mentalization; psychosis**

In primary process thinking, according to Freud, the id releases tension produced by the pleasure principle; unacceptable urges are deferred and a mental image of a desired *object* is substituted for the urge (the image can be expressed in dreams, hallucinations, fantasies or delusions). In this unconscious processing of the id, which uses symbols and metaphor, unfettered gratification of instinctual demands and drives is pursued. Primary process, activated by the drives, serves the pleasure principle and works to actualize psychic energy.

'Primary process' and 'secondary process', both terms used by Freud, describe two opposed but complementary modes of mental functioning. In secondary process thinking, energy is bound and in the service of the reality principle, where a system of control and regulation is established. In the first system, the primary process serves the purpose of freely discharging quantities of excitation, whereas in secondary process, the discharge is inhibited. Mental life is an ongoing balance and tension between these two processes, emerging (i.e. developmentally) over time, varying over time and differently experienced.

Researchers (Bazan *et al.*, 2013; Holt, 2008) have recently shown that primary process thinking, far from being a fiction of Freud's metapsychological ideas, is deeply rooted in our cognitive/neurobiological dynamics. Holt (2008) describes six understandings of both primary and secondary process thinking in psychoanalysis: dynamic, economic, topographic, structural, adaptive and genetic (2009, p. 5). Each of these in very different ways describes a quality of primary and secondary process. Primary process, Holt argues, can be empirically demonstrated using responses to Rorschach blots.

In her recent thinking on the subject, Irene Fast (2012) moves the discussion away from dichotomous thinking, primary and secondary processes, towards a more dialogical view. She writes that minds are not filled with early content determined by evolution but with patterned daily experience. Unlike Freud, Fast argues that the primitive qualities of our thought are better understood as moments of early nonintegration and nondifferentiation. Moreover, for Fast, we should see development not as a steady emergence of whole or stable object relations but as increasingly complex imagistic patterns, and the movement from behaviour to mental expression of thought and feeling produces not only logical/rational reasoning but also increasing availability of imagistic patterns. The outcome of development, for Fast, is a mentalizing mind capable of navigating the objective and impersonal worlds of rational thinking, alongside the personal and emotional, the one not replacing the other, leading to higher levels, but to equally valued expressions and experience. Where Fast sees evidence of so-called primitive mental characteristics in adult life (omnipotence, object impermanence, etc.), she does not infer a dichotomy between constitutionally deter-mined modes of thought, but developmental struggles (p. 196).

KEY TEXTS

- Bazan, A. *et al.* (2013) 'Empirical Evidence for Freud's Theory of Primary Process Mentation in Acute Psychosis', *Psychoanalytic Psychology*, 30 (1): pp. 57–74
- Fast, I. (2012) 'The Primary Processes Grow Up: Freud's More Radical View of the Mind', *Contemporary Psychoanalysis*, 48 (2): pp. 183–198
- Holt, R. R. (2008) *Primary Process Thinking: Theory, Measurement, and Research* (New York, NY: Jason Aronson)
- Suler, J. R. (1980) 'Primary Process Thinking and Creativity', *Psychological Bulletin*, 88 (1): pp. 144–165

projection

SEE ALSO **defence mechanisms**

Projection describes interaction between the inner and outer worlds. With projection, the subject expels or refuses to recognize or acknowledge qualities of the self: thought or feeling, or wish or internal objects. They are projected outwards and onto a person or thing. As a defence mechanism, projection is used to keep out of awareness undesirable aspects of the self by attributing feelings and thoughts (e.g. sexual, destructive) to others and thereby alto-gether avoid them. The projection of a thought or emotion enables the self to consider the disturbing nature of thoughts or feelings without having to know or feel that they truly belong to them. By disavowing what we do not want to acknowledge about the self we find in the external world feelings, thoughts or other quali-ties of objects, which have their origins in our own unconscious. Projection works by enabling the expression of desire or impulse, but in a form sufficiently modified that it cannot be recognized by the *ego*. The theory holds that it is easier to tolerate punishment from the outside than to accept impulses in conflict with moral standards or self-concept.

Projection may also produce a kind of erasure of the qualities in others, which we find disagreeable: by imagining that they are not unlike us, we are able to ignore the qualities that cause us discomfort.

Some have identified types of projection: neurotic, complementary and complimentary. Neurotic refers to the perception of others as operating in ways one unconsciously finds objectionable in the self. Complementary assumes that others act, feel and think in the same ways. Complimentary assumes that others can do things as well as the self.

Carl Jung argues that unacceptable parts of the self (represented by the 'shadow *archetype*') are most likely to produce projection.

points for reflection and practice
- Projection enables projectors to know something about their own mental states without feeling the discomfort of knowing their thoughts and emotions belong to them.
- Projection converts neurotic or moral *anxiety* into *real* anxiety, making it easier to manage.
- Projection, a common feature of paranoia, allows for the projection of disdain for the self onto others so the feeling is converted into others disliking them.
- Projection rationalizes unacceptable behaviour.

KEY TEXTS
- Olson, T *et al.* (2011) 'Addressing and Interpreting Defense Mechanisms in Psychotherapy: General Considerations', *Psychiatry: Interpersonal and Biological Processes*, 74 (2): pp. 142–165
- Sandler, J. (ed.) (2012) *Projection, Identification, Projective Identification* (London, UK: Karnac Books)

projective identification

SEE ALSO **anxiety; developmental stages; paranoid–schizoid; projection**

Projective identification, an intrapsychic and interpersonal process, is among the key ideas in the thinking and theory of Melanie Klein and later developed by her follower, Wilifred Bion, and more recently by Thomas Ogden. For Klein (1946), the early infant, in phantasy, splits parts of the self, or the whole self, and projects or inserts them into an external *object*, which then identifies with the split and projected parts. The aim is to harm, possess or control the external object. Projected phantasies may also be accompanied by provoking behaviours causing the recipient of the *projection* to act or feel in congruence with the projections. It is in the power of the phantasy of inhabiting the recipient (i.e. with feeling, attitude, behaviour) that the projector asserts control over the recipient; if there is receptivity to projections, the recipient is described as in counter-identification with the projector. When Klein writes about identification, she is referring to the particular manner in which the subject's self is projected. It is important to understand that Klein used this concept not only to understand fundamental developmental processes (i.e. primitive, pre-verbal modes of communicating and relating where the infant expresses feeling by relating to the mother through the experience of the feeling) but also how it served defensive purposes.

It is also important to understand how projection differs from projective identification. With projection, *ego* boundaries are maintained and the external object is not in the same way the target of control and manipulation. While projection involves a mostly intrapsychic process, projective identification describes a mostly interpersonal, dynamic mode of relating. Moreover, the feelings experienced by the projector are very different. Unlike projection, with projective identification, the projector may feel in synchrony with the other: 'I am you.' With projective identification, the recipient may also experience disturbing and difficult feelings.

Cashdan (1988) identified four patterns of projective identification, rooted in underlying dependency, power, sexuality and ingratiation. For Thomas Ogden (1982), in development and therapy, projective identification has three phases: (1) the projector first inserts or disposes unwanted bits; (2) the projector then inserts them into the receiver; (3) finally, the projector recovers a modified version of the projections. It is in the third phase where the bits are metabolized and made useful to the projector. Brenman (2006) shows how therapists feel hopelessness with excessive projective identification alongside the simultaneous need to tolerate and contain omnipotent and sometimes destructive actions.

Projective identification is associated with the *paranoid–schizoid* position. Betty Joseph (1987) argues that while projective identification is common to the paranoid–schizoid position, it is never entirely relinquished. With the *depressive position* projective identification becomes 'less absolute, more temporary, and more able to be drawn back into the individual's personality and thus the basis of *empathy*' (Joseph, 1988, p. 66; emphasis added).

In his work on *affect regulation*, Shore (2003) argues that our extant developmental models and understandings of therapeutic action now accept the fundamental view that projective identification is 'not unidirectional but instead is a bidirectional process in which both members of an emotionally communicating dyad act in a context of mutual reciprocal influence' (p. 65). He also agrees with Klein's view of projective identification as more than the transmission of negative states or emotions; it necessarily involves 'projection of a much-valued part of the self into another' (p. 64).

Finally, projective identification has been used by a range of scholars to think about the social and psychological dynamics of racism

and ethnic nationalism (see Rustin, Rasmussen and Salhani, 2010; Young-Bruehl, 1998).

points for reflection and practice
- Projective identification may be used to externalize chaotic or uncertain qualities of the self and after reflection re-internalized in acceptable forms:
- In the depressive position, projective identification may be used as a way of expressing unconscious hope for intrapsychic change.
- Projective identification may be used to insert good parts of the self into others for safe keeping.

KEY TEXTS
- Brenman, E. (2006) *Recovery of the Lost Good Object* (London, UK: Routledge)
- Cashdan, S. (1988) *Object Relations Therapy: Using the Relationship* (New York, NY: W. W. Norton & Company)
- Forrester, M. (2006) 'Projective Identification and Intersubjectivity', *Theory & Psychology*, 16 (6): pp. 783–802
- Frosh, S. (2013) 'Psychoanalysis, Colonialism, Racism', *Journal of Theoretical and Philosophical Psychology*, 33 (3): pp. 141–154
- Ogden, T. (2004) *Projective Identification and Psychotherapeutic Technique* (Lanham, MD: Rowman & Littlefield Publishers, Inc.)
- Rasmussen, B. and Salhani, D. (2010) 'A Contemporary Kleinian Contribution to Understanding Racism', *Social Service Review*, 84 (3): pp. 491–513

- Rustin, M. (1991) *The Good Society and the Inner World: Psychoanalysis, Politics, and Culture* (London, UK: Verso Books)
- Schore, A. (2003) *Affect Regulation and the Repair of the Self* (New York: W. W. Norton & Company)
- Young-Bruehl, E. (1998) *The Anatomy of Prejudices* (Cambridge, MA: Harvard University Press)

psychodynamic

SEE ALSO **conflict and compromise formation; defence mechanisms; ego**

The term 'psychodynamic' tends to have many referents. It may refer to a body of theory grounded in psychoanalytic ideas: the role of the unconscious in determining behaviour (i.e. psychic determinism or causality); internal conflicts and compromise formations; the use of *defence mechanisms* to protect against the expression of impulse or desire. It may also refer to the dynamic relationship among the agencies of the mind: id, *ego* and superego. Or it may more loosely refer to any approach borrowing from these ideas.

Or it may also refer to a particular approach to therapy. Some psychotherapists, not trained as psychoanalysts, who practice using ideas drawn from psychoanalysis, will describe their practice and work as psychodynamic. At other times the term may refer to less intensive (i.e. frequency) treatment approaches. Drew Weston (1998) identified five core principles of psychodynamic thought: (1) the role of the unconscious in mental functioning; (2) the role of cognitive and affective mechanisms in jointly producing conflicts among motive, thought and feeling, even with the same person or event alongside the defences modulating those conflicts; (3) the role early development in the formation of personality; (4) how mental representations of self and other contribute to the formation of personality and contribute to interpersonal behaviour; and (5) how movement from dependent states to mature autonomous ones produces healthy development.

KEY TEXTS
- Brandell, J. R. (2004) *Psychodynamic Social Work* (New York, NY: Columbia University Press)

- Goldstein, E. (2010) *Object Relations Theory and Self Psychology in Social Work* (New York, NY: Simon and Schuster)
- Mishna, F., Van Wert, M. and Asakura, K. (2013) 'The Best Kept Secret in Social Work: Empirical Support for Contemporary Psychodynamic Social Work Practice', *Journal of Social Work Practice*, 27 (3): pp. 289–303
- Safran, J. (2012) *Psychoanalysis and Psychoanalytic Therapies* (Washington, DC: American Psychological Association)
- Westen, D. (1998) 'The Scientific Legacy of Sigmund Freud: Toward a Psychodynamically Informed Psychological Science', *Psychological Bulletin*, 124 (3): pp. 333–371

psychosis

SEE ALSO **attacks on linking; neurosis; projective identification**

Early in the history of psychoanalysis, psychotic and neurotic phenomena were seen as categorically distinct. Over time, this categorical thinking gave way to a more dimensional understanding and a third category, the perversions, emerged. And much later borderline states presented complicating dilemmas: the potential for decompensation into *psychosis* during treatment (Kernberg, 1975).

Most often psychosis is associated with delusion, a break with reality, and the absence of consensual meaning-making. For Freud, the *ego*'s alienation from reality is the hallmark of psychotic disturbance. Through primary *narcissism*, the psychotic withdraws libido from objects and things and redirects them into the ego; while both *neurosis* and psychosis involve a withdrawal of *object*-cathexis, with neurosis, there is a reinvestment in the internal world and fantasized objects. With psychosis, the withdrawn cathexis is invested exclusively in the ego and at the expense of all other investments, including fantasy.

In object-relation theory, psychosis involves states of terror and powerlessness and feelings states (paranoia, feelings of persecution, etc.) associated with the disintegration of subjectivity; feelings of isolation and disconnectedness from relationships or engulfment and intrusion are seen as a breakdown in the ability to discriminate between self and non-self (me, not-me). Hanna Segal (2013) writes of the Kleinian approach to understanding psychotic phenomena:

It is our contention that psychotic illness is rooted in the pathology of early infancy, where the basic matrix of mental function is formed. By *projection* and introjection, by *splitting* of the object into good and bad, followed later by integration, by introjection and *identification* with good objects, the ego is gradually strengthened and so acquires a gradual capacity to differentiate between the external and the internal world; the beginnings of superego formation and relation to the external objects are laid down. It is at this time also, in the first year of life that symbol formation and the capacity to think and to speak develop. In psychosis, all these functions are disturbed or destroyed. The confusion between the external and the internal, the fragmentation of object relationships and of the ego, the deterioration of perception, the breakdown of *symbolic* proc-esses, and the disturbance of thinking, are all central features of psychosis. Understanding the genesis of the development of the ego and its object relationships and the kind of disturbance that can arise in the course of that development is thus essen-tial to understanding the mechanisms of psychotic states. (p. 3; emphases added)

Bion, in his very important work on psychosis, 'Differentiation of the Psychotic from the Non-psychotic Personalities' (1957), argues that the psychotic part of the self results from splitting the part of the mind concerned with awareness of internal and external reality; these split off fragments are then expelled, entering into or engulfing their objects. For Bion, the psychotic mind assem-bles a world of bizarre objects leading to an inability to think (see *attacks on linking*). And due to the destructive attacks on linking (i.e. thinking) the restoration of self and the object world is unimagi-nable. *Projective identification* plays the dominant role. However, for Bion, contact with reality is never entirely lost.

In relational psychoanalysis, psychosis is viewed as a human response to overpowering stressors and dangers; delusions and hallucinations, for example, function to communicate the fragmen-tation of the self and the attempt to hold onto reality. And disturbing experiences, delusions or hallucinations, are to be understood, affirmed and validated (Atwood, 2012) in the intersubjective fields where they are found to exist. Atwood writes that symptoms are 'not just outward signs of an inward illness; they were reactions to an ongoing experience of continuous abandonment and devastation at the hands of an uncomprehending world. – they were desperate cries for help' (p. 14).

For Lacan the difference between psychosis and neurosis is to be found in language. Lacan believed that theory fails to offer an adequate account of the differences between neurosis and psychosis: if the discourse of the psychotic can be interrupted on the same plane as the neurotic, he asked, how do we understand their differences? His answer was that psychosis presents a fundamentally different relationship to language: meanings for some are too fixed and for others too loose; they have a different relationship to speech and language than found in neurosis. Psychosis, then, is to be understood as a disruption in the subject's capacity to produce meaning (i.e. signifiers) across discursive contexts. Lacan uses the term 'foreclosure' to explain the essential difference between neurosis and psychosis: in psychosis, unlike neurosis, repression is not at work. This understanding of psychosis postulates an absolute and categorical difference between neurosis and psychosis. And Lacanians will argue that this rigid distinction is both diagnostically and clinically useful.

points for reflection and practice
- For Bion, it is important to identify the neurotic self, which he argued is concealed by the psychotic part of the mind, and know the psychotic part of the self, which exists in everyone.
- Attunement to the vicissitudes of psychotic phenomena and subjectivity is a necessary condition for effective treatment.

KEY TEXTS
- Atwood, G. (2012) *The Abyss of Madness* (New York, NY: Routledge)
- Atwood, G., Orange, D. and Stolorow, R. (2002) 'Shattered Worlds/ Psychotic States: A Post-Cartesian View of the Experience of Personal Annihilation', *Psychoanalytic Psychology*, 19 (2): pp. 281–306
- Katan, M. (1954) 'The Importance of the Non-psychotic Part of the Personality in Schizophrenia', *International Journal of Psychoanalysis*, 35 (2): pp. 119–128
- Kernberg, O. (1975) *Borderline Conditions and Pathological Narcissism* (New York, NY: Jason Aronson)
- Segal, H. (2013) 'The Psychoanalytic Approach to the Treatment of Psychotic Patients' in D. Bell (ed.), *Living on the Border: Psychotic Processes in the Individual, the Couple and the Group* (London, UK: Karnac Books), Chapter 1

- Steiner, J. (1993) *Psychic Retreats. Pathological Organizations in Psychotic, Neurotic and Borderline Patients* (New York, NY: Routledge)
- Vanheule S. (2011) *The Subject of Psychosis: A Lacanian Perspective* (London, UK: Palgrave)

r

real

SEE ALSO imaginary; Oedipal; symbolic

For Jacques Lacan the psyche is divided among three orders, domains or registers: the Real, the Imaginary and the *Symbolic*. Only neonates experience this relationship to nature, the Real, dominated by need and satisfaction. And for the infant the satisfaction of primal need is unfettered, outside language, and accomplished without separation of self from the outside world: pre-imaginary and pre-symbolic. It is also important to note that there is no absence in the Real. This is a register before culture and before the normative censorship enabled by belonging to a linguistic and social order: this state of nature (i.e. often described as a sense of fullness or completeness) resists representation or symbolization. Because we cannot ultimately know the *Real* (i.e. it is before language and cognition), throughout life we sense something absent, missing or lacking. And this is the source of motivation for our seeking wholeness or completion (i.e. *jouissance*). Life, however, is punctuated by moments during which the Real erupts and we are faced with the traumatic knowledge of our materiality.

Lionel Bailley (2012) writes that the Real must always be in a tension with the symbolic and the imaginary, 'for something to exist, its inverse must exist as well; and for existence to be, there must also be a state of nonbeing. Lacan borrowed a term from Heidegger when he said that the Real exists, because the Symbolic and Imaginary exist. More simply (and more usefully in psychoanalysis): for everything that comes into our field of *recognition* by means of a signifier, something of it must remain imperceptible, unsymbolised: this is the Real' (emphasis added).

points for reflection and practice
- In clinical practice, we learn how patients experience exclusion from the register or realm of the Real while at the same time, throughout life, the Real asserts itself.
- The patient and therapist might sense and share an unspeakable sense of reality, beyond language.
- Fantasy and language are never adequate in relationship to the Real. It is impossible to bring the Real into language and because of this it has a traumatic quality.
- Because the Real escapes language and resists symbolization, our patients will always feel and experience a sense of something missing or lacking (Lacan, 1977).

KEY TEXTS
- Declercq, F. (2002) 'The Real of the Body in Lacanian Theory', *Analysis*, (11): pp. 99–114
- Declercq, F. (2004) 'Lacan's Concept of the Real of Jouissance: Clinical Illustrations and Implications', *Psychoanalysis, Culture & Society*, 9 (2): pp. 237–251
- Lacan, J. (1977) *Écrits: A Selection* (A. Sheridan Trans.) (London, UK: Tavistock)
- Leader, D. and Groves, J. (2000) *Introducing Lacan* (Cambridge, UK: Icon Books)
- Bailly, L. (2012). *Lacan: A Beginner's Guide* (London: Oneworld Publications)

recognition

SEE ALSO **gender**

Recognition and misrecognition, in both their psychological and social, that is, normative dimensions, have been widely debated in social philosophy, social theory, psychology and psychoanalysis. There is no doubt that the recognition of another enables positive feeling, regard and respect (Honneth, 2007). It is important to note that recognition is more than a desire. For Honneth, we need recognition in multiple ways: in politics and the law, in everyday living, in culture and social life, in loving and family life. And for Jessica Benjamin (1998) and others in relational psychoanalysis it is the necessary condition for agency, the formation of subjectivity and *gender*, and the capacity to see and experience the Other as equal subject (Taylor, 1992).

Pride, *shame*, envy, resentment, compassion and contempt are more than affective states (Sayer, 2005): they entail normative claims and evaluative judgements about how people are treated, how their sense of self is produced, and how personal projects and concerns are assigned significance. Most theories of recognition share a fundamental assumption: our identity and ontological security depend on the reception and reaction of those in our immediate social surround and from the larger social order. And because identity is produced intersubjectively, that is, through dialogue and negotiation with what Taylor calls our 'significant others' (i.e. important people, parents and sibling, friends, teachers, colleagues), failure of recognition (i.e. negative evaluations or abject failure of seeing, hearing, noticing) in these relationships diminishes self-regard and respect and personal projects for those unrecognized remain beyond reach or incomplete. For Ikäheimo (2002), recognition requires more than being recognized by another; the person being recognized must know that the recognizer is qualified to confer recognition. (This points to the inherent reciprocity and mutuality necessary to acts of recognition.) It is in this way that recognition produces obligations.

Axel Honneth, a contemporary theorist of recognition, has postulated three spheres of interaction, all paired with recognition and the development of positive self-regard: love, rights and solidarity. In the mode of recognition, 'love', the subject builds self-confidence through primary relationships where physical and emotional needs are provided. 'Rights' refers to the development of moral responsibility: in this mode, the 'individual learns to see himself from the perspective of his [or her] partner in interaction as a bearer of equal rights' (Honneth, 1992, p. 194).

In her major psychoanalytic essay on this subject, Jessica Benjamin writes, 'denial of the mother's subjectivity, in theory and in practice, profoundly impedes our ability to see the world as inhabited by equal subjects' (1995, p. 31). Obviously, here, things can go terribly wrong: through forms of legal and social exclusion rights are often denied (i.e. gender-based discrimination, gay marriage, racial exclusion). In the mode 'solidarity', when individual traits and abilities are recognized, our self-esteem develops, and our personal difference is assigned social, historical and cultural value (Honneth, 1995, p. 122). For the development of positive self-regard we must be recognized in all spheres and the failure of recognition (i.e. nonrecognition or misrecognition) in any one of the spheres of self-formation (love, rights or solidarity) will cause psychic damage. For Benjamin, 'An intersubjective perspective helps us transcend the infantocentric viewpoint of intrapsychic theory by asking how a person becomes capable of enjoying recognition with an other. Logically, recognizing the parent as subject cannot be the result simply of internalizing her as mental *object*. This is a developmental process that has barely begun to be explicated. How does a child develop into a person who, as a parent, is able to recognize her or his own child? What are the internal processes, the psychic landmarks, of such development?' (1995, p. 16). For Phillip Bromberg, recognition has yet another intersubjective dimension: 'When [a therapist] gives up his attempts to "understand" his patient and allows himself to know his patient through the ongoing intersubjective field they are sharing at that moment, an act of recognition (not understanding) takes place in which words and thoughts come to symbolize experience instead of substitute for it' (2006, p. 11).

point for reflection and practice
- Jessica Benjamin writes about recognition: '[V]ery early on we find that recognition between persons – understanding and being understood, being in attunement – is becoming an end to itself. Recognition between persons is essentially mutual. By our very enjoyment of the other's confirming response, we recognize her in return. What the research on mother-infant interaction has uncovered about early reciprocity and mutual influence is best conceptualized as the development of the capacity for mutual recognition.'

KEY TEXTS
- Benjamin, J. (1992) 'Recognition and Destruction: An Outline of Intersubjectivity' in N. Skolnick and S. Warshaw (eds), *Relational Perspectives in Psychoanalysis* (Hillsdale, NJ: Analytic Press), pp. 43–60
- Benjamin, J. (1998) *The Bonds of Love: Psychoanalysis, Feminism, & the Problem of Domination* (New York, NY: Pantheon)
- Bromberg, P. (2006) *Awakening the Dreamer: Clinical Journeys* (Mahweh NJ: Analytic Press)
- Honneth, A. (2007) *Disrespect: The Normative Foundations of Critical Theory* (London, UK: Polity Press)

- Houston, S. (2009) 'Communication, Recognition and Social Work: Aligning the Ethical Theories of Habermas and Honneth', *British Journal of Social Work*, 39 (7): pp. 1274–1290
- Houston, S. (2010) 'Beyond Homo Economicus: Recognition, Self-Realization and Social Work', *British Journal of Social Work*, 40 (3): pp. 841–857
- Markell, P. (2009) *Bound by Recognition* (Princeton, NJ: Princeton University Press)
- Orange, D. M. (2008) 'Recognition as: Intersubjective Vulnerability in the Psychoanalytic Dialogue', *International Journal of Psychoanalytic Self Psychology*, 3 (2): pp. 178–194
- Sayer, A. (2005) 'Class, Moral Worth and Recognition', *Sociology*, 39 (5): pp. 947–963
- Taylor, C. (1989) *Sources of the Self: The Making of the Modern Identity* (Cambridge, MA: Harvard University Press)

reverie

SEE ALSO **alpha and beta elements (and functions); good enough mother (holding environment); mentalization**

Reverie refers to the maternal capacity for sensing and making sense of the infant's mental life and is, for Bion, essential to what he called alpha function (see *alpha and beta elements (and functions)*). Transformation of alpha elements (i.e. raw sensory experience, body feelings and relational experiences) requires what Bion called the 'alpha function', a function of the maternal mind (i.e. capacity for maternal reverie) necessary for containing the infant's chaotic, overwhelming, unbearable and inevitable frustrations. In a state of reverie the mother recognizes and holds projections and emphatically responds to these mental states so they can be returned to the infant in digestible and comprehensible forms.

In a similar way Daniel Stern, the *attachment* theorist, referred to attunement and Donald Winnicott talked of maternal preoccupation.

point for reflection and practice
- In therapy, 'reverie' is the hoped for state of the therapist, especially as a tool for responding to the patient's internal world.

KEY TEXTS

- Bion, W. (1962) *Learning from Experience* (Oxford, UK: Jason Aronson)
- Bion, W. (1963) *Elements of Psychoanalysis* (London, UK: Heinemann)
- Bion, W. (1965) *Transformations: Change from Learning to Growth* (London, UK: Heinemann)
- Ogden, T. (1999) *Reverie and Interpretation: Sensing Something Human* (London, UK: Karnac Books)

S

selfobject

SEE ALSO empathy; mirror stage (and mirroring); narcissism; object; recognition

The selfobject is a central concept in Heinz Kohut's self psychology. The selfobject, a person or object 'internal' to consciousness, is experienced as part of the self and functions for the self. This use of the concept, object, differs in significant ways from common understandings. For Freud the *object* is foremost the target of libidinal cathexis. For Kohut, the selfobject is invested with narcissistic energy and acts in the service of the self. In this way the term also denotes a process or movement from experiencing objects as external to the internalization of the perceived qualities of the other. Selfobjects, through empathic attunement (i.e. through mirroring and idealization), function to achieve a cohesive sense of self and throughout development remain crucial to the formation and maintenance of what Kohut calls 'healthy *narcissism*'. If the selfobject relationship is felt as soothing, it is likely that one will have a developed internal capacity for soothing. If this fails, some (i.e. mirror hungry) may seek and crave *recognition*. Others, ideal hungry, may seek the perfect parent. The alter-*ego* hungry may seek the perfect friend. And the merger hungry may seek selfobjects for need fulfilment.

Developmentally and clinically the selfobject refers to the actual experience of a person or object (animate or inanimate); selfobjects are, moreover, experienced as performing essential tasks: (1) admiration, praise and valuing. Kohut called this 'mirroring of grandiosity and exhibitionism'; (2) the experience of merger with figures or objects with force and power. Kohut called this 'idealized merger with omnipotent experience'; (3) 'essential alikeness', as twin (alter ego).

In 2005, Benai *et al.* conducted research to empirically validate key concepts in self-psychology. They were specifically interested in explaining individual differences in adult personality. Their

Selfobject Needs Inventory (SONI) has been used to establish selfobject needs for mirroring, idealization and twinship. Their findings also support 'the independence of the three selfobject needs; the orthogonality of a person's hunger for selfobject provisions and his or her defensive attempts to avoid acknowledging and satisfying selfobject needs; the motivational bases of narcissism; and the relation between selfobject needs and problems in interpersonal functioning, emotional adjustment, self-cohesion, and *affect regulation*' (p. 27; emphasis added).

point for reflection and practice
- The Selfobject Needs Inventory (SONI self-report scale), developed by Banai *et al.* (2005), has been used to test Kohut's key concepts. It is a 38-item instrument designed to measure: (1) approach orientation towards twinship (hunger), (2) avoidance orientation towards idealization and twinship (denial), (3) approach orientation for idealization (hunger), (4) approach orientation for mirroring (hunger) and (5) avoidance orientation towards the need for mirroring (denial).

KEY TEXTS
- Banai, E., Mikulincer, M. and Shaver, P. (2005) '"Selfobject" Needs in Kohut's Self Psychology: Links with Attachment, Self-Cohesion, Affect Regulation, and Adjustment', *Psychoanalytic Psychology*, 22 (2): pp. 224–260
- Kieffer, C. (2004) 'Selfobjects, Oedipal Objects, and Mutual Recognition: A Self-Psychological Reappraisal of the Female "Oedipal Victor"', *Annual of Psychoanalysis*, 32: pp. 69–80
- Kieffer, C. (2008) 'From Selfobjects to Mutual Recognition: Towards Optimal Responsiveness in Father-Daughter Relationships', *Psychoanalytic Inquiry*, 28 (1): pp. 76–91
- Kohut, H. and Wolf, E. (1978) 'The Disorders of the Self and Their Treatment: An Outline', *International Journal of Psychoanalysis*, 59 (4): pp. 413–425

self-states

SEE ALSO **affect regulation; dissociation**

In healthy development and psychic life, we are fleetingly and vaguely aware of what Bromberg (2003) calls self-states. These states are pieces in a 'functional whole, informed by a process of internal negotiation with the realities, values, affects, and perspectives' of others (Bromberg, 1996, p. 512); when all goes well self-states, even when in conflict with one another, function in relationship to other parts of the self to produce a sense of 'me-ness'. Troubling collisions among self-states, moreover, are inevitable and may lead to *affect* dysregulation. For Bromberg, each 'self-state has its own task and is dedicated to upholding its own version of truth. Each is a piece of a larger-than-life enterprise designed' (2012, p. 30) to sequester parts of the self. Bromberg sees *dissociation*, not as a defensive mechanism or a pathology, but as necessary to a sense of coherence and maintenance and continuity of the self.

Bromberg has not been without his critics, however, and one of the obvious questions about the relationship between the self and dissociation is: How do dissociation and the division of self-experience function to support integrity? Bromberg answers this question by arguing that 'self-experience originates in relatively unlinked self-states, each coherent in its own right, and that the experience of being a unitary self is an acquired, developmentally adaptive *illusion*' (1998, p. 182 emphasis added). Bromberg has further developed this argument by turning to mind/brain mechanisms and what he calls an anticipatory protective system, which functions proactively 'to shut down experiential access to self-states that are disjunctive with the dissociatively limited range of the state that is experienced as "me" at a given moment' (2012, p. 15).

points for reflection and practice
- Bromberg (1998) conceives of the unconscious in terms of dissociated *self-states*. He writes: 'What we call the unconscious we might usefully think of as the suspension or deterioration of linkages between self-states, preventing certain aspects of self – along with their respective constellations of affects, memories, values and cognitive capacities – from achieving access to the personality within the same state of consciousness' (p. 182).
- Some have elaborated on Bromberg's ideas to talk about multiple self-states (MSS) and the ability to shift among self-states while maintaining a continuous sense of self.
- The therapist must also be understood as a multiplicity of self-states.

KEY TEXTS

- Bromberg, P. (1998) *Standing in the Spaces: Essays on Clinical Process, Trauma, and Dissociation* (Hillsdale, NJ: Analytic Press)
- Bromberg, P. (2006) *Awakening the Dreamer: Clinical Journeys* (Mahweh, NJ: Analytic Press)
- Bromberg, P. (2012) *The Shadow of the Tsunami: And the Growth of the Relational Mind* (New York, NY: Routledge)
- Howell, E. (2013) *The Dissociative Mind* (New York, NY: Routledge)
- Sands, S. (2008) 'The Concept of Multiple Self States: Clinical Advantages', *International Journal of Psychoanalytic Self Psychology*, 4 (1): pp. 122–124

shame

SEE ALSO **developmental stages; guilt**

The 'Oxford English Dictionary' offers the following definition of shame, 'painful distress or humiliation', and mortification as 'great embarrassment and shame'. In clinical work shame can be imagined as a continuum (i.e. the social and psychological dynamics of shame) that runs from mild forms of embarrassment (i.e. mostly under cortical influence, language and meaning-making) to greater and greater disability, towards humiliation and finally, to mortification, that is, the wish to die or disappear (Kilbourne, 2002; Lansky, 1997, 2007). And each of these may be accompanied by specific symptoms. As one moves along this continuum, cognition, behaviour and emotion are increasingly under the influence of subcortical and somatic responses.

It would be almost impossible to consider our current understanding of shame without mentioning of the important contribution of the psychoanalyst, Helen Block Lewis. And even when her work remains unacknowledged (especially in fields unrelated to psychoanalysis), you can sense the large footprint of her ideas (Lansky, 2007). While there is now a very extensive and significant psychoanalytic literature on shame (Lansky, 2007; Mann, 2010; Kilbourne, 2002, 2003), it was first in her work that attention was finally and properly given to the role of shame in symptom formation, especially when it is repressed or denied (Lewis, 1971). Reminiscent of how anthropologists once regarded and generalized about cultural styles (i.e. *guilt* vs shame-based cultures) Lewis argued that we are governed by differing affective styles (i.e. shame-proneness or guilt-proneness) that yield degrees of shame or guilt experience; these, in turn, produce varying psychological symptoms.

In contemporary psychology, shame is counted among the so-called social emotions. June Price Tangney also refers to it as a moral emotion. Shame, guilt, embarrassment and pride belong to a family of social emotions: 'self-conscious emotions' that are evoked by self-reflection and self-evaluation. Self-evaluation, moreover, may be consciously experienced or outside awareness. And the degree to which it is out of awareness, the more likely it will be expressed in bodily ways and the more likely it will be anticipated and experienced in the clinical setting as the potential for increased exposure to shame and disengagement. Though not without controversy, researchers often describe two fundamental categories of emotion, basic and complex (Eckman, 1992; Griffiths, 1997).

Shame is foremost a somatic event. It is initially experienced and mediated through the automatic nervous system and signalled by the body: thus, the more it is perceived and observed, the more it is sensed, especially in the therapeutic setting (Dearing and Tangney, 2011). It appears that shame (Dickerson, Gruenewald and Kemeny, 2004; Shore, 1994), like fear (LeDoux, 2002, 2003), is processed through the primitive, subcortical part of the brain, the limbic system: amygdala, hypothalamus and thalamus. The shame response is easily moderated by conscious, intentional action. Acute shame forces us out of language and into the body. In short, one cannot talk oneself out of a shame state. And because both fear and shame are processed in these centres, they share a fundamental similarity: no cortical involvement, no *symbolic* representation, no words; there is only the bodily response of fight, flight or freeze, and hiding of pain and lament. Moreover, with pride the sympathetic nervous system is at work (i.e. high levels of arousal, activity, elation and decreased peristalsis), whereas with shame the parasympathetic nervous system dominates (i.e. low energy, gaze aversion, reduction in muscle tone (i.e. loss of smile), blushing and increased peristalsis). The brain shuts down the mind so that we are unable to clearly think or speak.

points for reflection and practice
- Glen Gabbard argues that shame is an important dynamic in *narcissism* and of the two subtypes of narcissism he describes,

'oblivious' (i.e. grandiose, arrogant and thick-skinned); it is with 'hypervigilant' (i.e. easily hurt, oversensitive) that shame plays an especially prominent role. Unlike the oblivious subtype, the second hides in shame; the weak internalized self hides in shame.

- Shame must be managed in the clinical process, from the beginning engagement through to the establishment of the alliance and into termination.
- Shame may be the central most important rate-limited factor in all therapeutic encounters.
- Dearing (2005) and colleagues have looked at the differential experience of shame and guilt in substance abuse. They argue that guilt, unlike shame, is more adaptive. Their research shows that shame-proneness is positively correlated with substance abuse, and guilt-proneness was inversely related. Clinically, this data suggests that 'shame and guilt should be considered separately in the prevention and treatment of substance misuse' (p. 1392).

KEY TEXTS
- Kilbourne, B. (2002) *Disappearing Persons: Shame and Appearance* (Albany, NY: SUNY Press)
- Lansky, M. and Morrison, A. (eds) (1997) *The Widening Scope of Shame* (Hillsdale, NJ: Analytic Press)
- Longhofer, J. (2013) 'Shame in the Clinical Process with LGBTQ Clients', *Clinical Social Work Journal*, 41 (3): pp. 297–301
- Mann, M. (2010) 'Shame Veiled and Unveiled: The Shame Affect and Its Re-Emergence in the Clinical Setting', *The American Journal of Psychoanalysis*, 70 (3): pp. 270–281
- Tangney, J. and Dearing, R. (2003) *Shame and Guilt* (New York, NY: Guilford Press)
- Wurmser, L. (1994) *The Mask of Shame* (New York, NY: Jason Aronson)

social constructivism (or anti-essentialism)

SEE ALSO **evidence-based practice; positivism and critical realism**

Today, we are left with several irreconcilable epistemological and ontological claims about the self and the related world of practice: positivism – and empirical realism and social constructivism (and anti-essentialism). We also face the equally troubling tendency to reduce the self to our concepts of self, or to dissolve the subject altogether into a language or discourse without referents (i.e. the self refers to nothing but language and concepts Jones, 2003).

Although constructivism has come to mean many things, most will agree that it stands in opposition to positivism, empiricism, essentialism (sometimes called foundationalism or objectivism) and various forms of reductionism ; in short, it is taken to be a critique of what some consider the dominant, modernist and 'scientific way of knowing'. Granvold argues that constructivism challenges one of positivism's central tenets, the correspondence theory of truth; he argues instead that constructivism refers not to validity but to viability (Granvold, 1996). For others, constructivism or constructionism refers to a type or quality of data (e.g. data generated in the clinical encounter may be seen as co-constructed in an unfolding and mutually determining narrative, sometimes called narrative data). Sometimes it refers to a method of collecting data (e.g. social construction or narrative research techniques). At other times the reference is to a type of textual analysis – narrative analysis (Reissman, 1990). Some refer to types of clinical intervention (constructivist, constructionist, intersubjective or narrative therapy), where, 'presenting problems are viewed as constructions, built through language and interaction. The goals in general are to co-create with clients a new "reality" through conversation with the therapist'. The 'emplotment, the activity and operation of a narrative, organizes the life events and experiences into a coherent, ever-evolving life story' (Neimeyer and Steward, 1996, p. 360). Brower describes the use of constructivism in small groups as a means of description of group process (1996, p. 36). Sometimes constructivists make more explicit reference to epistemological, ontological or theoretical assumptions (ways of knowing, what we take to be knowable, and our explanations of events, respectively).

For Holland and Kilpatrick 'narrative analysis is based on the theory of social constructivism' (1993, p. 302); here, it is assumed that narrative is a technique rooted in a social constructivist metatheory, or that social constructivism offers to practice an overarching paradigm or epistemology within which knowledge claims can be made (Franklin 1997). Granvold (1996, p. 346) and Guidano (1991) argue that the epistemology of constructivism is based on a motor theory of the mind, where 'the mind appears as an active, constructive system, capable of producing not only its output but also to a large extent the input it receives, including sensations that lie at the base of its own constructions' (Guidano, 1988, p. 309). Constructivism may also refer to the perceived tendency of nonconstructivists to pathologize or focus on the problem, rather than the solution or strengths (Held, 1995, p. 106; Gergen, 2000).

This claim for constructivism, however, poses a serious problem: What part of the reality is constructed and what part not? What are clients at liberty to remodel?

Some quite influential anti-essentialists in sociology and history have taken on the whole of developmental psychology, arguing that childhood itself is a mere social construction and psychic development a perilous fiction (Burman 2000). Burman, like others, confuses throughout her work the empirical phenomena, child development, with developmental psychology, the sense of self with the concepts of self, or what we know with how we know it. This problem Roy Bhaskar called the epistemic fallacy: 'to reduce questions about what there is (ontological questions) to questions about what we can know (epistemic questions)' (Collier, 1994, p. 36). What is remarkable about this kind of theorizing, often influenced by Foucault, is that nothing terribly revolutionary or new is said; Burman writes, for example, that 'children and childhood are "constructed"; we therefore have to study not only "the child", but also the context (that is, the interpersonal, cultural, historical and political situation) that produces her' (1994, p. 6). Although statements such as these – and many others in the debate – pretend to present an alternative to essentialist or structuralist accounts of human development, the alternative itself contains the very language from which it endeavours to escape: 'that is, the interpersonal, cultural, historical and political situation that *produces* [my emphasis] her.' Here, in what Margaret Archer calls downward conflation, 'the effects of socialization impress themselves upon people, seen as malleable "indeterminate material"' (2000, p. 5). Few, in their right minds, however, would disagree with the intent of Burman's theorization. To make us sensitive to history and context is surely the 'sine qua non' of good clinical practice or accurate and responsible explanatory accounts and necessary to the analysis of events or actions unfolding in 'open' systems.

Among the various social constructivist accounts of childhood one can easily discern a most conspicuous feature of anti-essentialism, that is, its emphasis on difference and reaction to any theory that fails to recognize difference. Gregor McLennan has argued that the emphasis on difference runs the risk of de-differentiation, to a point where difference itself is rendered devoid of meaning (McLennan, 1985; Buhle, 1998, pp. 349–350). Chris Jenks, one of the leading and new social constructivist sociologists of childhood and critics of developmental theory, argues that children, as a group, have been subjected to discourses that suppress difference and pathologize, homogenize and fix identities (1996, pp. 19–20).

Foremost among anti-essentialist arguments is the notion that agency and intentionality are dissolved, not by social or psychological forces, but by hegemonic social and psychological theory. This position, most forcefully argued by the late Rom Harré (1983), in his work, 'Personal Being', suggests that the self 'is a theoretical concept acquired in the course of human interactions'. For Harré, the self is 'rather like acquiring a personal organizer (a mental filofax)' without ontological depth (Archer, 2000, p. 96). Here, as with the new sociologists of childhood and the critics of human development, selves are mere constructions in discourse: there are no pre- or non-linguistic selves and intersubjectivity either replaces altogether or supersedes intrasubjectivity.

We are, in short, 'nothing beyond what society makes us, and it makes us what we are through our joining society's conversation' (Archer, 2000, p. 4). Thus, for the child, there are no prelinguistic sources for the development of a sense of self; bodies and psyches, moreover, have no properties or emergent powers of their own (Williams, 1999). The child, according to this view, simply joins the discursive community and through membership, the self, emotion, thought and memory are made possible. Here, ironically, the child, through socialization, is mere material to be worked on by the social order. One is left to wonder how with this downward conflation, as Margaret Archer calls it, agency is restored, when as noted above, the 'effects of socialization "impress" themselves upon people, seen as malleable "indeterminate material"' (2000, p. 5).

Andrew Sayer (1997) has argued that in our discussion of essentialism, social constructivists have missed the importance of understanding that some things have essences, while others do not. What is the significance of this very important insight? In short, even though language, social institutions and the psyche are constructed (and Freud would most certainly concur with this; despite detractors, his theory of psychic development entails social relatedness), they may also have, once constructed, essences, or generative properties.

Some properties of the self, moreover, may be seen as more essential than others, especially if a wider range of behaviours depend on the essential feature. Sayer argues, as well, that the concept essence may often be expected to do two different kinds of work: (1) 'identify the essence of an *object* in terms of properties which supposedly determine – or are indispensable for – what it can and cannot do; these are its "generative" properties', and (2) to identify the 'features of an object which enable us to distinguish it from other kinds of object; these are its distinguishing or identifying properties' (1997, p. 458). Though the two aspects, the generative properties and the distinguishing ones, may coincide, it may also be the case that 'scarcely any generative properties of an object may be unique to it and its distinguishing features may not tell us much about what enables it to do whatever it does' (1997, p. 458).

To have a common essence, thus, objects must have universally shared attributes. Yet when objects share some features, it does not necessarily mean that they are essential ones; they may be accidental. Thus, every object has characteristics, which coexist or interact, but could 'exist apart from those which could not exist without a certain other feature' (1997, p. 459). Instead, it is necessary to understand the attributes of an object and how they must exist in combination with other attributes. Then, one must ascertain which can exist without them. As well, their respective generative powers must be understood. For some, especially in so-called postmodern schools of thought, psychic agencies have no powers to generate effects, or they may be seen as dangerous fictions. However, what often substitutes for the 'fiction' of psychic agencies are the attributes of interpersonal relationships. One can easily detect the empiricism at work in many schools of relational, intersubjective or interpersonal psychologies, especially where emphasis, though often unstated, is given to the 'roles' of practitioner and client. What they take to be *real* and knowable (ontological) are those aspects of interrelating (hierarchical roles etc.) that lend themselves to direct observation or empirical investigation. Oddly, though many would think of themselves as existing in a tension with empiricism, their emphasis on the observable qualities of relationships lead them into radical forms of empiricism and the most modern of projects: their ontologies, inevitably flat and superficial, the self, transparent and superficially read.

KEY TEXTS

- Archer, M. (2000) *Being Human: The Problem of Agency* (Cambridge, UK: Cambridge University Press)
- Brower, Aaron M. (1996) 'Group Development as Constructed Social Reality: The Constructivism of Small Groups', *Families in Society: The Journal of Contemporary Human Services*, 77 (6): pp. 336–344
- Collier, A. (1994) *Critical Realism: An Introduction to Roy Bhaskar's Philosophy* (London, UK: Verso)
- Granvold, D. (1996) 'Constructivist Psychotherapy: Families in Society', *The Journal of Contemporary Human Services*, 77 (6): pp. 345–359
- Harré, R. (1983) *Personal Being: A Theory for Individual Psychology* (Oxford, UK: Blackwell)
- Jones, R. A. (2003) 'Between the Analytical and the Critical: Implications for Theorizing the Self', *Journal of Analytical Psychology*, 48 (3): pp. 355–370
- Neimeyer, R. and Stewart, A. (1996) 'Trauma, Healing, and the Narrative Emplotment of Loss', *Families in Society: The Journal of Contemporary Human Services*, 77 (6): pp. 360–375
- Reissman, C. (1990) *Narrative Analysis* (Thousand Oaks, CA: Sage)
- Sayer, A. (1997) 'Essentialism, Social Constructionism, and Beyond', *Sociological Review*, 45 (3): pp. 453–487

splitting

SEE ALSO **anxiety; bad object; borderline; defence mechanisms; depression; depressive position; diagnosis and the DSM; dissociation; projection; projective identification; selfobject**

Splitting is sometimes mistakenly described as black and white or all-or-nothing thinking. While splitting has this quality, it is not merely a cognitive process. One cannot simply think one's way into or out of splitting or into seeing another person as having both negative and positive aspects or treating them as a whole person with unique thoughts, feelings, desires, fears. Some, too, mistakenly see splitting solely as a defence, and while it may be used defensively, it is fore-most a way of experiencing the world, the self and other, feelings and thoughts, and as a necessary aspect of development. In the DSM (see entry, *diagnosis and the DSM*) splitting is among the differentiating criteria for diagnosis of *borderline* personality disorder: 'a pattern of unstable and intense interpersonal relationships characterized by alternating between extremes of idealization and devaluation.'

For Melanie Klein, the early infant *ego* experiences *anxiety* through internal, innate conflict between opposing life and death drives (i.e. manifested as destructive envy) alongside engagements with external reality. While good feelings are produced through the introjection of good objects, bad objects are removed by projecting bad feelings. It is through splitting that the *bad object* protects the good object and because fear of the bad object produces destructive feeling, aggression is often associated with splitting. Tolerating and integrating good and bad aspects is not easily accomplished and 'magical' omnipotent denial is used to neutralize the effects and power of persecuting bad objects.

For Ronald Fairbairn (1952), splitting is a function of schizoid phenomena, which is universal, foundational and structuring of the psyche, and it underlies all object relations. For Fairbairn, splitting begins with the infant's inability to integrate fulfilling qualities of the parent (i.e. the good object) with unresponsive actions and mental states of the caregivers (i.e. the unsatisfying object); the good and bad, instead, are separated.

For self psychology and Heniz Kohut, splitting results from disruptions in the modes of relating necessary to the maintenance of self-cohesion. With rupture, traumatic experience from childhood is relived along with the intensification of *affect* and intolerable rage. Splitting is used to preserve the *selfobject* connection to the frustrating object and conflicted needs.

More recently, some have argued that splitting and *dissociation* may describe the same mental process (Jiraskova, 2014).

points for reflection and practice
- For self psychologists, the correct therapeutic intervention ordinarily is to try to understand what caused the rupture, what the intrapsychic and behavioural consequences were, what predisposed the patient to the injury and what led to the unique defences and then to repair the rapport.
- Akhtar and Bryne (1983) describe five clinical manifestations of splitting: (1) inability to experience *ambivalence*; (2) marked

and convincing oscillations of self-esteem; (3) intensification of affects; (4) reckless decision-making; and (5) ego-syntonic loss of impulse control (e.g. promiscuity, kleptomania) that produces little *guilt.*

KEY TEXTS

- Akhtar, S. and Byrne, J. (1983) 'The Concept of Splitting and Its Clinical Relevance', *American Journal of Psychiatry*, 140 (8): pp. 1013–1016
- Grotstein, J. (1981) *Splitting and Projective Identification* (Northvale NJ: Jason Aronson)
- Jiraskova, T. (2014) 'Splitting of the Mind and Unconscious Dynamics', *The Journal for Neurocognitive Research*, 56 (1–2): pp. 24–27

sublimation

SEE ALSO **defence mechanisms; ego; recognition**

Sublimation is most often thought of as a defence mechanism, and it is often counted among the so-called mature or higher level defences. It is mature because it is said to enable substitution, modification or transfer of unacceptable wish or raw impulse to socially acceptable ones. For some, sublimation is seen as a channelling of libido into nonsexual activities (i.e. artistic creation or intellectual activity). While the impulse is repudiated in its original form, sublimation grants a measure of gratification to it. In short, the aim and *object* of the impulse are altered without impeding appropriate measures of discharge. In other words, substitution (Goebel, 2012) allows for partial gratification (i.e. with social approval) of a more direct one, which would otherwise violate a person's ideals or normative social standards. Others, especially *ego* psychologists, argue that with sublimation, the ego is no longer in the service of the id: the ego allows the id to find a means of external expression by changing form. Unlike repression, 'the unacceptable' is in this way modified such that gratification can be achieved without disapproval or disapprobation. And especially important in Freud's thinking about the conditions necessary for social life, sublimation serves an essential purpose in the increase of civilization. In this way sublimation serves a far greater purpose than mere channelling of impulse into acceptable behaviour. Joel Whitebook (1996) describes what he calls the twofold clinical significance of sublimation: 'From the side of the patient, it would be difficult to conceptualize an alternative fate for the drives that are unloosed from their habitual moorings in the course of an analysis, and hence the nature and course of the "cure", without a theory of sublimation. And from the other side of the couch, only a concept of the analyst's sublimation can allow us to identify what he or she has to offer to the treatment beyond *countertransference* to the patient' (p. 218; emphasis added).

In 1988, Hans Loewald reimagined the concept. For him, sublimation is not a mere transformation or conversion of lower unconscious processes into higher ones. He argued that sublimation involves linking two fundamental human experiences of the world: unity and differentiation. Loewald writes: 'It is the original unity that is in the process of being restored ... in sublimation; there is a *symbolic* linkage which constitutes what we call meaning ... the transmutations of sublimation reveal an unfolding into differentiated elements of a oneness of instinctual-spiritual experience: oneness stays alive as connection' (1988, p. 453).

For Lacan, sublimation does not refer to a redirection of the *drive* towards a different and nonsexual object. What is especially important and consequential for Lacan is the role of social *recognition*: the drives are sublimated only because the social order and shared values make this demand. Most importantly, for Lacan, what changes is the position of the object, not the object itself, in what he calls the structure of fantasy. Sublimation does not, thus, require redirection of the drive to an alternative object; instead, while the drive pursues its direction and course, the object remains unchanged.

For Harry Stack Sullivan (1973), sublimation refers to much more than the direct satisfaction of the drive or need. It is for him the 'unwitting substitution of a partial satisfaction with social approval for the pursuit of a direct satisfaction which would be contrary to one's ideals or to the judgment of social censors and other important people who surround one' (1973, p. 14).

Goebel (2012), in his comprehensive work on the topic of sublimation, argues that

the drives themselves are not transformed, but rather their objects are changed. The richness and consistency of Freud's remarks, not to mention the phenomenon of an enduring discontent within civilization, become clear only when one recognizes that the aim of sublimation is substitution. Through the theory of the sexual drives' plasticity, the theory of the amalgamation of the sexual and ego drives, and finally through the doctrine of productive *identification*, it becomes both possible and plausible to conceive of sublimation as work on the object of the drive. To think of sublimation as a transformation of the drive itself would render incomprehensible Freud's lifelong concern with the fact of desublimation, of regression. (2012, p. 144)

KEY TEXTS

- Chasseguet-Smirgel, J. (1974) 'Perversion, Idealization and Sublimation', *International Journal of Psychoanalysis*, 55 (3): pp. 349–357
- Goebel, E. (2012) *Beyond Discontent: 'Sublimation' from Goethe to Lacan* (New York, NY: Continuum International Publishing Group)
- Hartmann, H. (1955) 'Notes on the Theory of Sublimation', *The Psychoanalytic Study of the Child*, 10: pp. 9–29
- Loewald, H. (1988) *Sublimation: Inquiries into Theoretical Psychoanalysis* (New Haven: Yale University Press)
- Sullivan, H. S. (1973) *Clinical Studies in Psychiatry* (Vol. 2) (New York, NY: W. W. Norton & Company)
- Whitebook, J. (1996) *Perversion and Utopia: A Study in Psychoanalysis and Critical Theory* (Boston, MA: MIT Press)

symbolic

SEE ALSO **imaginary; Oedipal; real**

For Jacques Lacan, the psyche is divided among three orders, domains or registers: the *Real*, the *Imaginary*, and the *Symbolic*. In the symbolic register (i.e. the 'big Other') language, symbol, metaphor and narrative dominate and determine our subjectivity. For Lacan, because speaking and language (i.e. langue and parole) are the same, one can speak only with the expectation of an answer and in this way the big Other is already implied. Moreover, it is the larger social order, the community, which is addressed, without which there would be no speaking.

No longer in a world of equations and identifications that dominate in the imaginary, the child enters a linguistic order, not only to reconcile to rules and social convention but to enter and manage a growing world of others. And because the child must now accept and use language to negotiate the world, it must align with powerful linguistic others. This was how Lacan viewed the *Oedipal* event. Entrance into the symbolic requires compliance with, and socialization into, what Lacan called the 'Name of the Father': laws, rules of discourse and conventions that control desire and modes of communication: 'It is in the "name of the father" that we must recognize the support of the symbolic function which, from the dawn of history, has identified his person with the figure of the law' (quoted in Roof, 1996, p. 106). Unlike the *Real* (governed by need) and the Imaginary (governed by demand), in the symbolic order desire rules and once in the linguistic or Symbolic order desire is essentially and necessarily grounded in the play of language. Nevertheless, it is important to know that the Real and Imaginary always exert a force on human desire and within the symbolic order.

KEY TEXTS
- Fink, B. (1997) *A Clinical Introduction to Lacanian Psychoanalysis: Theory and Technique* (Cambridge, MA: Harvard University Press)
- Fink, B. (2007) *Fundamentals of Psychoanalytic Technique: A Lacanian Approach for Practitioners* (New York, NY: W. W. Norton & Company)
- Miller, M. J. (2011) *Lacanian Psychotherapy: Theory and Practical Applications* (London, UK: Routledge)
- Parker, I. (2010) *Lacanian Psychoanalysis: Revolutions in Subjectivity* (London, UK: Routledge)
- Roof, J. (1996) 'A Verdict on the Paternal Function: Law, the Paternal Metaphor, and Paternity Law' in W. Apollon and R. Feldstein (eds), *Law Politics and Aesthetics* (Albany, NY: SUNY Press), pp. 101–126

symptom, symptom formation

SEE ALSO evidence-based practice; psychodynamic; recognition

Most often the term 'symptom' refers to observable or behavioural manifestations of an underlying condition. In *psychodynamic* theory, they are generally explained by looking into internal, mental or emotional factors, not visible to the naked eye. During treatment, attention is given to internal mental states.

Debate about the meanings of symptoms has become contentious in modern psychiatry, psychology and psychoanalysis. In the language of the DSM, especially after the second and third editions, complex and dynamic ways of thinking about symptoms were replaced by a language of diseases, disorders and syndromes, as in clinical medicine: tumours, warts, body temperature, blood pressure. Psychic symptoms, under the hegemony of the DSM, came to share with symptoms in clinical medicine the same qualities: empirically discrete, describable entities. In much, if not most, of contemporary psychology symptoms are treated as natural kinds (i.e. rocks, soil, oxygen); in short, they are not dependent on human action, meaning-making or intersubjectivity. And modern science, especially positivism and biological reductionism, promises that we will eventually establish the foundation of mental life in natural kinds and that if all goes well, our classificatory systems (i.e. DSM) will eventually correspond to natural kinds. And where it is assumed that these *real* and independent kinds of things exist we may be justified in our pursuit of 'science'. Yet over half of the symptoms that patients bring to us cannot be neatly placed within DSM categories and most fit into several categories (Messer, 2001). To make matters even more complicated, there is little, if any, connection between the diagnostic categories and relevant treatments. Over time, as social work and psychology have been taken up by positivist science and methodology (i.e. what can be seen, measured, operationalized) and the descriptive nosology (i.e. DSM), and the human brain has become the essential basis for understanding (human action, motivation, emotion and cognition), a broader and deeper understanding of symptoms has almost disappeared. Thomas Insel (2013), Director of the US National Institute of Mental Health, recently proclaimed that all mental disorders must be understood just as we've understood malignant tumours. He writes on his blog: 'But patients and families should welcome this change as a first step towards "precision medicine", the movement that has transformed cancer diagnosis and treatment. RDoC is nothing less than a plan to transform clinical practice by bringing a new generation of research to inform how we diagnose and treat mental disorders.' And even where there may be clear organic (brain or body) bases for understanding a symptom, we also tend to strip away the meanings even those symptoms have under any particular circumstance or description.

What exactly does the symptom refer to? Freud had his take on the nature and quality of the symptom: symptoms refer to emotion, thought, behaviour or body states caused by a return of the repressed; repressed desires may be expressed in many ways, towards satisfaction, and manifest as symptoms. In Freud's words, 'A symptom is a sign of, and a substitute for, an instinctual satisfaction which has remained in abeyance; it is a consequence of the process of repression' ('Inhibitions, Symptoms and Anxiety' 20.91). In the worst cases, such symptoms 'can result in an extraordinary impoverishment of the subject in regard to the mental energy available to him and so in paralysing him for all the important tasks of life' ('Introductory Lectures' 16.358).

Freud often used 'symptom formation' to refer to a process (i.e. psychical working out) leading to psychoneurotic symptoms. The formation of a symptom shifts the focus of attention to the specific and significant moments in the production of neurotic phenomena. Moreover, Freud differentiated the moment of symptom formation from the moment of defence; symptom formation he grounds in the return of the repressed and defence he saw an altogether different process.

For Winnicott, symptoms were troubling because they were not sufficiently functioning and disturbance/abnormality resulted from limitations and rigidity: 'it is not the symptoms that are the trouble; it is the fact that the symptoms are not doing their job, and are as much a nuisance to the child as to the mother' (Winnicott, 1964, p. 103). Abnormality shows in a "limitation" and a "rigidity" in the child's capacity to employ symptoms and a relative lack of relationship between the symptoms and what can be expected in the way of help' (p. 127).

Lander describes the functions of symptoms for Lacan. First, there is the clinical symptom (i.e. a demand for help to the Other). The second, the analytic symptom, where there is no appeal to the Other. In the first instance, the symptom (e.g. obsession) is seen as something out of the patient's control; thus, the patient petitions the therapist for a cure, for elimination of the intruding force. The therapist has the knowledge and authority to remove it much as a surgeon removes a tumour. Over time, patients come to realize that they have control over the symptom and that there is an underlying desire to the suffering and that they must be able to act in accordance with their desire and that the symptom is not to be eliminated or excised. Lacan is famous for having said about the symptom that it comes not from the present but from the future. Also, for Lacan, the symptom, because it is a floating signifier, becomes meaningful (to the patient and therapist) only with the work of interpretation, in the narrative about the symptom, and in interactions with the analyst. With an interpretation (which symbolizes and recognizes the desire expressed through the symptom) the symptom is relieved. There is a paradox here: the *recognition* of the desire simultaneously fulfils the desire. In sum, the unconscious desire, expressed through the symptom is always a desire for recognition (see entry, *recognition*), and our desires are inevitably linked to the desires of the Other and relations with them. Soler describes the symptom for Lacan as 'a mode of satisfaction. It can be deciphered like a message, but it is not only a way of speaking, it is also above all a form of *jouissance*, the key of its rebus being always the *drive* which is secretly satisfied' (p. 87).

For Žižek, a contemporary social philosopher and psychoanalyst, there is a false belief at the heart of psychoanalysis and the attempt to grasp the meaning of symptoms: the analyst Other knows the meaning of the symptom. For Žižek, it is only through sustaining this false belief that analysis has potential and motion, and with this transference belief that the symptom can finally be interpreted and understood by the analyst. In short, also for Žižek, there is a paradox at work: the symptom only has meaning in relationship to the analyst interpreter (Other) (1989, p. 73). For Lacan and Žižek, the transference itself presupposes a knowing Other capable of revealing the truth of behaviour, action, feeling and thought.

point for reflection and practice
- In Lacanian therapy the goal of the work is the recognition that the patient is the subject of desire.

KEY TEXTS
- Freud, S. (1915) *Repression*. Standard Edition, 14
- Insel, T. (2013) 'Director's Blog: Transforming Diagnosis'. Available at http://www.nimh.nih.gov/about/director/2013/transforming-diagnosis.shtml
- Lander, R. and Filc, J. (2006) *Subjective Experience and the Logic of the Other* (New York, NY: Other Press)
- Verhaeghe, P. (2004) *On Being Normal and Other Disorders: A Manual for Clinical Psychodiagnostics* (New York, NY: Other Press)

- Žižek, Slavoj (1992) *Enjoy Your Symptom! Jacques Lacan in Hollywood* (London, UK: Routledge)

synchronicity

SEE ALSO archetype

Jung used the term 'synchronicity' to describe the coincidence (or equivalence) of events, psychic and physical states. Jung called these, 'temporally coincident occurrences of acausal events'. Jung writes, 'the meaningful coincidence or equivalence of a psychic and a physical state that have no causal relationship to one another means, in general terms, that it is a modality without a cause, an "acausal orderedness"'(2010, p. 138). He had always been interested in coincidences, especially the remarkable ones unexplained by positivist science. For Jung, positivist science makes the assumption that causality must be understood in terms of temporal relations between cause and effect (i.e. if A precedes B and C in time, A must be the cause or somehow causally related to A): causes precede effects in a constant conjunction of events in shared time and space. Most importantly, Jung argued that the constant conjunction of events (i.e. statistical regularity among variables and prediction) does not offer adequate explanatory accounts in the human sciences (i.e. psychology, sociology, anthropology, economics). Jung was especially interested in what he called "inconstant" relationships. He writes: 'the philosophical principle that underlies our conception of natural law is causality. But if the connection between cause and effect turns out to be only statistically valid and only relatively true, then the causal principle is only of relative use for explaining natural processes and therefore presupposes the existence of one or more other factors which would be necessary for an explanation' (Jung, 2010, p. 7).

Events are synchronous when meaningful connections or associations among them can be established; in short, synchronicity is not the result of chance occurrences. Moreover, for Jung, events that are synchronistic involve archetypes (i.e. aspects of the *collective unconscious* that inform human action and behaviour). It is the *archetype* that ultimately enables synchronous connections among events.

KEY TEXTS

- Bright, G. (1997) 'Synchronicity as a Basis of Analytic Attitude, *Journal of Analytical Psychology*, 42 (4): pp. 613–635
- Cambray, J. (2002) 'Synchronicity and Emergence', *American Imago*, 59 (4): pp. 409–434
- Frey-Wehrlin, C. (1976) 'Reflections on CG Jung's Concept of Synchronicity', *Journal of Analytical Psychology*, 21 (1): pp. 37–49
- Jung, C. G. (1955) *Synchronicity: An Acausal Connecting Principle* (London, UK: Routledge)
- Keutzer, C. (1982) 'Archetypes, Synchronicity and the Theory of Formative Causation', *Journal of Analytical Psychology*, 27 (3): pp. 255–262
- Main, R. (2007) 'Synchronicity and Analysis: Jung and After', *European Journal of Psychotherapy and Counseling*, 9 (4): pp. 359–371
- Main, R. (2011) 'Synchronicity and the Limits of Re-Enchantment', *International Journal of Jungian Studies*, 3 (2): pp. 144–158

t

transitional space/transitional phenomena/
transitional object

SEE ALSO good enough mother (holding environment); illusion;
selfobject

For Winnicott, it is through the infant's movement from the illusory
sense of merger with and omnipotent control over the mother that
psychic structure is very gradually shaped. The process involves a
steady development towards *recognition* of the 'me' and the 'not-me',
the internal and the external world. The 'transitional object' (e.g.
teddy bear, security blanket, thumb) is the first 'not-me' possession:
it is neither the infant nor the object; moreover, the first 'not-me'
possessions are universal and variable.

While the objects are *real* they are not yet experienced or perceived
as altogether external. In the child's engagements with the object, a
transition occurs. Gradually the child gives up omnipotent control
over the object; the object is no longer destroyed or banished but
comes instead to survive destructive impulse and gains a sense of
its own independent existence. The transitional object enables the
child to maintain an illusory symbiotic relationship with the mother
and a related sense of imagining that what is has been created by
the infant in reality. This prevents a sense of disillusionment and
enables the child to establish differences among inner and outer,
fact and fantasy, similarity and difference.

While the child is interacting with the object, the 'good enough'
mother is also relating to the infant while gradually establishing
herself as a separate person. Soon, the child experiences a growing
sense of its own subjective agency. Very gradually, the child aban-
dons the dynamic shifts in mental states between controlling and
being controlled. It simultaneously learns not to aggressively and

destructively act on the object world and people around it. The child learns instead to create and play with those sample people and objects. Winnicott describes this in-between space as transitional and transitional phenomenon describes how one experiences the space between the inner and outer. In this space, the child first comes to understand that the maternal figure is not an extension of the self and that the absent mother will reappear. And it is in this space that creativity emerges (Winnicott calls this primary creativity). He is also interested here in how the child manages object loss and unresponsive caregiving environments.

While Lacan shares with Winnicott a concern about the separation of the infant from the mother, for him the separation is always and necessarily traumatic. And for Lacan, unlike Winnicott, it is the father who interrupts the relationship between the mother and infant.

Winnicott's concepts, *transitional space* and phenomena, have been used across a wide array of disciplines to think about the creative process (e.g. Kuhn, 2013; Magruder, 2011; Pedder, 1979; Sabbadini, 2011; Sagan, 2008) in theatre, the Internet, music, gerontology, film and learning. Finally, many have conceptualized the analytic space as a transitional space.

KEY TEXT
• Winnicott, D. W. (1971) *Playing and Reality* (London, UK: Tavistock)

true/false self

SEE ALSO developmental stages; good enough mother (holding environment)

Although Winnicott offered little clear definition of the sense of the true self, in general he describes a state of feeling connected, whole, *real*, alive and spontaneous. This is a feeling of being real and alive in the mind and body: it is a state that produces the necessary conditions for intimacy and creativity. Winnicott did not imagine, however, that these were categorical distinctions, and because the true and false selves are potential states for everyone, he placed them along a continuum.

The false self maintains relationships through the continual anticipation of the demands of others. And if the caregiver fails to respond to the child's states, the false self may emerge as an adaptation to the maternal situation. Winnicott describes what he calls impinging and traumatizing maternal environments where there is a failure to respond to a child's needs in appropriate and integrated ways; under these developmental conditions the false self emerges as a defence against unsafe or overwhelming environments (i.e. excessive discomfort and distress) and the failure of attuned caregiving. With compliance and conforming behaviour, the infant is motivated to please the caregiver; the result is an inhibition of spontaneous expression of authentic feeling and thought. This may also occur when one conforms or complies with social codes, conventions or rules: over time mental life and relational patterns are organized around compliant adaptation to the environment.

Using ideas developed by Winnicott and others, contemporary researchers in academic psychology have described what has been called state authenticity. Authentic states result when 'enduring propensities (e.g. attitudes, values, beliefs, personality) match cognition or action. Others have argued that self-concordant (i.e. authentic) results from a match between situational goal strivings and personal values' (Schlegel *et al.*, 2009, p. 990).

KEY TEXTS

- Schlegel, R. and Hicks, J. (2011) 'The True Self and Psychological Health: Emerging Evidence and Future Directions', *Social and Personality Psychology Compass*, 5 (12): pp. 989–1003
- Schlegel, R. *et al.* (2009) 'Thine Own Self: True Self-Concept Accessibility and Meaning in Life', *Journal of Personality and Social Psychology*, 96 (2): pp. 473–490
- Winnicott, D. W. (1958) 'Primary Maternal Preoccupation' in D. W. Winnicott (ed.), *Collected Papers: Through Paediatrics to Psycho-Analysis* (London, UK: Tavistock), pp. 300–305

W

working alliance/therapeutic alliance

SEE ALSO evidence-based practice

In 2010, in a remarkable move for the mostly anti-*psychodynamic* and prestigious academic journal, the 'American Psychologist', Jonathan Shedler reported findings from a large meta-analytic study (i.e. meta-analysis is a statistical method used to contrast and combine results from many studies to identify patterns among study results, sources of disagreement or other relationships revealed in the context of multiple sources of research findings) showing the efficacy of psychodynamic approaches. Shedler examined results from 80 studies published in top tier academic journals. The findings were indisputable: effect sizes for psychodynamic therapy were as large as those reported for so-called empirically supported or evidence-based ones. The data, moreover, showed that the effects of psychodynamic therapy were not only long-lasting, but improvement also continued after termination (Shedler, 2010). Most important for understanding the significance of the concepts, 'working or therapeutic alliance', is the conclusion reached by Shedler and now widely debated well beyond the scope of psychodynamic practice. The research suggests that the effectiveness of most therapeutic approaches to human sufferings include the effect of the therapy relationship on treatment (i.e. transference and *countertransference*, empathic attunement, all fundamental to the outcomes of all treatment and central to the formation and maintenance of a therapeutic alliance): exploration of the underlying emotional motivations for behaviour, feeling and thought (i.e. self-exploration) and understanding relational patterns. Several studies of *depression* (with data from recorded therapy sessions) show how, though therapists were not explicitly deploying psychodynamic technique, positive outcomes were related to methods derived from psychodynamic theory. The US National Institute of Mental Health Treatment of Depression Collaborative Research Program (Krupnick *et al.*, 1996) showed that the therapeutic alliance was a strong predictor of efficacy for cognitive behavioural and interpersonal psychotherapy for depression and also for medication and placebo.

The working alliance refers to both intrapersonal (i.e. client perceptions of the relationship between him/herself and the therapist) and interpersonal dimensions (i.e. therapist and client collaboratively reaching for mutually understood and valued goals (Horvath, 2006). Both have been shown to be related to treatment outcomes. Research also suggests a relationship between *attachment* styles (i.e. more secure attachment leads to positive engagement) and the formation of the alliance (Smith, Msetfi and Golding, 2010). The achievement of a collaborative relationship is not only an emerging consensus and willingness of both, therapist and client, to engage in and work towards improvement. It also describes the quality of the partnership and its dynamic in time and content (Horvath, 1991).

There is no doubt that one of the greatest challenges for psychodynamic practice is the pressure to demonstrate the effectiveness of psychodynamic psychotherapy. It is also clear that research shows that all therapies depend for their effectiveness on ideas and practices, mostly unacknowledged, derived from psychoanalytic theory. Among those ideas, the working alliance, developed and popularized more recently by Horvath (1991), is firmly grounded in psychoanalytic ideas and practice. The concept, therapeutic alliance, first discussed in the 1950s by Zetzel (1956) and further developed by Greenson (1965) cannot be used interchangeably with its current and most popular derivative: working alliance. The working alliance literature and theory, unlike the therapeutic alliance, tends to altogether elide the importance of the unconscious dimensions of the patient–therapist interactions. Moreover, for Horvath, the working alliance is based on the *real* relationship, not the transference relationship. Luborksy and Bordin, in the 1970s, began to apply ideas developed by Zetzel, Greenson and others in psychoanalysis to the formation and maintenance of all helping relationships. Bordin (1979) proposed that the alliance is reality based (i.e. in the 'here and now' relationship between client and therapist) and composed of three essential elements: (1) a positive bond between the client and patient; (2) agreement about the therapeutic tasks; and (3) agreement about the goals.

Jeremy Safran, a psychodynamic psychologist and alliance researcher, has looked into ruptures in the alliance. For Safran and Moran (2006) ruptures (i.e. tensions or breakdowns in the collaborative relationship) vary in intensity from relatively minor (with differing degrees of therapist and patient awareness) to major disruptions in collaboration, understanding and communication.

points for reflection and practice

- In using the Working Alliance Inventory (WAI) and related instruments, it is important to consider two areas: training therapists to create and maintain a working alliance (focus on the interpersonal nature of the alliance) and understanding how the alliance works differently with each client (i.e. the focus shifts to intrapersonal dimensions of the alliance).
- The WAI is now widely used across areas of practice (education, medicine and nursing, consumer relations, social work, case management).
- The WAI can be downloaded at Horvath's website: http://wai. profhorvath.com/history-long
- Colli and Lingiardi (2009) have developed observer-based methods for understanding alliance ruptures and resolutions: the Collaborative Interaction Scale (CIS).
- Safran and his colleagues, using research on ruptures, suggest that therapists should be aware that many patients have *anxiety* about directly addressing the relationship in fear of the therapist reaction and that the practitioner should be aware that clients often have negative feelings about therapy and the relationship.
- Practitioners should be attuned to the potential for ruptures and be especially open to exploring this dynamic in the relationship.

KEY TEXTS

- Colli, A. and Lingiardi, V. (2009) 'The Collaborative Interactions Scale: A New Transcript-Based Method for the Assessment of Therapeutic Alliance Ruptures and Resolutions in Psychotherapy', *Psychotherapy Research*, 19 (6): pp. 718–734
- Horvath, A. and Symonds, B. (1991) 'Relation between Working Alliance and Outcome in Psychotherapy: A Meta-Analysis', *Journal of Counseling Psychology*, 38 (2): pp. 139–149

- Krupnick, J. *et al.* (1996) 'The Role of the Therapeutic Alliance in Psychotherapy and Pharmacotherapy Outcome: Findings in the National Institute of Mental Health Treatment of Depression Collaborative Research Program', *Journal of Consulting and Clinical Psychology*, 64 (3): pp. 532–539
- Meissner, W. (1996) *The Therapeutic Alliance* (New Haven, CT: Yale University Press)
- Safran, J. (2000) *Therapeutic Alliance* (New York, NY: John Wiley & Sons)
- Safran, J. and Muran, J. (1996) 'The Resolution of Ruptures in the Therapeutic Alliance', *Journal of Consulting and Clinical Psychology*, 64 (3):p. 447
- Safran, J. and Muran, J. (2000) *Negotiating the Therapeutic Alliance: A Relational Treatment Guide* (New York, NY: Guilford Press)
- Safran, J. and Muran, J. (2006) 'Has the Concept of the Therapeutic Alliance Outlived Its Usefulness?' *Psychotherapy: Theory, Research, Practice, Training*, 43 (3): pp. 286–291
- Safran, J., Muran, J. and Eubanks-Carter, C. (2011) 'Repairing Alliance Ruptures', *Psychotherapy*, 48 (1): p. 80
- Smith, A., Msetfi, R. and Golding, L. (2010) 'Client Self Rated Adult Attachment Patterns and the Therapeutic Alliance: A Systematic Review', *Clinical Psychology Review*, 30 (3): pp. 326–337
- Sterba, R. (1934) 'The Fate of the Ego in Analytic Therapy', *International Journal of Psychoanalysis*, 15: pp. 117–126
- Zetzel, E. (1956) 'Current Concepts of Transference', *International Journal of Psychoanalysis*, 37: pp. 369–375

wounded healer

SEE ALSO **archetype; empathy; working alliance/therapeutic alliance**

The wounded healer was a concept used by Jung to understand the underlying motivations of those who offer the self for healing purposes. The *archetype* of the wounded healer was used to imagine how personal experience of the healer produces empathy in the helping relationship. For Jung 'only the wounded healer can truly heal' (1963, p. 125). While it is through the healer's capacity for *empathy* that the healer relates to another's suffering, the healer must of necessity confront his or her own need for healing, the need for continual self-reflection, personal therapy or analysis, and the work of self-reflection is an ongoing and lifelong process. Zerubavel and

Wright (2012) write that 'the wounded healer paradigm suggests that "wounded" and "healer" can be represented as a duality rather than a dichotomy. Woundedness lies on a continuum, and the wounded healer paradigm focuses not on the degree of woundedness but on the ability to draw on woundedness in the service of healing' (p. 482).

points for reflection and practice
- Therapists, to be effective, must be aware of their personal wounds. There are times during treatment when specific wounds are activated, especially when the patients' wounds not unlike those of the therapist.
- The wounds of the patient and those of the therapist may be mutually affecting both.
- Impaired professionals and wounded healers should be carefully differentiated (Zerubavel and Wright, 2012).

KEY TEXTS
- Barnett, M. (2007) 'What Brings You Here? an Exploration of the Unconscious Motivations of Those Who Choose to Train and Work as Psychotherapists and Counsellors', *Psychodynamic Practice*, 13 (3): pp. 257–274
- Conchar, C. and Repper, J. (2014) '"Walking Wounded or Wounded Healer?" Does Personal Experience of Mental Health Problems Help or Hinder Mental Health Practice? A Review of the Literature', *Mental Health and Social Inclusion*, 18 (1): pp. 35–44
- Dunne, C. (2000) *Carl Jung Wounded Healer of the Soul: An Illustrated Biography* (New York, NY: Parabola Books)
- Martin, P. (2011) 'Celebrating the Wounded Healer', *Counseling Psychology Review*, 26 (1): pp. 10–19
- Richard, A. (2012) 'The Wounded Healer: Can We Do Better Than Survive as Therapist?' *International Journal of Psychoanalytic Self Psychology*, 7 (1): pp. 131–138
- Zerubavel, N. and Wright, M. O. D. (2012) 'The Dilemma of the Wounded Healer', *Psychotherapy*, 49 (4): pp. 482–491

appendix 1: timeline

1856

Freud born on 6 May, Freiberg, Moravia.

1859

Freud family moves from Freiberg to Leipzig.
Darwin publishes 'The Origin of Species'.

1860

Freud family settles in Vienna.

1867

Karl Marx publishes Volume I, 'Capital'.

1875

Carl Jung born, Kesswill, Switzerland.

1877

Freud's first publications on intersexuality in eels.

1885–1986

Freud studies under Charcot at the Salpêtrière Hospital, Paris.
Charcot provides new insight into hysteria and uses hypnosis.

1891

Freud publishes 'On Aphasia' (language disorders and neurology).

1892

Josef Breuer describes the case of Anna O to Freud.
Harry Stack Sullivan born.

1893–1896

Freud works with Josef Breuer on case histories (including that of 'Anna O') which later become 'Studies on Hysteria' (1895). Introduces the idea that the symptoms of hysteria were symbolic representations of traumatic memories, often of a sexual nature.

1895

Anna Freud born, Vienna.

1896

First use of the term 'psychoanalysis'.
D. W. Winnicott born.

1897

Freud's self-analysis begins, leading to the abandonment of the trauma theory of neurosis (developed with Breuer), recognition of infantile sexuality and the Oedipus complex.

1900

Freud publishes 'The Interpretation of Dreams'.

1901

Freud publishes 'The Psychopathology of Everyday Life'.
Jacques Lacan born, Paris.

1902

Erik Erikson born, Frankfurt, Germany.

1904

B. F. Skinner born.

1905

Freud publishes 'Three Essays on the Theory of Sexuality', 'Dora' (case dates from 1899) and 'Jokes and Their Relation to the Unconscious'.

1906

'The Journal of Abnormal Psychology' founded by Morton Prince. Jung initiates correspondence with Sigmund Freud and visits in 1907.

1907

Formation of the Vienna Psychoanalytic Society.

1908

Salzburg: first International Meeting of Psychoanalysts. In this year, Freud meets Hungarian psychoanalyst Sándor Ferenczi. The two begin professional and personal relationship, recorded in more than 1200 letters.

1909

Freud and Jung travel to the US to deliver Clark Lectures: first lectures on psychoanalysis in America.
Freud publishes his study of five-year-old 'Little Hans', the first such analytic observation of a child.

1910

Karl Abraham, close friend and colleague of Freud, establishes the Berlin Psychoanalytic Society.

1911

Alfred Adler left Freud's Psychoanalytic Group to form separate organization, accusing Freud of overemphasizing sexuality and basing theory on his own childhood.

1912–1913

Freud publishes 'Totem and Taboo' (explores how culture and society are rooted in the prohibition against incest, an assertion contrary to the development of Jung's studies).

1913

Jung breaks from Freud.
Heinz Kohut born, Vienna.
Jung publishes 'On the Importance of the Unconscious in Psychopathology'.

1914

Melanie Klein begins analysis with Sándor Ferenczi.
Jung publishes 'Seven Sermons of the Dead' (outlines his most essential ideas, including the conflict of opposites and the concept of individuation).

1917

Freud publishes 'Mourning and Melancholia'.

1918

Melanie Klein attends the Fifth Psychoanalytic Congress at the Hungarian Academy of Sciences, Budapest, where she hears Freud read paper.

1919

Freud observes soldiers traumatized by the war.
Freud publishes 'Beyond the Pleasure Principle'.
Melanie Klein presents her study of her five-year-old son Erich to the Hungarian Psychoanalytic Society.

1920

Freud experiences death of daughter, Sophie.
Freud publishes 'Beyond the Pleasure Principle' (new theories of the 'compulsion to repeat' and the concept of the 'death drive', as well as a revision of the 1900 theory of dreams as wish fulfilments).

Melanie Klein attends the first International Congress since the war.

1921

Freud publishes 'Group Psychology and the Analysis of the Ego'.
Jung publishes 'Psychological Types' (introduces concepts, introverted and extroverted).

1922

Anna Freud presents paper 'Beating Fantasies and Daydreams' to Vienna Psychoanalytic Society and becomes member.

1923

Freud publishes 'The Ego and the Id' (new account of the structure of the mind, revising the 'conscious/pre-conscious/unconscious' distinction introduced in 'The Interpretation of Dreams').

1923

Great Depression in Germany and Austria.
Ruhr occupied by France and Belgium. Jung visits Pueblo Indians in North America.

1924

Melanie Klein asks Karl Abraham to analyse her.
Karen Horney publishes 'On the Genesis of the Castration Complex in Women'.

1925

Hitler's 'Mein Kampf' published.

1926

Freud publishes 'Inhibitions, Symptoms and Anxiety' (anxiety enters as central concept of his developmental theory).
The London Clinic for Psychoanalysis opens on 6th May, Freud's 70th birthday.

Ernest Jones encourages Melanie Klein's move to London.
Karen Horney publishes 'The Flight from Womanhood'.

1927

Freud publishes 'The Future of an Illusion: A Consideration of the Origins and Function of Religion'.
Anna Freud addresses the Berlin Society on the subject of child analytic technique, an attack on Melanie Klein's approach to psychoanalysis.
Anna Freud publishes 'Introduction to the Technique of Child Analysis'.
Winnicott starts his analytic training.

1928

Erik Erikson begins studying and working with Anna Freud.

1929

Joan Riviere publishes 'Womanliness as a Masquerade'.

1930

Freud publishes 'Civilization and Its Discontents', his thinking about the irreconcilability of personal drives and the demands of society.

1932

Lacan beings analysis with Rudolph Loewenstein.

1933

Erik Erikson receives diploma from the Vienna Psychoanalytic Institute. This and his Montessori diploma are his only academic credentials.

1935

Karen Horney publishes 'The Problem of Feminine Masochism'.

1936

Freud's 8oth birthday.

Anna Freud publishes 'The Ego and the Mechanisms of Defense'. Lacan presents paper on the mirror stage at the International Psychoanalytical Association conference.

1937

Michael Balint publishes 'Primary Object Love'.

1938

Freud finishes 'Moses and Monotheism' and 'An Outline of Psychoanalysis'.
Erik Erikson invited to observe the education of native Sioux children on the Pine Ridge Reservation in South Dakota.
Sigmund and Anna Freud flee Vienna after Nazi's invasion.

1939

Freud dies in London, 23 September.
Melanie Klein re-works 'Mourning and Its Relation to Manic-Depressive States'.

1941

Karen Horney founds the American Institute for Psychoanalysis.
Eric Fromm publishes 'Escape from Freedom'.

1942

The first of the British Society's Extraordinary Meetings takes place on 25 February, after months and years of increasing discord and infighting among its members. They are heated and often venomously personal battles between the opposing groups in the Society – the Kleinians and Viennese Freudians.

1944

Melanie delivers paper for the Controversial Discussion, 'The Emotional Life of the Infant'.
Helene Deutsche, 1944–1955, publishes her two-volume work, 'The Psychology of Women'.

Theodor Adorno and Max Horkheimer publish 'Dialectic of the Enlightenment'.

1946

Melanie Klein delivers paper, 'Notes on Some Schizoid Mechanisms'.
Wilfred Bion publishes important paper, 'Leaderless Group Project', Bulletin of the Menninger Clinic.

1948

B. F. Skinner publishes 'Walden Two'. This was a fictional account of a Utopia based on Skinner's behavioural idea.

1950

Erik Erikson publishes 'Childhood and Society'.
Theodor Adorno publishes 'The Authoritarian Personality'.

1951

D. W. Winnicott publishes 'Transitional Objects and Transitional Phenomena'.
Lacan Seminar on Freud's case of the Wolf Man.
Lacan gives a seminar on Freud's Wolf-Man case.
Hannah Arendt publishes 'The Origins of Totalitarianism'.

1952

'The Diagnostic and Statistical Manual of Mental Disorders' was published by the American Psychiatric Association, marking the beginning of modern mental illness classification.

1953

Harry Stack Sullivan publishes 'The Interpersonal Theory of Psychiatry'.
Mary Ainswort and John Bowlby publish major paper, 'Research Strategy in the Study of Mother–Child Separation'.

B.F. Skinner publishes 'The Science of Learning and the Art of Teaching'.

Harry Stack Sullivan publishes 'The Psychiatric Interview'.

1955

Herbert Marcuse publishes 'Eros and Civilization: A Philosophical Inquiry into Freud'.

1956

Eric Fromm publishes 'The Art of Loving'.

1957

Melanie Klein publishes controversial 'Envy and Gratitude'.

Hanna Segal publishes 'Notes on Symbol Formation'.

1958

'Man and His Symbols' begun, completed and published in 1961, after Jung's death.

Hannah Arendt publishes 'The Human Condition'.

1959

Melanie Klein delivers paper, 'On the Sense of Loneliness' at the Copenhagen Congress.

Selma Fraiberg publishes 'The Magic Years: Understanding and Handling the Problems of Early Childhood'.

Noam Chomsky publishes controversial and fatal critique of behaviourism, 'A Review of B. F. Skinner's Verbal Behavior'.

Hans Loewald publishes 'On the Therapeutic Action of Psycho-Analysis'.

1960

Melanie Klein dies, 22 September.

1962

Harry Stack Sullivan publishes 'Schizophrenia as a Human Process'.

1963

Hannah Arendt publishes 'Eichmann in Jerusalem: A Report on the Banality of Evil'.
Irving Bieber and colleagues published 'Homosexuality: A Psychoanalytic Study' (influential in its portrayal of a pathogenic family type).

1964

Herbert Marcuse publishes 'One-Dimensional Man'.

1967

Aaron Beck publishes psychological model of depression, 'The Diagnosis and Management of Depression'.
Mary Ainsworth publishes 'Infancy in Uganda: Infant Care and the Growth of Love'.

1968

Erik Erikson publishes 'Identity: Youth and Crisis'.
'DSM II' published by the American Psychiatric Association.
Michael Balint publishes 'The Basic Fault: Therapeutic Aspects of Regression'.

1971

Winnicott dies in London, 25 January.
Heinz Kohut publishes 'The Analysis of the Self: A Systematic Approach to the Psychoanalytic Treatment of Narcissistic Personality Disorders'. Here, he discuses concept of 'self-object transferences'.
Hans Loewald publishes 'On Motivation and Instinct Theory'.

1972

Jurgen Habermas publishes 'Knowledge and Human Interests'. (Like Lacan, Habermas argues that the unconscious is linguistic in nature.)

1973

Hans Loewald publishes 'On Internalization'.
Margaret Mahler and colleagues publish 'The Psychological Birth of the Human Infant'.
The American Psychiatric Association (APA) removed homosexuality from its official 'Diagnostic and Statistical Manual of Mental Disorders'.

1974

Luce Irigaray publishes 'Speculum of the Other Woman'.

1975

Cornelius Castoriadis publishes 'The Imaginary Institution of Society'.

1977

Heinz Kohut publishes 'The Restoration of the Self'.
Lacan publishes, English translation, 'Écrits: A Selection'.
Luce Irigaray publishes 'This Sex Which Is Not One'.

1978

Nancy Chodorow publishes 'The Reproduction of Mothering: Psychoanalysis and the Sociology of Gender'.

1979

Hans Loewald publishes 'The Waning of the Oedipus Complex'.

1982

Betty Joseph publishes 'Addiction to Near-Death'.
Julia Kristeva publishes 'Powers of Horror: An Essay on Abjection'.

1984

Janine Chasseguet-Smirgel publishes 'Creativity and Perversion'.

1985

Betty Joseph publishes 'Transference: The Total Situation'.
Juliet Mitchell publishes, edited volume, 'Feminine Sexuality: Jacques Lacan and the École Freudienne'.

1986

Betty Joseph publishes 'Envy in Everyday Life'.

1988

Steven Mitchell publishes 'Relational Concepts in Psychoanalysis'.

1989

Betty Joseph publishes, selection of papers, 'Psychic Equilibrium and Psychic Change'.
Joyce McDougall publishes 'Theatre of the Body: A Psychoanalytic Approach to Psychosomatic Illness'.

1993

Andre Green publishes 'The Dead Mother'.

1999

Eric Kandel, first psychiatrist to win the Nobel Prize, publishes controversial article in 'The American Journal of Psychiatry', calling for a synthesis of neuro and cognitive science with key ideas in psychoanalysis.

2000

The International Neuropsychoanalysis Society was founded in London to promote interdisciplinary work between the fields of psychoanalysis and neuroscience.

2008

Paul Verhaeghe, a Belgian Lacanian, publishes seminal work on diagnostics 'On Being Normal and Other Disorders: A Manual for Clinical Psychodiagnostics'.

2014

Eric Laurent, a French Lacanian, publishes critique of the turn to cognitive and neuroscience in psychoanalysis, 'Lost in Cognition'.

appendix 2: brief
biography of Freud

Freud in 'fin de siècle' Vienna. Here I will very briefly consider the life and work of Sigmund Freud (1856–1939), the founder and leading figure in the psychoanalytic movement, by placing him, his work and his followers in the Victorian era (1837–1901), a period in history marked by the birth and death of the British monarch, Victoria. While it is important to get a sense of the entire period, I will focus especially on Vienna in what is commonly known as the 'fin de siècle': 1890–1910. The entire nineteenth century saw cataclysmic shifts in economic life, revolutionary movements and radically new ideologies. In a remarkable trilogy of books, Eric Hobsbawm describes them as ages: 'Age of Revolution: 1789–1848', 'Age of Capital: 1848–1875', and 'Age of Empire: 1875–1914'. There were unprecedented movements of people from the countryside to the city. Hobsbawm writes that 'between 1846 and 1875 considerably more than 9 million people left Europe, by far the greater part of these for the United States' (p. 228). During the 'Age of Capital' even the middle classes were on the move. Freud's family, for example, moved from Freiberg, Moravia, to Vienna. London at the beginning of the Victorian era was a city of only two million; by the end it was a massive urban centre with more than six million. Between 1870 and 1910 the population of Vienna more than doubled – from 900,000 to more than two million. Before the 1860 emancipation, 6200 Jews (2.2% of the population) lived in Vienna. By 1870, there were 40,200 (6.6%), and 72,600 (10.1%) in 1880. In the Vienna of 1867, one could finally own property, choose a place of residence, gain access to employment as civil servants, and a university education, without restriction. An immediate consequence of this extension of rights and the emancipation was a surge of Jewish migrants.

The Vienna of 1860, the year the Freud family arrived, was well before the collapse of the liberal project. Sigmund was four. Two older brothers, from his father's first wife, had migrated to Manchester, England. In Vienna, the Freuds had four daughters (Rosa, Marie, Adolfine and Paula) and a son, Alexander. Sigmund finished the gymnasium with honours and entered the University of Vienna at 17, where he studied natural sciences and philosophy. He studied philosophy and phenomenology under Franz Brentano (Tauber, 2010), physiology under Ernst Brücke and zoology under Carl Claus. In 1881 he finished his medical degree. It was in neurology, however, where Freud found early interest and enthusiasm and where he worked on the central nervous systems of lower vertebrates and humans. He published three papers describing the structure and function of the medulla oblongata and a pioneering work on cocaine's use as an anaesthetic. Freud also wrote four major texts describing neurological disorders. His final work in neurology, 'Infantile Cerebral Paralysis', was published in 1897. His work under Brentano, among the foremost phenomenologists, did not leave (Tauber, 2010, pp. 29, 40) the same visible mark on Freud's thinking.

'Fin de siècle' Vienna was the capital of the Austro-Hungarian Empire, a complex multi-ethnic and multi-faith state forever faced with political challenge and instability (Schorkse, 1980). The Empire had a wide reach: 15 states and 50 million inhabitants. The Empire at the 'fin de siècle' was held together by a mostly symbolic figure, Emperor Franz Joseph I (1848–1916), and a highly efficient bureaucratic state. With the First World War, the Empire was in shambles. From 1890 to 1910, however, Vienna was the centre of modernism: Freud's psychoanalysis, Arnold Schoenberg's 12-tone music, Arthur Schnitzler's 'soul-scapes', and Richard's Strauss's highly discordant Salome, an opera based on a play of the same title by Oscar Wilde (Gilman, 1988; Ross, 2007). For Gordon Craig,

The rise of modernism in Vienna was conditioned by the break-down, at the end of the 1870s, of the political ascendancy of the Liberal Party and the rise of new forms of mass politics. This shook the confidence of the liberal elite and weakened the cohesion of its cultural tradition, that synthesis of aesthetic cultivation inherited from the baroque and of rationalist political and

academic dedication inherited from the Enlightenment which
Schorske calls the union of Grace and the Word. Tolerance of
opposing points of view became less frequent, the search for
culprits on whom to blame the disarray of the times became more
common, the tie between generations broke down. Indeed, the
evolution of modernism was marked by a series of Oedipal revolts
by the sons against the fathers. (Craig, 1998, pp. 8–20)

Europe and the United States saw unprecedented concentrations of
wealth and equally significant social and economic upheaval. Steam
and electricity, sometimes called 'motive powers', transformed our
relationships to nature and society. In physics there was a shift of
emphasis from matter to energy and major leaps in our understud-
ying of electricity and magnetism. Faraday, in the 1830s, visualized
electric and magnetic fields as flux emanating from charged bodies
and magnets. When Freud was nine years old, in 1865, James
Maxwell published 'A Dynamical Theory of the Electromagnetic
Field', and the equations necessary for understanding the relationship between electric and magnetic forces. It was in this age
of electricity and the emerging physics of electromagnetism that
Freud was born, educated and developed many of his most influential and lasting ideas (see key idea entry, *drive*). He was especially
influenced by the work of Helmholz on the conservation of energy;
and under the influence of Ernst Brücke at the University of Vienna
he embraced the view that living organisms were energy systems
governed by the principle of conservation (i.e. the total amount of
energy in a system is constant, that energy quanta can be changed
but not annihilated and when energy moves from one part of the
system, it must reappear in another). The conservation of energy
for Freud became the basis for much of his theorizing about the
special qualities of psychic energies and agencies and their functions in mental life. The aim of analytic work, then, was to understand how psychic energies and their transformations occur and
shape the life of the mind.

The power of the microscope to magnify and to look into nature
made possible close observation of tissues and the development of
what was called cell theory: cells are the fundamental unit of all
living things and are produced from other cells, and that change
in cell function is the ultimate cause of disease (Mazzarello, 1999).

Freud was especially interested in nerve cells and used these new technologies to investigate their properties and function, histology, neuroanatomy and neuropathology; his first microscopic study was the testis of the eel (Tauber, 2010, pp. 120–121; Triarhou, 2009; Rovainen and Yan, 1985).

In the social sciences, too, sociology and psychology emerged as distinct disciplines of knowledge. Karl Marx offered a powerful critique and philosophy to think about the growing influence of industrial capitalism and new logics of economic life. It was in this context and these revolutions in ways of knowing and understanding the physical and social world that Freud began his studies. And like Marx, Freud argued for the existence of unseen but knowable causal forces. For Marx, there was the hidden force of labour power, necessary for commodities to have exchangeable values. For Freud, the unconscious and the drives, both unavailable to our direct awareness, like gravity or labour power, could be known only through the effects produced. In short, labour power, for Marx, and the drives, for Freud, could not be directly measured or apprehended through sensory experience. It was also during this time, late nineteenth century, when social reformers began to imagine the application of knowledge produced in the emerging social sciences to the problems of everyday life. And it was in the crises of urban, industrial capitalism that social work as a distinct area of practice and knowledge began to emerge (Skocpol, 1992).

Moreover, there were in Vienna the beginnings of one of the most important movements in modern philosophy: the Vienna Circle. Formally organized in 1922, its members included famous names: Wittgenstein, Frank, Hahn, Neurath, Schlick, Carnap, Feigl, Gödel, Kraft, Neurath, Waismann. The Circle organized and promoted what became to be known as 'logical positivism' (Weideman, 2013), one, if not the most important, of the philosophies of science in the twentieth century and beyond. And it was out of this movement that one of Freud's earliest critics emerged: Karl Popper's 'Open Society' (Grant and Harari, 2005; Popper, 1945), and it is also out of positivism that the governing epistemology and methodologies of our current time have emerged: what is that which we can see (i.e. ontology, empiricism) and the statistical regularity (i.e. prediction) among events provides an adequate causal or explanatory account (i.e. epistemology, positivism).

Freud's first major psychoanalytic work, 'The Interpretation of Dreams', did not appear until 1900, when Freud was 44. Eight editions were published in his lifetime. In 1932, Adolf Hitler came to power in Germany. In 1933, Freud's books were publicly burned by the Nazis. In 1936, Freud celebrated his 80th birthday in Vienna. In 1938, when the Nazis annexed Austria, Freud, along with his family, fled to England. On 23 September 1939, he died after a painful and debilitating struggle with cancer (Edmundson, 2007).

appendix 3: the major

psychodynamic/analytic

dictionaries

Abram, J. (2007) *The Language of Winnicott: A Dictionary of Winnicott's Use of Words* (London, UK: Karnac Books)

Akhtar, S. (2009) *Comprehensive Dictionary of Psychoanalysis* (London, UK: Karnac Books)

Auchincloss, E. and Samberg, E. (eds) (2012) *Psychoanalytic Terms and Concepts* (New Haven, CT: Yale University Press)

Cohen, J. (2005) *How to Read Freud* (London, UK: Granta)

Etchegoyen, R. (2005) *The Fundamentals of Psychoanalytic Technique* (London, UK: Karnac Books)

Evans, D. (2006) *An Introductory Dictionary of Lacanian Psychoanalysis* (London: Routledge)

Fink, B. (2011) *Fundamentals of Psychoanalytic Technique: A Lacanian Approach for Practitioners* (New York, NY: W. W. Norton & Company)

Green, A. (2012) *Key Ideas for a Contemporary Psychoanalysis: Misrecognition and Recognition of the Unconscious* (London, UK: Routledge)

Jean-Michel, R. (ed.) (2003) *The Cambridge Companion to Lacan* (Cambridge, UK: Cambridge University Press)

Laplanche, J. and Pontalis, J. (1988) *The Language of Psychoanalysis* (London, UK: Karnac Books)

Loose, R. (2010) *The Edinburgh International Encyclopaedia of Psychoanalysis* (Edinburgh: Edinburgh University Press)

López-Corvo, R. (2003) *The Dictionary of the Work of W.R. Bion* (London, UK: Karnac Books)

Mitchell, S. (1988) *Relational Concepts in Psychoanalysis* (Cambridge, MA: Harvard University Press)

Moore, B. and Fine, B. (eds) (1990) *Psychoanalytic Terms and Concepts* (New Haven, CT: Yale University Press)

Rycroft, C. (1995) *A Critical Dictionary of Psychoanalysis* (London, UK: Puffin)

Samuels, A., Shorter, B. and Plaut, F. (1986) *A Critical Dictionary of Jungian Analysis* (New York, NY: Routledge)

Sandler P. (2005) *The Language of Bion: A Dictionary of Concepts* (London, UK: Karnac Books)

Spillius, E. *et al.* (2011) *The New Dictionary of Kleinian Thought* (New York, NY: Routledge)

Wright, E. (1992) *Feminism and Psychoanalysis: A Critical Dictionary* (Oxford, UK: Oxford University Press)

Žižek, S. (2006) *How to Read Lacan* (London, UK: Granta)

appendix 4: the defence
mechanisms

Major Defence Mechanisms:

- Repression: removal from consciousness of unwelcome idea, affect or desire.
- Reaction formation: fixation in consciousness of ideas, affects or desires opposed to unwanted unconscious impulse.
- Projection: unwanted feelings attributed to another person.
- Regression: return means of gratification belonging to earlier phase, due to conflicts at later and more developed stages.
- Rationalization: substitution of the true, but threatening cause of behaviour for a safe and reasonable account.
- Denial: the conscious refusal to perceive disturbing facts. Deprives the individual of the necessary awareness to cope with external challenges and the employment of adequate strategies for survival.
- Displacement: redirection of impulse towards substitute.
- Undoing: is achieved through an act, which goal is the cancellation of a prior unpleasant experience.
- Introjection: intimately related to identification, aims at solving some emotional difficulty of the individual by means of introjecting personality characteristics of someone else.
- Sublimation: part of the energy invested in sexual impulses is shifted to the pursuit of socially valuable achievements, such as artistic or scientific endeavours.

appendix 5: Erik Erikson's
developmental stages

1   basic trust vs basic mistrust (0–2 years)

The crisis for the infant at this stage, for Erikson, overlaps with the oral stage. The infant depends on others to meet its most fundamental needs. If needs are met in a predictable and reliable manner, the child develops a sense of trust. If unresolved, a sense of mistrust may be carried in into adult relationships. If the basic mistrust is significant, psychosis may result (i.e. a break with reality).

2   autonomy vs shame and doubt (2–3 years)

Here, the child gradually establishes a sense of independence as it becomes mobile in the world. If the child receives predictable and consistent support and encouragement in the social surround, the child will move towards autonomous action, feeling and thought. In the absence of support and inconsistency, the child will experience and feel shame and doubt. When adults insist on bowel mastery before a child is ready or impose punitive interventions, power struggles will follow.

3   initiative vs guilt (4–5 years)

Some associate this stage with Freud's phallic period. Here, the child explores and experiments. With support from the parents and social surround, experimentation and trial and error lead to initiative. If the parent punishes or in some way inhibits exploratory activity, a sense of guilt will follow.

4   industry vs inferiority (6–12 years)

As a child enters school, it must contend with new social roles and seeking approval from peers. This is accomplished, in part, by facing the challenge of performing new tasks. If this is not accomplished (i.e. competent performance), a child may not feel accepted and may develop a sense of inferiority.

5   identity vs identity confusion (12–18 years)

This crisis corresponds roughly to Freud's genital stage. For Erikson, this is a moment marked by a search for social and sexual identities. Here, with the integration of prior stages and experience, earlier crises are resolved, and a strong ego identity results. With a strong ego, there is less confusion over identity.

6   intimacy vs isolation (19–25 years)

Here the crisis is organized around the need for intimacy. If there is difficulty at this stage, some find themselves unable to form intimate relationships and develop feelings of isolation.

7   generativity vs stagnation (26–40 years)

Here, intimacy is by itself insufficient. Generativity requires a capacity to look beyond the self to the surrounding world and to contribute to it. Difficulties arise when at during this period one is self-centred or self-absorbed. The result is a sense of stagnation and questioning about the relevance of past to current life experience.

8   ego integrity vs despair (41– years)

During this period, we reflect on the lives we've lived and feel a sense of fulfilment and accomplishment. Or we live with a sense of regret and despair.

appendix 6: selected resources: biographies, histories, criticism, philosophy of mind

Wilfred Bion

Bleandonu, G. (1994) *Wilfred Bion: His Life and Works* (London, UK: Free Association Books)

Sigmund Freud

Atwood, G. E. and Stolorow, R. D. (eds) (1994) *Faces in a Cloud: Intersubjectivity in Personality Theory* (Oxford, UK: Jason Aronson)

Breger, L. (2000) *Freud: Darkness in the Midst of Vision* (New York, NY: John Wiley & Sons)

Edmundson, M. (2007) *The Death of Sigmund Freud: The Legacy of His Last Days* (New York, NY: Bloomsbury)

Freud, S. (1963) *An Autobiographical Study* (New York, NY: W. W. Norton & Company)

Gay, P. (1996) *The Naked Heart: The Bourgeois Experience Victoria to Freud (The Bourgeois Experience: Victoria to Freud)* (Vol. 4) (New York, NY: W. W. Norton & Company)

Gay, P. (1998) *Freud: A Life for Our Time* (New York, NY: W. W. Norton & Company)

Jones, E. (1953) *The Life and Work of Sigmund Freud, Vol. 1: The Formative Years and the Great Discoveries, 1856–1900* (New York, NY: Basic Books)

Jones, E. (1955) *The Life and Work of Sigmund Freud, Vol. 2: Years of Maturity, 1901–1919* (New York, NY: Basic Books)

Jones, E. (1957) *The Life and Work of Sigmund Freud, Vol. 3: The Last Phase, 1919–1939* (New York, NY: Basic Books)

Lear, J. (2005) *Freud* (London, UK: Routledge)

Mitchell, S. (1995) *Freud and Beyond: A History of Modern Psychoanalytic Thought* (New York, NY: Basic Books)

Phillips, A. (2014) *Becoming Freud* (New Haven, CT: Yale University Press)

Roazen, P. (1992) *Freud and His Followers* (New York, NY: Da Capo Press)

Robinson, P. (1993) *Freud and His Critics* (Berkeley, CA: University of California Press)

Rieff, P. (1979) *Freud: The Mind of the Moralist* (Chicago, IL: University of Chicago Press)

Anna Freud

Britzman, D. P. (2012) *After-Education: Anna Freud, Melanie Klein, and Psychoanalytic Histories of Learning* (Albany, NY: SUNY Press)

Coles, R. (1992) *Anna Freud: The Dream of Psychoanalysis* (New York, NY: Basic Books)

Dyer, R. (1983) *Her Father's Daughter: The Work of Anna Freud* (New York, NY: Jason Aronson)

Peters, U. H. (1985) *Anna Freud: A Life Dedicated to Children* (New York, NY: Schocken Books)

Pollak, R. (1998) *The Creation of Doctor B: A Biography of Bruno Bettelheim* (New York, NY: Simon and Schuster)

Sayers, J. (1993) *Mothers of Psychoanalysis: Helene Deutsch, Karen Horney, Anna Freud, and Melanie Klein* (New York, NY: W. W. Norton & Company)

Young-Bruehl, E. (2008) *Anna Freud: A Biography* (New Haven, CT: Yale University Press)

Erik Erikson

Coles, R. (1970) *Erik H. Erikson: The Growth of His Work* (Boston, MA: Little, Brown)

Friedman, L. J. (2000) *Identity's Architect: A Biography of Erik H. Erikson* (Cambridge, MA: Harvard University Press)

Hoover, K. (ed.) (2004) *The Future of Identity: Centennial Reflections on the Legacy of Erik Erikson* (Oxford, UK: Lexington Books)

Roazen, P. (1997) *Erik H. Erikson: The Power and Limits of a Vision* (New York, NY: Free Press)

Robert Fairbairn

Britton, R. (1989) *The Oedipus Complex Today: Clinical Implications* (Sterling, VA: Stylus Publishing)

Sutherland, J. D. (1989) *Fairbairn's Journey into the Interior* (Oxford, UK: Free Association Books)

Karen Horney

Hitchcock, S. T. (2004) *Karen Horney: Pioneer of Feminist Psychology* (New York: Chelsea House Publishers)

O'Connell, A. N. (1990) 'Karen Horney (1885–1952)' in A. N. O'Connell and N. F. Russo (eds), *Women in Psychology: A Bio- Bibliographic Sourcebook* (Westport, CT: Greenwood Press), pp. 184–190

Paris, B. (1994) *Karen Horney: A Psychoanalyst's Search for Self-Understanding* (New Haven, CT: Yale University Press)

Quinn, S. (1987) *A Mind of Her Own: The Life of Karen Horney* (New York, NY: Summit Books)

Rubins, J. L. (1978) *Karen Horney: Gentle Rebel of Psychoanalysis* (New York, NY: The Dial Press)

Sayers, J. (1991) *Mothers of Psychoanalysis: Helene Deutsch, Karen Horney, Anna Freud, Melanie Klein* (New York, NY: W. W. Norton & Company)

Carl Gustav Jung

Hannah, B. (1976) *Jung, His Life and Work: A Biographical Memoir* (New York, NY: Putnam)

Dunne, C. (2002) *Carl Jung: Wounded Healer of the Soul: An Illustrated Biography* (New York, NY: Bloomsbury)

Smith, R. (1997) *The Wounded Jung: Effects of Jung's Relationships on His Life and Work* (Evanston, IL: Northwestern University Press)

Wehr, G. and Weeks, D. (1987) *Jung: A Biography* (Boston, MA: Shambhala Publications)

Melaine Klein

Britzman, D. (2012) *After-Education: Anna Freud, Melanie Klein, and Psychoanalytic Histories of Learning* (Albany, NY: SUNY Press)

Frank, C. (2009) *Melanie Klein in Berlin: Her First Psychoanalyses of Children* (London, UK: Routledge)

Grosskurth, P. (2013) *Melanie Klein* (New York, NY: Random House)

Holder, A. (2005) *Anna Freud, Melanie Klein, and the Psychoanalysis of Children and Adolescents* (London, UK: Karnac Books)

King, P. and Steiner, R. (eds) (1991) *The Freud-Klein Controversies, 1941–45* (Vol. II) (London, UK: Routledge)

Kristeva, J. (2013) *Melanie Klein* (Columbia, SC: Columbia University Press)

Sayers, J. (2000) *Kleinians: Psychoanalysis Inside Out* (New York, NY: John Wiley & Sons)

Sayers, J. (1993) *Mothers of Psychoanalysis: Helene Deutsch, Karen Horney, Anna Freud, and Melanie Klein* (New York, NY: W. W. Norton & Company)

Segal, H. (1989) *Klein* (Sterling, VA: Stylus Publishing) Heinz Kohut

Kohut, H. (1994) *The Curve of Life: Correspondence of Heinz Kohut, 1923–1981* (Chicago, CL: University of Chicago Press)

Siegel, A. M. (1996) *Heinz Kohut and the Psychology of the Self* (New York, NY: Psychology Press)

Strozier, C. B. (2001) *Heinz Kohut: The Making of a Psychoanalyst* (New York, NY: Palgrave Macmillan)

Jacques Lacan

Felman, S. (1987) *Jacques Lacan and the Adventure of Insight: Psychoanalysis in Contemporary Culture* (Cambridge, MA: Harvard University Press)

Homer, S. (2005) *Jacques Lacan* (New York, NY: Psychology Press)

Marini, M. and Tomiche, A. T. (1992) *Jacques Lacan: The French Context* (New Brunswick, NJ: Rutgers University Press)

Roudinesco, E. and Bray, B. (1997) *Jacques Lacan* (Columbia, SC: Columbia University Press)

Roudinesco, E. (1990) *Jacques Lacan & Co: A History of Psychoanalysis in France, 1925–1985* (Chicago, IL: University of Chicago Press)

Clément, C. and Goldhammer, A. (1983) *The Lives and Legends of Jacques Lacan* (New York, NY: Columbia University Press)

Harry Stack Sullivan

Chapman, A. H. (1976) *Harry Stack Sullivan: His Life and His Work* (New York, NY: Putnam)

Perry, H. S. (1982) *Psychiatrist of America, The Life of Harry Stack Sullivan* (Cambridge, MA: Belknap Press)

D. W. Winnicott

Brett Kahr (1996) *D. W. Winnicott: A Biographical Portrait* (Sterling, VA: Stylus Publishing)

Phillips, A. (2007) *Winnicott* (London, UK: Penguin)

Rodman, F. R. (2004) *Winnicott: Life and Work* (Da Capo Press)

psychoanalysis and philosophy, philosophy of mind

Cavell, M. (1996) *The Psychoanalytic Mind: From Freud to Philosophy* (Cambridge, MA: Harvard University Press)

Lear, J. (ed.) (1990) *Love and Its Place in Nature: A Philosophical Interpretation of Freudian Psychoanalysis* (New Haven, CT: Yale University Press)

Ricoeur, P. (2008) *Freud and Philosophy: An Essay on Interpretation* (New Delhi, India: Motilal Banarsidass Publisher)

Karlsson, G. (2010) *Psychoanalysis in a New Light* (Cambridge, UK: Cambridge University Press)

Lear, J. (1998) *Open Minded: Working Out the Logic of the Soul* (Cambridge, MA: Harvard University Press)

Lohmar, D. and Brudzinska, J. (2011) *Founding Psychoanalysis Phenomenologically: Phenomenological Theory of Subjectivity and the Psychoanalytic Experience* (Vol. 199) (Dordrecht: Springer)

other titles

Alexander, F., Eisenstein, S. and Grotjahn, M. (eds) (1995) *Psychoanalytic Pioneers* (Piscataway, NJ: Transaction Publishers)

Aron, L. E. and Harris, A. E. (1993) *The Legacy of Sandor Ferenczi* (New Jersey, NJ: Analytic Press)

Banissy, M. and Ward, J. (2007) 'Mirror-Touch Synesthesia Is Linked with Em-pathy', *Nature Neuroscience*, 10 (7): pp. 815–816

Bowlby, R. and King, P. (2004) *Fifty Years of Attachment Theory* (London, UK: Karnac Books)

Baruch, E. H. (1991) *Women Analyze Women: In France, England, and the United States* (New York, NY: New York University Press)

Hazell, J. (1996) *HJS Guntrip: A Psychoanalytical Biography* (London, UK: Free Association Books)

Hirschmüller, A. (1989) *The Life and Work of Josef Breuer: Physiology and Psychoanalysis* (New York, NY: New York University Press)

Kristeva, J. (2001) *Hannah Arendt: Life Is a Narrative* (Toronto: University of Toronto Press)

Petocz, A. (1999) *Freud, Psychoanalysis and Symbolism* (Cambridge, UK: Cambridge University Press)

Pollak, R. (1998) *The Creation of Doctor B: A Biography of Bruno Bettelheim* (New York, NY: Simon and Schuster)

Roazen, P. (1993) *Meeting Freud's Family* (Amherst, MA: University of Massachusetts Press)

Roazen, P. (1985) *Helene Deutsch: A Psychoanalyst's Life* (New York, NY: Doubleday)

Rudnytsky, P. L., Giampieri-Deutsch, P. and Bokay, A. (eds) (2000) *Ferenczi's Turn in Psychoanalysis* (New York, NY: New York University Press)

Stepansky, P. E. (2009) *Psychoanalysis at the Margins* (New York, NY: Other Press)

Stolorow, R. D. and Atwood, G. E. (2014) *Contexts of Being: The Intersubjective Foundations of Psychological Life* (New York, NY: Routledge)

Young-Bruehl, E. (1998) *Subject to Biography: Psychoanalysis, Feminism, and Writing Women's Lives* (Cambridge, MA: Harvard University Press)

Zaretsky, E. (2005) *Secrets of the Soul: A Social and Cultural History of Psychoanalysis* (New York, NY: Random House)

selected critics

Crews, F. C. (1998) *Unauthorized Freud: Doubters Confront a Legend* (New York, NY: Viking)

Crews, F. C. (2006) *Follies of the Wise: Dissenting Essays* (Emeryville, CA: Shoemaker & Hoard)

Grunbaum, A. (1985) *The Foundations of Psychoanalysis: A Philosophical Critique* (Berkeley, CA: University of California Press)

Masson, J. M. (1985) *The Assault on Truth: Freud's Suppression of the Seduction Theory* (London, UK: Penguin Press)

Popper, K. (1963) *Conjectures and Refutations: The Growth of Scientific Knowledge* (London, UK: Routledge & Kegan Paul)

Sulloway, F. (1992) *Freud, Biologist of the Mind: Beyond the Psychoanalytic Legend* (Cambridge, MA: Harvard University Press)

Varela, C. R. (1995) 'Ethogenic Theory and Psychoanalysis: The Unconscious as a Social Construction and a Failed Explanatory Concept', *Journal for the Theory of Social Behaviour*, 25 (4): pp. 363–385

Watters, E. and Ofshe, R. (1999) *Therapy's Delusions: The Myth of the Unconscious and the Exploitation of Today's Walking Worried* (New York, NY: Scribner)

Webster, R. (1996) *Why Freud Was Wrong: Sin, Science, and Psychoanalysis* (New York, NY: Basic Books)

references

Aguayo, J. (2009) 'On Understanding Projective Identification in the Treatment of Psychotic States of Mind: The Publishing Cohort of H. Rosenfeld, H. Segal and W. Bion (1946–1957)', *International Journal of Psychoanalysis*, 90 (1): pp. 69–92

Ainsworth, M. S. and Bowlby, J. (1991) 'An Ethological Approach to Personality Development', *American Psychologist*, 46 (4): pp. 333–341

Akhtar, S. (2012) *Psychoanalytic Listening: Methods, Limits, and Innovations* (London, UK: Karnac Books)

Akhtar, S. and Byrne, J. (1983) 'The Concept of Splitting and Its Clinical Relevance', *American Journal of Psychiatry*, 140 (8): pp. 1013–1016

Alizade, A. M. (ed.) (2006) *Motherhood in the Twenty-First Century* (London, UK: Karnac Books)

Allen, J. G. and Fonagy, P. (2002) The Development of Mentalizing and Its Role in Psychopathology and Psychotherapy. Technical Report No. 02–0048 (Topeka, KS: Menninger Clinic, Research Department). Available at https://docs.google.com/document/edit?id=1dgfo64AaKCaO8v – PLeAS2pMyK4uiwyaaX_oTbzdbb8

Anderson, R. and Segal, H. (eds) (2004) *Clinical Lectures on Klein and Bion* (*The New Library of Psychoanalysis* (Book 14)) (London, UK: Routledge)

Andrews, G., Singh, M. and Bond, M. (1993) 'The Defense Style Questionnaire', *The Journal of Nervous and Mental Disease*, 181 (4): pp. 246–256

Anzieu, D. and Turner, C. (1989) *The Skin Ego* (New Haven, CT: Yale University Press)

Arlow, J. (1995) 'Stilted Listening: Psychoanalysis as Discourse', *The Psychoanalytic Quarterly*, 64 (2): pp. 215–233

Arnett, J. J. (2004) *Emerging Adulthood: The Winding Road from the Late Teens through the Twenties* (Oxford, UK: Oxford University Press)

Arnett, J. J. (2007) 'Suffering, Selfish, Slackers? Myths and Reality about Emerging Adults', *Journal of Youth and Adolescence*, 36 (1): pp. 23–29

Arnett, J. J. and Tanner, J. (eds) (2006) *Emerging Adults in America: Coming of Age in the 21st Century* (Washington, DC: American Psychological Association), pp. 3–19

Arnold, K. (2006) 'Reik's Theory of Psychoanalytic Listening', *Psychoanalytic Psychology*, 23 (4): pp. 754–765

Atwood, G. (2012) *The Abyss of Madness* (New York, NY: Routledge)

Atwood, G., Orange, D. and Stolorow, R. (2002) 'Shattered Worlds/ Psychotic States: A Post-Cartesian View of the Experience of Personal Annihilation', *Psychoanalytic Psychology*, 19 (2): pp. 281–306

Baldwin, E. N. (2014) 'Recognizing Guilt and Shame: Therapeutic Ruptures with Parents of Children in Psychotherapy', *Psychoanalytic Social Work*, 21 (1–2): pp. 2–18

Banai, E., Mikulincer, M. and Shaver, P. (2005) '"Selfobject" Needs in Kohut's Self Psychology: Links with Attachment, Self-Cohesion, Affect Regulation, and Adjustment', *Psychoanalytic Psychology*, 22 (2): pp. 224–260

Bargh, J. A. and Chartrand, T. (1999) 'The Unbearable Automaticity of Being', *American Psychologist*, 54 (7): pp. 462–479

Bargh, J. A. and Morsella, E. (2008) 'The Unconscious Mind', *Perspectives on Psychological Science*, 3 (1): pp. 73–79

Barnett, M. (2007) 'What Brings You Here? An Exploration of the Unconscious Motivations of Those Who Choose to Train and Work as Psychotherapists and Counsellors', *Psychodynamic Practice*, 13 (3): pp. 257–274

Bateman, A. and Fonagy, P. (2004) 'Mentalization-Based Treatment of BPD', *Journal of Personality Disorders*, 18 (1): pp. 36–51

Bateman, A. and Fonagy, P. (2006) *Mentalization Based Treatment: A Practical Guide* (Oxford, UK: Oxford University Press)

Bauman, Z. (1991) *Modernity and Ambivalence* (New York, NY: John Wiley & Sons)

Baumrind, D. (1966) 'Effects of Authoritative Parental Control on Child Behavior', *Child Development*, 37 (4): pp. 887–907

Bazan, A. *et al.* (2013) 'Empirical Evidence for Freud's Theory of Primary Process Mentation in Acute Psychosis', *Psychoanalytic Psychology*, 30 (1): pp. 57–74

Benedek, T. (1959) 'Parenthood as a Developmental Phase: A Contribution to the Libido Theory', *Journal of the American Psychoanalytic Association*, 7 (3): pp. 389–417

Benedek, T. (1977) 'Ambivalence, Passion, and Love', *Journal of the American Psychoanalytic Association*, 25 (1): pp. 53–79

Benjamin, J. (1992) 'Recognition and Destruction: An Outline of Intersubjectivity' in N. Skolnick and S. Warshaw (eds), *Relational Perspectives in Psychoanalysis* (Hillsdale, NJ: Analytic Press), pp. 43–60

Benjamin, J. (1995) *Like Subjects, Love Objects: Essays on Recognition and Sexual Difference* (New Haven, CT: Yale University Press)

Benjamin, J. (1998) *The Bonds of Love: Psychoanalysis, Feminism, & the Problem of Domination* (New York, NY: Pantheon Books)

Benjamin, J. (2013) 'The Bonds of Love: Looking Backward', *Studies in Gender and Sexuality*, 14 (1): pp. 1–15

Bettelheim, B. (1983) *Freud and Man's Soul* (New York, NY: Vintage Press)

Bhaskar, R. (2010) *Reclaiming Reality: A Critical Introduction to Contemporary Philosophy* (New York, NY: Taylor & Francis)

Bick, E. (1986) 'Further Considerations on the Function of the Skin in Early Object Relations', *British Journal of Psychotherapy*, 2 (4): pp. 292–299

Billig, M. (1997) 'The Dialogic Unconscious: Psychoanalysis, Discursive Psychology and the Nature of Repression', *British Journal of Social Psychology*, 36 (2): pp. 139–159

Billig, M. (1999) *Freudian Repression: Conversation Creating the Unconscious* (Cambridge, UK: Cambridge University Press)

Bion, W. R. (1957) 'Differentiation of the Psychotic from Non-Psychotic Personalities', *International Journal of Psychoanalysis*, 38 (3–4): pp. 266–275

Bion, W. R. (1959) 'Attacks on Linking', *International Journal of Psychoanalysis*, 40 (5–6): p. 308

Bion, W. R. (1962) *Learning from Experience* (New York, NY: Basic Books)

Bion, W. R. (1963) *Elements of Psychoanalysis* (London, UK: Heinemann)

Bion, W. R. (1965) *Transformations: Change from Learning to Growth* (London, UK: Heinemann)

Bion, W. R. (1967) *A Theory of Thinking: Selected Papers on Psychoanalysis* (New York, NY: Jason Aronson)

Bion, W. R. (1970) *Attention and Interpretation* (London, UK: Tavistock)

Blass, R. (2002) *The Meaning of the Dream in Psychoanalysis* (Albany, NY: SUNY Press)

Blatt, S., Corveleyn, J. and Luyten, P. (2006) 'Minding the Gap between Positivism and Hermeneutics in Psychoanalytic Research', *Journal of the American Psychoanalytic Association*, 54 (2): pp. 571–610

Blechner, M. J. (1995) 'The Patient's Dreams and the Countertransference', *Psychoanalytic Dialogues*, 5 (1): pp. 1–25

Blechner, M. J. (2001) *The Dream Frontier* (New York, NY: Routledge)

Blechner, M. J. (2005) 'The Grammar of Irrationality: What Psychoanalytic Dream Study Can Tell Us about the Brain', *Contemporary Psychoanalysis*, 41 (2): pp. 203–221

Blechner, M. J. (2013) 'What Are Dreams Like and How Does the Brain Make Them That Way?' *Contemporary Psychoanalysis*, 49 (2): 165–175

Bleuler, E. (1952) *Dementia Praecox* (Joseph Zinkin, Trans.) (New York, NY: International Universities Press; original work published in 1911)

Blévis, M. (2009) *Jealousy: True Stories of Love's Favorite Decoy* (New York, NY: Other Press)

Blos, P. (1967) 'The Second Individuation Process of Adolescence', *The Psychoanalytic Study of the Child*, 22: pp. 162–186

Bollas, C. (2002) *Free Association* (Cambridge, UK: Icon Books)

Bornstein, R. F. (2007) 'Nomothetic Psychoanalysis', *Psychoanalytic Psychology*, 24 (4): pp. 590–602

Bosma, H. A. and Kunnen, E. S. (2001) 'Determinants and Mechanisms in Ego Identity Development: A Review and Synthesis', *Developmental Review*, 21 (1): pp. 39–66

Bott Spillius, E. (2001) 'Freud and Klein on the Concept of Phantasy', *International Journal of Psychoanalysis*, 82 (2): pp. 361–373

Bowie, M. (1993) *Lacan* (Cambridge, MA: Harvard University Press)

Bowlby, J. (1982) 'Attachment and Loss: Retrospect and Prospect', *American Journal of Orthopsychiatry*, 52 (4): pp. 664–678

Braddock, L. (2011) 'Psychological Identification, Imagination and Psychoanalysis', *Philosophical Psychology*, 24 (5): pp. 639–657

Bradley, R. and Westen, D. (2005) 'The Psychodynamics of Borderline Personality Disorder: A View from Developmental Psychopathology', *Development and Psychopathology*, 17 (4): pp. 927–957

Brandell, J. R. (2004) *Psychodynamic Social Work* (New York, NY: Columbia University Press)

Brenman, E. (2006) *Recovery of the Lost Good Object* (London, UK: Routledge)

Brenner, C. (2002) 'Conflict, Compromise Formation, and Structural Theory', *The Psychoanalytic Quarterly*, 71 (3): pp. 397–417

Bretherton, I. (1999) 'Updating the Internal Working Model's Construct: Some Reflections', *Attachment & Human Development*, 1 (3): pp. 343–357

Bright, G. (1997) 'Synchronicity as a Basis of Analytic Attitude', *Journal of Analytical Psychology*, 42 (4): pp. 613–635

Bromberg, P. (1994) '"Speak! That I May See You"; Some Reflections on Dissociation, Reality, and Psychoanalytic Listening', *Psychoanalytic Dialogues*, 4 (4): pp. 517–547

Bromberg, P. (1998) *Standing in the Spaces: Essays on Clinical Process, Trauma, and Dissociation* (Hillsdale, NJ: Analytic Press)

Bromberg, P. (2006) *Awakening the Dreamer: Clinical Journeys* (New York, NY: Analytic Press)

Bromberg, P. (2012) *The Shadow of the Tsunami: And the Growth of the Relational Mind* (New York, NY: Routledge)

Bronstein, C. (2001) *Kleinian Theory: A Contemporary Perspective* (London, UK: Whurr Publishers/Wiley)

Brown, E. R. (1979) *Rockefeller Medicine Men: Medicine and Capitalism in America* (Berkeley, CA: University of California Press)

Brown, K. W. and Ryan, R. M. (2003) 'The Benefits of Being Present: Mindfulness and Its Role in Psychological Well-Being', *Journal of Personality and Social Psychology*, 84 (4): pp. 822–848

Brown, L. (2013) 'The Development of Bion's Concept of Container and Contained' in H .B. Levine and L. J. Brown (eds), *Growth and Turbulence in the Container/Contained: Bion's Continuing Legacy* (London, UK: Routledge), pp. 7–22

Bucholtz, M. (2002) 'Youth and Cultural Practice', *Annual Review of Anthropology*, 31: pp. 525–552

Buie, D. (1981) 'Empathy: Its Nature and Limitation', *Journal of the American Psychoanalytic Association*, 29 (2): pp. 281–307

Busch, F. (1995) *The Ego at the Center of Clinical Technique* (Lanham, MD: Jason Aronson)

Busch, F. and Joseph, B. (2004) 'A Missing Link in Psychoanalytic Technique: Psychoanalytic Consciousness', *International Journal of Psychoanalysis*, 85 (3): pp. 567–577

Butler, J. (1993) *Bodies That Matter* (New York, NY: Routledge)

Caldwell, L. and Joyce, A. (eds) (2011) *Reading Winnicott* (London, UK: Routledge)

Cambray, J. (2002) 'Synchronicity and Emergence', *American Imago*, 59 (4): pp. 409–434

Carnì, S. *et al.* (2013) 'Intrapsychic and Interpersonal Guilt: A Critical Review of the Recent Literature', *Cognitive Processing*, 14 (4): pp. 333–346

Cartwright, D. (2009) *Containing States of Mind: Exploring Bion's Container Model in Psychoanalytic Psychotherapy* (London, UK: Routledge)

Cartwright, D. (2013) 'Clinical Features of the Container Function', *Psychoanalytic Psychotherapy in South Africa*, 21 (2): pp. 73–104

Cartwright, N. (2007) 'Are RCTs the Gold Standard?' *BioSocieties*, 2 (1): pp. 11–20

Cartwright, N. (2011) 'A Philosopher's View of the Long Road from RCTs to Effectiveness', *The Lancet*, 377 (9775): pp. 1400–1401

Cartwright, N. and Hardie, J. (2012) *Evidence-Based Policy: A Practical Guide to Doing It Better* (Oxford, UK: Oxford University Press)

Carveth, D. L. (2010) 'Superego, Conscience, and the Nature and Types of Guilt', *Modern Psychoanalysis*, 35 (1): pp. 106–130

Carveth, D. L. (2013) *The Still Small Voice: Psychoanalytic Reflections on Guilt and Conscience* (London, UK: Karnac Books)

Cashdan, S. (1988) *Object Relations Therapy: Using the Relationship* (New York, NY: W. W. Norton & Company)

Castoriadis, C. (1975) *The Imaginary Institution of Society* (Boston, MA: MIT Press)

Cavell, M. (1993) *The Psychoanalytic Mind: From Freud to Philosophy* (Cambridge, MA: Harvard University Press)

Charles, M. (2011) *Working with Trauma: Lessons from Bion and Lacan* (New York, NY: Jason Aronson)

Charon, R. (2001) 'Narrative Medicine', *The Journal of the American Medical Association*, 286 (15): pp. 1897–1902

Chasseguet-Smirgel, J. (1974) 'Perversion, Idealization and Sublimation', *International Journal of Psychoanalysis*, 55 (3): pp. 349–357

Chodorow, N. (1994) *Femininities, Masculinities, Sexualities* (Lexington, KY: University Press of Kentucky)

Chodorow, N. (2012) 'Analytic Listening and the Five Senses', *Journal of the American Psychoanalytic Association*, 60 (4): pp. 747–758

Chomsky, N. (1959) 'A Review of B. F. Skinner's Verbal Behavior', *Language*, 35 (1): pp. 26–58

Clarke, G. (2005) 'The Preconscious and Psychic Change in Fairbairn's Model of Mind', *International Journal of Psychoanalysis*, 86 (1): pp. 61–77

Clarke, G. (2007) 'Fairbairn and Macmurray: Psychoanalytic Studies and Critical Realism', *Journal of Critical Realism*, 2 (1): pp. 7–36

Clarke, G. S. and Scharff, D. E. (2014) *Fairbairn and the Object-Relations Tradition* (London, UK: Karnac Books)

Clarke, S. (2000) 'Psychoanalysis, Psychoexistentialism and Racism', *Psychoanalytic Studies*, 2 (4): pp. 343–355

Clarke, S. (2002) 'On Strangers: Phantasy, Terror and the Human Imagination', *Journal of Human Rights*, 1 (3): pp. 345–355

Clarke, S. (2003) 'Psychoanalytic Sociology and the Interpretation of Emotion', *Journal for the Theory of Social Behavior*, 33 (2): pp. 145–163

Clarkin, J. *et al.* (2004) 'The Personality Disorders Institute/Borderline Personality Disorder Research Foundation Randomized Control Trial for Borderline Personality Disorder: Rationale, Methods, and Patient Characteristics', *Journal of Personality Disorders*, 18 (1): pp. 52–72

Cohen, O. (1998) 'Parental Narcissism and the Disengagement of the Non-custodial Father after Divorce', *Clinical Social Work Journal*, 26 (2): pp. 195–215

Cohler, B. J. and Galatzer-Levy, R. M. (2000) *The Course of Gay and Lesbian Lives: Social and Psychoanalytic Perspectives* (Chicago, IL: University of Chicago Press)

Colby, K. and Stoller, R. (2013) *Cognitive Science and Psychoanalysis* (London, UK: Routledge)

Colli, A. and Lingiardi, V. (2009) 'The Collaborative Interactions Scale: A New Transcript-Based Method for the Assessment of Therapeutic Alliance Ruptures and Resolutions in Psychotherapy', *Psychotherapy Research*, 19 (6): pp. 718–734

Collier, A. (1994) *Critical Realism: An Introduction to Roy Bhaskar's Philosophy* (London, UK: Verso Books)

Conchar, C. and Repper, J. (2014) '"Walking Wounded or Wounded Healer?" Does Personal Experience of Mental Health Problems Help or Hinder Mental Health Practice? A Review of the Literature', *Mental Health and Social Inclusion*, 18 (1): pp. 35–44

Coole, D. *et al.* (2010) *New Materialisms: Ontology, Agency, and Politics* (Durham, NC: Duke University Press)

Corbett, K. (1997) 'It Is Time to Distinguish Gender from Health: Reflections on Lothsteins's "Pantyhose Fetishism and Self Cohesion: A Paraphilic Solution?"' *Gender & Psychoanalysis*, 2: pp. 259–271

Corbett, K. (2001) 'Faggot = Loser', *Studies in Gender & Sexuality*, 2 (1): pp. 3–28

Corbett, K. (2001a) 'More Life: Centrality and Marginality in Human Development', *Psychoanalytic Dialogues*, 11 (3): pp. 313–335

Corbett, K. (2009) *Boyhoods: Rethinking Masculinities* (New Haven: Yale University Press)

Craig, G. A. (1998) 'The Good, the Bad, and the Bourgeois', *New York Review of Books*, 45, 13 (August): pp. 8–20

Cramer, P. (2000) 'Defense Mechanisms in Psychology Today: Further Processes for Adaptation', *American Psychologist*, 55 (6): pp. 637–646

Cramer, P. (2006) *Protecting the Self: Defense Mechanisms in Action* (New York, NY: The Guilford Press)

Crews, F. C. (1998) *Unauthorized Freud: Doubters Confront a Legend* (New York, NY: Viking)

Damasio, A. (1999) *The Feeling of What Happens: Body, Emotion and the Making of Consciousness* (London, UK: Heineman)

Darling, N. and Steinberg, L. (1993) 'Parenting Style as Context: An Integrative Model', *Psychological Bulletin*, 113 (3): pp. 487–496

Davies, J. M. (2004) 'Whose Bad Objects Are We Anyway? Repetition and Our Elusive Love Affair with Evil', *Psychoanalytic Dialogues*, 14 (6): pp. 711–732

Dearing, R. L., Stuewig, J. and Tangney, J. P. (2005) 'On the Importance of Distinguishing Shame from Guilt: Relations to Problematic Alcohol and Drug Use', *Addictive Behaviors*, 30 (7): pp. 1392–1404

Declercq, F. (2002) 'The Real of the Body in Lacanian Theory', *Analysis*, (11): pp. 99–114

Declercq, F. (2004) 'Lacan's Concept of the Real of Jouissance: Clinical Illustrations and Implications', *Psychoanalysis, Culture & Society*, 9 (2): pp. 237–251

Demick, J. (2002) 'Stages of Parental Development', *Handbook of Parenting*, 3: pp. 389–413

DeWall, F. (2010) *The Age of Empathy: Nature's Lesson from a Kinder Society* (New York: Random House)

Diamond, N. (2013) *Between Skins: The Body in Psychoanalysis-Contemporary Developments* (New York, NY: John Wiley & Sons)

Diem-Wille, G. (2011) *The Early Years of Life: Psychoanalytical Development Theory According to Freud, Klein, and Bion* (London, NY: Karnac Books)

Dor, J. (1998) *The Clinical Lacan* (New York, NY: Other Press)

Dorpat, T. (1976) 'Structural Conflict and Object Relations Conflict', *Journal of the American Psychoanalytic Association*, 24 (4): pp. 855–874

Drisko, J. W. and Grady, M. D. (2012) *Evidence-Based Practice in Clinical Social Work* (New York, NY: Springer)

Dunne, C. (2000) *Carl Jung Wounded Healer of the Soul: An Illustrated Biography* (New York, NY: Parabola Books)

Dyer, R. (1983) *Her Father's Daughter: The Work of Anna Freud* (New York, NY: Jason Aronson)

Edmundson, M. (2007) *The Death of Sigmund Freud: The Legacy of His Last Days* (New York, NY: Bloomsbury)

Eissler, K. (1971) 'Death Drive, Ambivalence, and Narcissism', *Psychoanalytic Study of the Child*, 26: pp. 25–78

Ekman, P. (1993) 'Facial Expression and Emotion', *American Psychologist*, 48 (4): pp. 384–392

Elder-Vass, D. (2010) *The Causal Power of Social Structures: Emergence, Structure and Agency* (Cambridge, UK: Cambridge University Press)

Elder-Vass, D. (2013) *The Reality of Social Construction* (Cambridge, UK: Cambridge University Press)

Elliott, A. (1992) *Social Theory and Psychoanalysis in Transition: Self and Society from Freud to Kristeva* (Oxford, UK: Blackwell)

Elliott, A. (2007) *Concepts of the Self* (Cambridge, UK: Polity Press)

Engle, D. and Arkowitz, H. (2006) *Ambivalence in Psychotherapy: Facilitating Readiness to Change* (New York, NY: Guilford Press)

Epstein, S. (1994) 'Integration of the Cognitive and the Psychodynamic Unconscious', *American Psychologist*, 49 (8): p. 709

Erdelyi, M. H. and Goldberg, B. (1979) 'Let's Not Sweep Repression under the Rug: Toward a Cognitive Psychology of Repression' in J. F. Kihlstrom and F. J. Evans (eds), *Functional Disorders of Memory* (Hillsdale, NJ: Erlbaum Associates), pp. 355–402

Erikson, E. (1950) *Childhood and Society* (New York, NY: W. W. Norton & Company)

Erikson, E. (1963) *Childhood and Society* (New York, NY: John Wiley & Sons)

Erikson, E. (1968) *Identity: Youth and Crisis* (New York, NY: W. W. Norton & Company)

Etchegoyen, R. H. (1985) 'Identification and Its Vicissitudes', *International Journal of Psychoanalysis*, 66 (1): pp. 3–18

Evans, D. (1996) *An Introductory Dictionary of Lacanian Psychoanalysis* (London, UK: Routledge)

Fairbairn, W. (1954) *An Object-Relations Theory of the Personality* (New York, NY: Basic Books)

Fast, I. (1984) *Gender Identity* (Hillsdale, NJ: Analytic Press)

Fast, I. (2012) 'The Primary Processes Grow Up: Freud's More Radical View of the Mind', *Contemporary Psychoanalysis*, 48 (2): pp. 183–198

Fink, B. (1997) *A Clinical Introduction to Lacanian Psychoanalysis: Theory and Technique* (Cambridge, MA: Harvard University Press)

Fink, B. (2007) *Fundamentals of Psychoanalytic Technique: A Lacanian Approach for Practitioners* (New York, NY: W. W. Norton & Company)

Fonagy, P. (2013) 'There Is Room for Even More Doublethink: The Perilous Status of Psychoanalytic Research', *Psychoanalytic Dialogues*, 23 (1): pp. 116–122

Fonagy, P. and Bateman, A. (2006) 'Progress in the Treatment of Borderline Personality Disorder', *The British Journal of Psychiatry*, 188 (1): pp. 1–3

Fonagy, P. and Target, M. (1995) 'Dissociation and Trauma', *Current Opinion in Psychiatry*, 8 (3): pp. 161–166

Fonagy, P. and Target, M. (1996) 'Predictors of Outcome in Child Psychoanalysis: A Retrospective Study of 763 Cases at the Anna Freud Centre', *Journal of the American Psychoanalytic Association*, 44 (1): pp. 27–77

Fonagy, P. and Target, M. (2003) *Psychoanalytic Theories: Perspectives from Developmental Psychopathology* (London, UK: Routledge)

Fonagy, P., Target, M. and Gergely, G. (2000) 'Attachment and Borderline Personality Disorder', *Psychiatric Clinics of North America*, 23: pp. 103–122

Fonagy, P. *et al.* (2002) *Affect Regulation, Mentalization, and the Development of the Self* (New York, NY: Other Press)

Fonagy, P. *et al.* (eds) (2012) *The Significance of Dreams: Bridging Clinical and Extraclinical Research in Psychoanalysis* (London, UK: Karnac Books)

Forrester, M. (2006) 'Projective Identification and Intersubjectivity', *Theory & Psychology*, 16 (6): pp. 783–802

Fosshage, J. L. (2013) 'The Dream Narrative: Unconscious Organizing Activity in Context', *Contemporary Psychoanalysis*, 49 (2): pp. 253–258

Fraiberg, S. H. (1959) *The Magic Years: Understanding and Handling the Problems of Early Childhood* (New York, NY: Fireside)

Fraiberg, S. H., Adelson, E. and Shapiro, V. (1975) 'Ghosts in the Nursery: A Psychoanalytic Approach to the Problems of Impaired Infant-Mother Relationships', *Journal of the American Academy of Child Psychiatry*, 14 (3): pp. 387–421

Frankland, A. (2010) *The Little Psychotherapy Book: Object Relations in Practice* (Oxford, UK: Oxford University Press)

Freud, A. (1963) 'The Concept of Developmental Lines', *The Psychoanalytic Study of the Child*, 18: pp. 245–265

Freud, A. (1993) *The Ego and the Mechanisms of Defense* (London, UK: Karnac Books)

Freud, S. (1895) *Studies in Hysteria*. Standard Edition, p. 2

Freud, S. (1900) *The Interpretation of Dreams*. Standard Edition, pp. 4–5

Freud, S. (1901) *The Psychopathology of Everyday Life*. Standard Edition, p. 6

Freud, S. (1915–1917) *Introductory Lectures on Psychoanalysis*. Standard Edition, pp. 15–16

Freud, S. (1915) *Instincts and Their Vicissitudes*. Standard Edition, p. 14

Freud, S. (1915a) *Repression*. Standard Edition, p. 14

Freud, S. (1917) Mourning and Melancholia. Standard Edition, p. 14

Freud, S. (1920) *Beyond the Pleasure Principle*. Standard Edition, p. 18

Freud, S. (1923) *The Ego and the Id*. Standard Edition, p. 19

Freud, S. (1926) *Inhibitions, Symptoms and Anxiety*. Standard Edition, p. 20

Freud, S. (1953–74) *The Standard Edition of the Complete Psychological Works of Sigmund Freud* (James Strachey, Trans.) (24 Vols) (London, UK: Hogarth Press)

Freud, S. (1963) *Elements of Psychoanalysis* (London, UK: Heinemann)

Freud, S. (1997) *Sexuality and the Psychology of Love* (New York, NY: Simon and Schuster)

Frey-Wehrlin, C. (1976) 'Reflections on CG Jung's Concept of Synchronicity', *Journal of Analytical Psychology*, 21 (1): pp. 37–49

Frosh, S. (1987) *The Politics of Psychoanalysis: An Introduction to Freudian and Post-Freudian Theory* (New Haven, CT: Yale University Press)

Frosh, S. (2013) 'Psychoanalysis, Colonialism, Racism', *Journal of Theoretical and Philosophical Psychology*, 33 (3): pp. 141–154

Fuchs, T. (2007) 'Fragmented Selves: Temporality and Identity in Borderline Personality Disorder', *Psychopathology*, 40 (6): pp. 379–387

Furman, E. (1985) 'On Fusion, Integration, and Feeling Good', *Psychoanalytic Study of the Child*, 40: pp. 81–110

Furman, E. (1994) 'Early Aspects of Mothering: What Makes It So Hard to Be There to Be Left', *Journal of Child Psychotherapy*, 20 (2): pp. 149–164

Furman, E. (2001) *On Being and Having a Mother* (Madison, CT: International Universities Press)

Furman, R. A. and Furman, E. (1984) 'Intermittent Decathexis: A Type of Parental Dysfunction', *International Journal of Psychoanalysis*, 65: pp. 423–433

Gabbard, G. (1993) 'An Overview of Countertransference with Borderline Patients', *The Journal of Psychotherapy Practice and Research*, 2 (1): pp. 7–18

Gabbard, G. (1995) 'Countertransference: The Emerging Common Ground', *International Journal of Psychoanalysis*, 76: pp. 475–486

Gabbard, G. and Westen, D. (2003) 'Rethinking Therapeutic Action', *International Journal of Psychoanalysis*, 84: pp. 823–841

Gazolla, V., Aziz-Zadeh, L. and Keysers, C. (2006) 'Empathy and the Soma-totopic Auditory Mirror System in Humans', *Current Biology*, 16 (8): pp. 1824–1829

Gibbons, S. (2011) 'Understanding Empathy as a Complex Construct: A Review of the Literature', *Clinical Social Work Journal*, 39 (3): pp. 243–252

Gilligan, J. (2003) 'Shame, Guilt, and Violence', *Social Research: An International Quarterly*, 70 (4): pp. 1149–1180

Gilman, S. L. (1988) 'Strauss, the Pervert, and Avant Garde Opera of the Fin de Siècle', *New German Critique*, (43): pp. 35–68

Gleser, G. and Ihilevich, D. (1969) 'An Objective Instrument for Measuring Defense Mechanisms', *Journal of Consulting and Clinical Psychology*, 33 (1): pp. 51–60

Goebel, E. (2012) *Beyond Discontent: 'Sublimation' from Goethe to Lacan* (New York, NY: Continuum International Publishing Group)

Goldstein, E. (1995) *Ego Psychology and Social Work Practice* (New York, NY: Simon and Schuster)

Goldstein, E. (2010) *Object Relations Theory and Self Psychology in Social Work* (New York, NY: Simon and Schuster)

Goldwyn, R. and Hugh-Jones, S. (2011) 'Using the Adult Attachment Interview to Understand Reactive Attachment Disorder: Findings from a 10-Case Adolescent Sample', *Attachment & Human Development*, 13 (2): pp. 169–191

Goodwyn, E. (2010) 'Approaching Archetypes: Reconsidering Innateness', *Journal of Analytical Psychology*, 55 (4): pp. 502–521

Gordon, R. M. (2006) 'Psychodynamic Diagnostic Manual', *Corsini Encyclopedia of Psychology*

Gradmann, C. (2009) *Laboratory Disease: Robert Koch's Medical Bacteriology* (Elborg Forster, Trans.) (Baltimore, MD: Johns Hopkins University Press)

Grant, D. C. and Harari, E. (2005) 'Psychoanalysis, Science and the Seductive Theory of Karl Popper', *Australian and New Zealand Journal of Psychiatry*, 39 (6): pp. 446–452

Grant, D. C. and Harari, E. (2011) 'Empathy in Psychoanalytic Theory and Practice', *Psychoanalytic Inquiry*, 31 (1): pp. 3–16

Gray, M., Plath, D. and Webb, S. A. (2009) *Evidence-Based Social Work: A Critical Stance* (London: Routledge)

Gray, P. (1973) 'Psychoanalytic Technique and the Ego's Capacity for Viewing Intrapsychic Activity', *Journal American Psychoanalytic Association*, 21, 474–494

Gray, P. (1990) 'The Nature of Therapeutic Action in Psychoanalysis', *Journal of the American Psychoanalytic Association*, 38 (4): pp. 1083–1097

Gray, P. (2005) *The Ego and Analysis of Defense* (Oxford, UK: Rowman & Littlefield)

Green, A. (1999) *Fabric of Affect in the Psychoanalytic Discourse* (London, UK: Routledge)

Green, A. (2005) *Key Ideas for a Contemporary Psychoanalysis: Misrecognition and Recognition of the Unconscious* (London, UK: Routledge)

Greenberg, G. (2010) *Manufacturing Depression: The Secret History of a Modern Disease* (New York, NY: Simon & Schuster)

Greenberg, J. (1991) 'Countertransference and Reality', *Psychoanalytic Dialogues*, 1 (1): pp. 52–73

Greenberg, S. and Mitchell, J. (1983) *Object Relations in Psychoanalytic Theory* (Cambridge, MA: Harvard University Press)

Greenson, R. (1960) 'Empathy and Its Vicissitudes', *International Journal of Psychoanalysis*, 41: pp. 418–424

Grinberg, L., Sor, D. and de Bianchedi, E. (1991) *New Introduction to the Work of Bion* (Northvale, NJ: Jason Aronson)

Grotstein, J. (1978) 'Inner Space: Its Dimensions and Its Coordinates', *International Journal of Psychoanalysis*, 59: pp. 55–61

Grotstein, J. (1981) *Splitting and Projective Identification* (Northvale, NJ: Jason Aronson)

Grotstein, J. (1997) '"Internal Objects" or "Chimerical Monsters?": The Demonic "Third Forms" of the Internal World', *Journal of Analytical Psychology*, 42 (1): pp. 47–80

Grotstein, J. (2008) 'The Overarching Role of Unconscious Phantasy', *Psychoanalytic Inquiry*, 28 (2): pp. 190–205

Grünbaum, A. (1979) 'Is Freudian Psychoanalytic Theory Pseudo-Scientific by Karl Popper's Criterion of Demarcation?' *American Philosophical Quarterly*, 16 (2): pp. 131–141

Guralnik, O. and Simeon, D. (2010) 'Depersonalization: Standing in the Spaces between Recognition and Interpellation', *Psychoanalytic Dialogues*, 20 (4): pp. 400–416

Gut, E. (1989) *Productive and Unproductive Depression: Success or Failure of a Vital Process* (New York, NY: Basic Books)

Hall, J. (2008) 'Relinquishing Orthodoxy: One Freudian Analyst's Personal Journey', *The Psychoanalytic Review*, 95 (5): pp. 845–871

Halpern, J. (2001) *From Detached Concern to Empathy: Humanizing Medical Practice* (New York, NY: Oxford University Press)

Halpern, J. (2003) 'What Is Clinical Empathy?' *Journal of General Internal Medicine*, 18 (8): pp. 670–674

Hamer, F. (2012) 'Evocative Space Where Listening Begins', *Journal of the American Psychoanalytic Association*, 60 (4): pp. 781–789

Harari, R. (2013) *Lacan's Seminar on Anxiety: An Introduction* (New York, NY: Other Press)

Harder, S. and Folke, S. (2012) 'Affect Regulation and Metacognition in Psychotherapy of Psychosis: An Integrative Approach', *Journal of Psychotherapy Integration*, 22 (4): pp. 330–343

Harris, A. (2005) *Gender as Soft Assembly* (Hillsdale, NJ: Analytic Press)

Hartmann, H. (1955) 'Notes on the Theory of Sublimation', *The Psychoanalytic Study of the Child*, 10: pp. 9–29

Hartmann, H. (1964) *Essays on Ego Psychology: Selected Problems in Psychoanalytic Theory* (Madison, CT: International Universities Press)

Hartmann, H. (1985) 'Psychoanalysis as a Scientific Theory (1959)' in C. F. Settlage and R. Brockbank (eds), *New Ideas in Psychoanalysis: The Process of Change in Humanistic Science* (Hillsdale, NJ: The Analytic Press), pp. 101–126

Haslam, N. (2000) 'Psychiatric Categories as Natural Kinds: Essentialist Thinking about Mental Disorder', *Social Research*, 67 (4): pp. 1031–1058

Hassin, R., Uleman, J. and Bargh, J. (eds) (2005) *The New Unconscious* (New York, NY: Oxford University Press)

Healy, D. (1997) *The Antidepressant Era* (Cambridge, MA: Harvard University Press)

Healy, D. (2012) *Pharmageddon* (Berkeley, CA: University of California Press)

Hentschel, U. *et al.* (eds) (2004) 'Defense Mechanisms: Theoretical, Research and Clinical Perspectives' in G. E. Stelmach (ed.), *Advances in Psychology* (Holland, Amsterdam: Elsevier), p. 136

Herdt, G. and Stoller, R. (1992) *Intimate Communications: Erotics and the Study of Culture* (New York, NY: Columbia University Press)

Hinshelwood, R. (1999) 'Countertransference and the Therapeutic Relationship: Recent Kleinian Developments in Technique'. Available at http://dspp.com/papers/hinshelwood.htm

Hinshelwood, R. (2007) 'The Kleinian Theory of Therapeutic Action', *The Psychoanalytic Quarterly*, 76 (S1): pp. 1479–1498

Hinshelwood, R. (2013) *Research on the Couch: Single-Case Studies, Subjectivity and Psychoanalytic Knowledge* (London, UK: Routledge)

Hobsbawm, E. J. (1962) *Age of Revolution* (London, UK: Weidenfeld & Nicolson)

Hobsbawm, E. J. (1975) *Age of Capital* (London, UK: Weidenfeld & Nicolson)

Hobsbawm, E. J. (1994) *The Age of Extremes: A History of the World, 1914–1991* (New York, NY: Pantheon Books)

Hoffer, A. and Youngren, V. (2004) 'Is Free Association Still at the Core of Psychoanalysis?' *International Journal of Psychoanalysis*, 85 (6): pp. 1489–1492

Hoffman, I. (2009) 'Doublethinking Our Way to "Scientific" Legitimacy: The Desiccation of Human Experience', *Journal of the American Psychoanalytic Association*, 57 (5): pp. 1043–1069

Hoffman, L. (2003) 'Mothers' Ambivalence with Their Babies and Toddlers: Manifestations of Conflicts with Aggression', *Journal of the American Psychoanalytic Association*, 51 (4): pp. 1219–1240

Hofmann, S. and Weinberger, J. (eds) (2007) *The Art and Science of Psychotherapy* (New York, NY: Routledge)

Hollan, D. (2008) 'Being There: On the Imaginative Aspects of Understanding Others and Being Understood', *Ethos*, 36 (4): pp. 475–489

Hollan, D. and Throop, C. (2008) '"Whatever Happened to Empathy?": Introduction', *Ethos*, 36 (4): pp. 385–401

Holt, R. (2008) *Primary Process Thinking: Theory, Measurement, and Research* (New York, NY: Jason Aronson)

Holtzman, D. and Kulish, N. (2000) 'The Femininization of the Female Oedipal Complex, Part I: A Reconsideration of the Significance of Separation Issues', *Journal of the American Psychoanalytic Association*, 48 (4): pp. 1413–1437

Honneth, A. (2006) 'The Work of Negativity. A Psychoanalytical Revision of the Theory of Recognition', *Critical Horizons*, 7: pp. 101–111

Honneth, A. (2007) *Disrespect: The Normative Foundations of Critical Theory* (London, UK: Polity Press)

Hopper, E. (2003) *The Social Unconscious: Selected Papers* (London, UK: Jessica Kingsley Publishers)

Hopper, E. and Weinberg, H. (eds) (2011) *The Social Unconscious in Persons, Groups and Societies: Mainly Theory* (Vol. 1) (London, UK: Karnac Books)

Horvath, A. and Symonds, B. (1991) 'Relation between Working Alliance and Outcome in Psychotherapy: A Meta-Analysis', *Journal of Counseling Psychology*, 38 (2): pp. 139–149

Horwitz, A. and Wakefield, J. (2007) *The Loss of Sadness* (New York, NY: Oxford University Press)

Houston, S. (2005) 'Philosophy, Theory and Method in Social Work Challenging Empiricism's Claim on Evidence-Based Practice', *Journal of Social Work*, 5 (1): pp. 7–20

Houston, S. (2009) 'Communication, Recognition and Social Work: Aligning the Ethical Theories of Habermas and Honneth', *British Journal of Social Work*, 39 (7): pp. 1274–1290

Houston, S. (2010) 'Beyond Homo Economicus: Recognition, Self-Realization and Social Work', *British Journal of Social Work*, 40 (3): pp. 841–857

Howell, E. (2013) *The Dissociative Mind* (New York, NY: Routledge)

Hughes, J. (2007) *Guilt and Its Vicissitudes: Psychoanalytic Reflections on Morality* (London, UK: Routledge)

Hunt, H. (2012) 'A Collective Unconscious Reconsidered: Jung's Archetypal Imagination in the Light of Contemporary Psychology and Social Science', *Journal of Analytical Psychology*, 57 (1): pp. 76–98

Hurvich, M. (1989) 'Traumatic Moment, Basic Dangers, and Annihilation Anxiety', *Psychoanalytic Psychology*, 6 (3): pp. 309–323

Hurvich, M. (2000) 'Fear of Being Overwhelmed and Psychoanalytic Theories of Anxiety', *Psychoanalytic Review*, 87 (5): pp. 615–649

Hurvich, M. (2003) 'The Place of Annihilation Anxieties in Psychoanalytic Theory', *Journal of the American Psychoanalytic Association*, 51 (2): pp. 579–616

Hyphantis, T. *et al.* (2011) 'Assessing Ego Defense Mechanisms by Questionnaire: Psychometric Properties and Psychopathological Correlates of the Greek Version of the Plutchik's Life Style Index', *Journal of Personality Assessment*, 93 (6): pp. 605–617

Iacoboni, M. (2009) 'Imitation, Empathy, and Mirror Neurons', *Annual Review of Psychology*, 60: pp. 653–670

Ihde, D. (2007) *Listening and Voice: Phenomenologies of Sound* (Albany, NY: SUNY Press)

Ingenhoven, T. and Abraham, R. (2010) 'Making Diagnosis More Meaningful. The Developmental Profile: A Psychodynamic Assessment of Personality', *American Journal of Psychotherapy*, 64 (3): pp. 215–238

Insel, T. (2013) Available at http://www.nimh.nih.gov/about/director/2013/transforming-diagnosis.shtml

Irigaray, L. (1985) *Speculum of the Other Woman* (Ithaca, NY: Cornell University Press)

Irigaray, L. (1985a) *This Sex Which Is Not One* (Ithaca, NY: Cornell University Press)

Isaacs, S. (1943) 'The Nature and Function of Phantasy', *International Journal of Psychoanalysis*, 29 (1948): pp. 73–97

Izenberg, G. (2000) *Modernism and Masculinity: Mann, Wedekind, Kandinsky through World War I* (Chicago, IL: University of Chicago Press)

Jacobs, T. (1999) 'Countertransference Past and Present: A Review of the Concept', *International Journal of Psychoanalysis*, 80 (3): pp. 575–594

Jacoby, M. (2013) *Individuation and Narcissism: The Psychology of Self in Jung and Kohut* (London, UK: Routledge)

James, A. (2007) 'Giving Voice to Children's Voices: Practices and Problems, Pitfalls and Potentials', *American Anthropologist*, 109 (2): pp. 261–272

Jean-Michel, R. (ed.) (2003) *The Cambridge Companion to Lacan* (Cambridge, UK: Cambridge University Press)

Jiménez, J. P. (2009) 'Grasping Psychoanalysts' Practice in Its Own Merits', *International Journal of Psychoanalysis*, 90 (2): pp. 231–248

Jiraskova, T. (2014) 'Splitting of the Mind and Unconscious Dynamics', *The Journal for Neurocognitive Research*, 56 (1–2): pp. 24–27

Johnston, A. and Malabou, C. (2013) *Self and Emotional Life: Philosophy, Psychoanalysis, and Neuroscience* (New York, NY: Columbia University Press)

Jones, J. (1995) *Affects as Process: An Inquiry into the Centrality of Affect in Psychological Life* (Hillsdale, NJ: The Analytic Press)

Jones, R. A. (2002) 'The Necessity of the Unconscious', *Journal for the Theory of Social Behaviour*, 32 (3): pp. 344–365

Jones, R. A. (2003) 'Between the Analytical and the Critical: Implications for Theorizing the Self', *Journal of Analytical Psychology*, 48 (3): pp. 355–370

Jones, R. A. *et al.* (eds) (2008) *Education and Imagination: Post-Jungian Perspectives* (London, UK: Routledge)

Jonsson, S. (2000) *Subject without Nation: Robert Musil and the History of Modern Identity* (Durham, NC: Duke University Press)

Julien, P. (1996) *Jacques Lacan's Return to Freud: The Real, the Symbolic and the Imaginary* (New York, NY: New York University Press)

Jung, C. G. (1955) *Synchronicity: An Acausal Connecting Principle* (London, UK: Routledge)

Jung, C. G. (1963) *Memories, Dreams, Reflections* (Glasgow, Scotland: Random House)

Jung, C. G. (1964) *Man and His Symbols* (New York, NY: Doubleday and Company, Inc)

Jung, C. G. (2010) *Synchronicity: An Acausal Connecting Principle* (Princeton: Princeton University Press)

Jurist, E., Slade, A. and Bergner, S. (2008) *Mind to Mind: Infant Research, Neuroscience, and Psychoanalysis* (New York, NY: Other Press)

Kabat-Zinn, J. (2003) 'Mindfulness-Based Interventions in Context: Past, Present, and Future', *Clinical Psychology: Science and Practice*, 10 (2): pp. 144–156

Kabat-Zinn, J. (2005) *Coming to Our Senses* (New York, NY: Hyperion)

Kandel, E. (1999) 'Biology and the Future of Psychoanalysis: A New Intellectual Framework for Psychiatry Revisited', *American Journal of Psychiatry*, 156 (4): pp. 505–524

Katan, M. (1954) 'The Importance of the Non-Psychotic Part of the Personality in Schizophrenia', *International Journal of Psychoanalysis*, 35 (2): pp. 119–128

Keller, E. F. (2010) 'Goodbye Nature vs Nurture Debate', *New Scientist*, 207 (2778): pp. 28–29

Keller, E. F. (2011) 'Genes, Genomes, and Genomics', *Biological Theory*, 6 (2): pp. 132–140

Kernberg, O. (1975) *Borderline Conditions and Pathological Narcissism* (New York, NY: Jason Aronson)

Kernberg, O. (1995) *Object Relations Theory and Clinical Psychoanalysis* (New York, NY: Jason Aronson)

Kernberg, O. (2001) 'Object Relations, Affects, and Drives: Toward a New Synthesis', *Psychoanalytic Inquiry*, 21 (5): pp. 604–619

Kernberg, O. (2012) *The Inseparable Nature of Love and Aggression: Clinical and Theoretical Perspectives* (New York, NY: American Psychiatric Publishing)

Keutzer, C. (1982) 'Archetypes, Synchronicity and the Theory of Formative Causation', *Journal of Analytical Psychology*, 27 (3): pp. 255–262

Kieffer, C. (2004) 'Selfobjects, Oedipal Objects, and Mutual Recognition: A Self-Psychological Reappraisal of the Female "Oedipal Victor"', *Annual of Psychoanalysis*, 32: pp. 69–80

Kieffer, C. (2008) 'From Selfobjects to Mutual Recognition: Towards Optimal Responsiveness in Father-Daughter Relationships', *Psychoanalytic Inquiry*, 28 (1): pp. 76–91

Kihlstrom, J. (1987) 'The Cognitive Unconscious', *Science*, 237 (4821): pp. 1445–1452

Kihlstrom, J. (2013) 'Unconscious Processes' in D. Reisberg (ed.), *Oxford Handbook of Cognitive Psychology* (Oxford, UK: Oxford University Press), pp. 176–186

Kilborne, B. (2002) *Disappearing Persons: Shame and Appearance* (Albany, NY: SUNY Press)

Kim, J. (2011) *Philosophy of Mind* (Boulder, CO: Westview Press)

Kirshner, L. (2005) 'Rethinking Desire: The Objet Petit a in Lacanian Theory', *Journal of the American Psychoanalytic Association*, 53 (1): pp. 83–102

Kirshner, L. (2013) 'Trauma and Psychosis: A Review and Framework for Psychoanalytic Understanding', *International Forum of Psychoanalysis*. Published online 4 June. DOI: 10.1080/0803706X.2013.778422

Kirshner, L. (ed.) (2011) *Between Winnicott and Lacan: A Clinical Engagement* (New York, NY: Taylor & Francis)

Kirshner, L. (2004) *Having a Life: Self-Pathology after Lacan* (New York, NY: Analytic Press)

Klein, M. (1932) *The Psychoanalysis of Children* (London, UK: Hogarth Press)

Klein, M. (1940) 'Mourning and Its Relationship to Manic-Depressive States', *International Journal of Psychoanalysis*, 21: pp. 125–153

Klein, M. (1957) *Envy and Gratitude: A Study of Unconscious Forces* (London, UK: Hogarth Press)

Klein, M. (1975) *Love, Guilt and Reparation and Other Works 1921–1945* (London, UK: Karnac Books)

Kleinginna, P. R. and Kleinginna, A. M. (1981) 'A Categorized List of Emotion Definitions, with Suggestions for a Consensual Definition', *Motivation and Emotion*, 5 (4): pp. 345–379

Knight, R. (1953) 'Borderline States', *Bulletin of the Menninger Clinic*, 17: pp. 1–12

Kohut, H. (1959) 'Introspection, Empathy, and Psychoanalysis', *Journal of the American Psychoanalytic Association*, 7 (3): pp. 459–483

Kohut, H. (1968) 'The Psychoanalytic Treatment of Narcissistic Personality Disorders: Outline of a Systematic Approach', *The Psychoanalytic Study of the Child*, 23: pp. 86–113

Kohut, H. (1971) *The Analysis of the Self: A Systematic Approach to the Psychoanalytic Treatment of Narcissistic Personality Disorders* (Chicago, IL: University of Chicago Press)

Kohut, H. and Wolf, E. (1978) 'The Disorders of the Self and Their Treatment: An Outline', *International Journal of Psychoanalysis*, 59 (4): pp. 413–425

Korbin, J. E. and Anderson-Fye, E. P. (2011) 'Adolescence Matters: Practice – and Policy-Relevant Research and Engagement in Psychological Anthropology', *Ethos*, 39 (4): pp. 415–425

Kovacevic, F. (2013) 'A Lacanian Approach to Dream Interpretation', *Dreaming*, 23 (1): pp. 78–89

Kramer, U. (2010) 'Coping and Defense Mechanisms: What's the Difference? Second Act', *Psychology and Psychotherapy: Theory, Research and Practice*, 83 (2): pp. 207–221

Kran, A. P. (2010) 'Comparing Causality in Freudian Reasoning and Critical Realism', *Journal of Critical Realism*, 9 (1): pp. 5–32

Kris, A. (1992) 'Interpretation and the Method of Free Association', *Psychoanalytic Inquiry*, 12 (2): pp. 208–224

Kris, A. (1996) *Free Association: Methods and Process* (revised and updated revision of the Yale University Press, 1982) (Hillsdale, NJ: The Analytic Press)

Kris, E. (1975) 'The Nature of Psychoanalytic Propositions and Their Validation' in L. M. Newman (ed.), *The Selected Papers of Ernst Kris* (New Haven, CT: Yale University Press), pp. 3–23

Kristeva, J. (1980) *Desire in Language: A Semiotic Approach to Literature and Art* (New York, NY: Columbia University Press)

Krupnick, J. *et al.* (1996) 'The Role of the Therapeutic Alliance in Psychotherapy and Pharmacotherapy Outcome: Findings in the National Institute of Mental Health Treatment of Depression Collaborative Research Program', *Journal of Consulting and Clinical Psychology*, 64 (3): pp. 532–539

Kuhn, A. (ed.) (2013) *Little Madnesses: Winnicott, Transitional Phenomena and Cultural Experience* (London, UK: I. B. Tauris)

Kulish, N. (2010) 'Clinical Implications of Contemporary Gender Theory', *Journal of the American Psychoanalytic Association*, 58 (2): pp. 231–258

Kulish, N. and Holtzman, D. (2008) *A Story of Her Own: The Female Oedipus Complex Reexamined and Renamed* (New York, NY: Jason Aronson)

Lacan, J. (1977) 'The Subversion of the Subject and the Dialectic of Desire in the Freudian Unconscious' in *Ecrits: A Selection* (A. Sheridan, Trans.) (London, UK: Tavistock), pp. 292–325

Lacan, J. (1977a) *Écrits: A Selection* (A. Sheridan, Trans.) (London, UK: Tavistock)

Lacan, J. (1977b) 'The Mirror Stage as Formative in the Function of the I as Revealed in Psychoanalytic Experience' in *Écrits: A Selection* (A. Sheridan, Trans.) (London, UK: Tavistock), pp. 1–7

Lacan, J. (1992) *The Ethics of Psychoanalysis 1959–1960: The Seminar of Jacques Lacan Book VII* (Ed. Jacques-Alain Miller and D. Porter, Trans.) (New York, NY: W. W. Norton & Company)

Lacan, J. (1992a) *The Seminar of Jacques Lacan. Book 7: The Ethics of Psychoanalysis 1959–1960* (Dennis Porter, Trans.) (New York, NY: W. W. Norton & Company)

Lacan, J. (2011) *Ecrits: The First Complete Edition in English* (B. Fink Trans., in collaboration with H. Fink and R. Grigg) (New York, NY: W. W. Norton & Company)

Lander, R. and Filc, J. (2006) *Subjective Experience and the Logic of the Other* (New York, NY: Other Press)

Landes, D. S. (1969) *The Unbound Prometheus: Technological Change and Industrial Development in Western Europe from 1750 to the Present* (Cambridge, UK: Cambridge University Press)

Lanier, J. (2010) *You Are Not a Gadget* (New York, NY: Vintage Books)

Lansky, M. and Morrison, A. (eds) (1997) *The Widening Scope of Shame* (Hillsdale, NJ: Analytic Press)

Laplanche, J. (2004) 'The So-Called "Death Drive": A Sexual Drive', *British Journal of Psychotherapy*, 20 (4): pp. 455–471

Laplanche, J. and Pontalis, J. (1988) *The Language of Psychoanalysis* (London, UK: Karnac Books)

Larsen, J. T., McGraw, A. P. and Cacioppo, J. T. (2001) 'Can People Feel Happy and Sad at the Same Time?' *Journal of Personality and Social Psychology*, 81 (4): pp. 684–696

Lasch, C. (1991) *The Culture of Narcissism: American Life in an Age of Diminishing Expectations* (New York, NY: W. W. Norton & Company)

Laufer, M. and Laufer, M. (2011) *Adolescence and Developmental Breakdown: A Psychoanalytic View* (London, UK: Karnac Books)

Layton, L. (2013) *Who's That Girl? Who's That Boy? Clinical Practice Meets Postmodern Gender Theory* (Vol. 2) (London, UK: Routledge)

Le Rider, J. and Robertson, R. (1993) *Modernity and Crises of Identity: Culture and Society in Fin-de-Siècle Vienna* (R. Morris, Trans.) (Cambridge, UK: Polity Press)

Leader, D. (2008) *The New Black: Mourning, Melancholia and Depression* (London, UK: Penguin)

Leader, D. and Groves, J. (2000) *Introducing Lacan* (Cambridge, UK: Icon Books)

Levine, H. (1997) 'The Capacity for Countertransference', *Psychoanalytic Inquiry*, 17 (1): pp. 44–68

Lewontin, R. C. (1991) 'Facts and the Factitious in Natural Sciences', *Critical Inquiry*, 18 (1): pp. 140–153

Lewontin, R. C. (2011) 'It's Even Less in Your Genes', *New York Review of Books*, 26 May. http://www.nybooks.com/articles/archives/2011/may/26/its-even-less-your-genes/

Little, M. (1960) 'On Basic Unity', *International Journal of Psychoanalysis*, 41: pp. 377–384

Loden, S. (2003) 'The Fate of the Dream in Contemporary Psychoanalysis', *Journal of the American Psychoanalytic Association*, 51 (1): pp. 43–70

Loewald, H. W. (1971) 'On Motivation and Instinct Theory', *The Psychoanalytic Study of the Child*, 26: pp. 91–128

Loewald, H. W. (1979) 'The Waning of the Oedipus Complex', *Journal of the American Psychoanalytic Association*, 27 (4): pp. 751–775

Loewald, H. W. (1988) *Sublimation: Inquiries into Theoretical Psychoanalysis* (New Haven, CT: Yale University Press)

Lombardi, R. (2009) 'Symmetric Frenzy and Catastrophic Change: A Consideration of Primitive Mental States in the Wake of Bion and Matte Blanco', *International Journal of Psychoanalysis*, 90 (3): pp. 529–549

Lombardozzi, A. (2010) 'The Use of the Alpha Function in Analytical Construction', *International Journal of Psychoanalysis*, 91 (5): pp. 1268–1271

Longhofer, J. (2013) 'Shame in the Clinical Process with LGBTQ Clients', *Clinical Social Work Journal*, 41 (3): pp. 297–301

Lunbeck, E. (2014) *The Americanization of Narcissism* (Cambridge, MA: Harvard University Press)

Magee, M. and Miller, D. (2013) *Lesbian Lives: Psychoanalytic Narratives Old and New* (London, UK: Routledge)

Magruder, M. T. (2011) 'Transitional Space (S): Creation, Collaboration and Improvisation within Shared Virtual/Physical Environments', *International Journal of Performance Arts and Digital Media*, 7 (2): pp. 189–204

Mahler, M. S. (1974) 'Symbiosis and Individuation: The Psychological Birth of the Human Infant', *Psychoanalytic Study of the Child*, 29, 89–106

Main, R. (2007) 'Synchronicity and Analysis: Jung and After', *European Journal of Psychotherapy and Counseling*, 9 (4): pp. 359–371

Main, R. (2011) 'Synchronicity and the Limits of Re-Enchantment', *International Journal of Jungian Studies*, 3 (2): pp. 144–158

Malin, B. D. (2011) 'Kohut and Lacan: Mirror Opposites', *Psychoanalytic Inquiry*, 31 (1): pp. 58–74

Mann, M. (2010) 'Shame Veiled and Unveiled: The Shame Affect and Its Re-Emergence in the Clinical Setting', *The American Journal of Psychoanalysis*, 70 (3): pp. 270–281

Mantilla Lagos, C. (2007) 'The Theory of Thinking and the Capacity to Mentalize: A Comparison of Fonagy's and Bion's Models', *The Spanish Journal of Psychology*, 10 (1): pp. 189–198

Markell, P. (2009) *Bound by Recognition* (Princeton, NJ: Princeton University Press)

Markstrom, C. and Marshall, S. (2007) 'The Psychosocial Inventory of Ego Strengths: Examination of Theory and Psychometric Properties', *Journal of Adolescence*, 30 (1): pp. 63–79

Martin, P. (2011) 'Celebrating the Wounded Healer', *Counseling Psychology Review*, 26 (1): pp. 10–19

Martindale, B. and Summers, A. (2013) 'The Psychodynamics of Psychosis. *Advances in Psychiatric Treatment*, 19 (2): pp. 124–131

Massumi, B. (2002) *Parables for the Virtual: Movement, Affect, Sensation* (Durham, NC: Duke University Press)

Mazzarello, P. (1999) 'A Unifying Concept: The History of Cell Theory', *Nature Cell Biology*, 1 (1): pp. E13–E15

McDermott, V. (2003) 'Is Free Association Still Fundamental?' *Journal of the American Psychoanalytic Association*, 51 (4): pp. 1349–1356

McLeod, J. (2013) 'Increasing the Rigor of Case Study Evidence in Therapy Research', *Pragmatic Case Studies in Psychotherapy*, 9 (4): pp. 382–402

McWilliams, N. (1999) *Psychoanalytic Case Formulation* (New York, NY: Guilford Press)

McWilliams, N. (2011) *Psychoanalytic Diagnosis: Understanding Personality Structure in the Clinical Process* (New York, NY: Guilford Press)

Mead, M. (1954) *Coming of Age in Samoa: A Study of Adolescence and Sex in Primitive Societies* (London, UK: Penguin Books)

Meissner, W. (1996) *The Therapeutic Alliance* (New Haven, CT: Yale University Press)

Meissner, W. (1970) 'Notes on Identification: Origins in Freud', *The Psychoanalytic Quarterly*, 39 (4): pp. 563–589

Meissner, W. (2000) 'On Analytic Listening', *The Psychoanalytic Quarterly*, 69 (2): pp. 317–367

Meltzer, D. (2008) *The Claustrum: An Investigation of Claustrophobic Phenomena* (London, UK: Karnac Books)

Meltzer, D. *et al.* (1982) 'The Conceptual Distinction between Projective Identification (Klein) and Container-Contained (Bion)', *Journal of Child Psychotherapy*, 8 (2): pp. 185–202

Mendell, D. and Turrini, P. (eds) (2003) *The Inner World of the Mother* (Madison, CT: Psychosocial Press)

Merchant, J. (2009) 'A Reappraisal of Classical Archetype Theory and Its Implications for Theory and Practice', *Journal of Analytical Psychology*, 54 (3): pp. 339–358

Messer, S. and Wolitzky, D. (2007) 'The Psychoanalytic Approach to Case Formulation' in T. D. Eells (ed.), *Handbook of Psychotherapy Case Formulation* (New York, NY: Guilford Press), pp. 67–104

Midgley, N. and Kennedy, E. (2011) 'Psychodynamic Psychotherapy for Children and Adolescents: A Critical Review of the Evidence Base', *Journal of Child Psychotherapy*, 37 (3): pp. 232–260

Miller, G. and Baldwin D. (1987) 'Implications of the Wounded-Healer Paradigm for the Use of the Self in Therapy', *Journal of Psychotherapy & the Family*, 3 (1): pp. 139– 151

Miller, M. J. (2011) *Lacanian Psychotherapy: Theory and Practical Applications* (London, UK: Routledge)

Mishna, F., Van Wert, M. and Asakura, K. (2013) 'The Best Kept Secret in Social Work: Empirical Support for Contemporary Psychodynamic Social Work Practice', *Journal of Social Work Practice*, 27 (3): pp. 289–303

Mitchell, J. and Rose, J. (eds) (1983) *Feminine Sexuality: Jacques Lacan and the école freudienne* (London, UK: Palgrave)

Mitchell, S. A. (1981) 'The Origin and Nature of the "Object" in the Theories of Klein and Fairbairn', *Contemporary Psychoanalysis*, 17 (3): pp. 374–398

Mitchell, S. A. (1984) 'Object Relations Theories and the Developmental Tilt', *Contemporary Psychoanalysis*, 20 (4): pp. 473–499

Mitchell, S. A. (1986) 'The Wings of Icarus: Illusion and the Problem of Narcissism', *Contemporary Psychoanalysis*, 22 (1): pp. 107–132

Mitchell, S. A. (1988) 'The Intrapsychic and the Interpersonal: Different Theories, Different Domains, or Historical Artifacts?' *Psychoanalytic Inquiry*, 8 (4): pp. 472–496

Mitrani, J. (2008) *A Framework for the Imaginary: Clinical Explorations in Primitive States of Being* (London, UK: Karnac Books)

Mitrani, J. (2011) 'Excogitating Bion's Cogitations: Further Implications for Technique', *The Psychoanalytic Quarterly*, 80 (3): pp. 671–698

Modell, A. (2003) *Imagination and the Meaningful Brain* (Boston, MA: MIT Press)

Moncayo, R. (2012) *The Emptiness of Oedipus: Identification and Non-Identification in Lacanian Psychoanalysis* (London, UK: Routledge)

Moors, A. and De Houwer, J. (2006) 'Automaticity: A Theoretical and Conceptual Analysis', *Psychological Bulletin*, 132 (2): p. 297

Muller, J. (1985) 'Lacan's Mirror Stage', *Psychoanalytic Inquiry*, 5 (2): pp. 233–252

Neu, J. (ed.) (1991) *The Cambridge Companion to Freud* (Cambridge, UK: Cambridge University Press)

Neubauer, P. (1984) 'Anna Freud's Concept of Developmental Lines', *The Psychoanalytic Study of the Child*, 39: pp. 15–29

Nilsson, M. (2006) 'To Be the Sole Therapist: Children and Parents in Simultaneous Psychotherapy', *Journal of Infant, Child, and Adolescent Psychotherapy*, 5 (2): pp. 206–225

Novick, K. K. and Novick, J. (2010) *Emotional Muscle: Strong Parents, Strong Children* (USA: Xlibris Corporation)

O'Brien, G. and Jureidini, J. (2002) 'Dispensing with the Dynamic Unconscious', *Philosophy, Psychiatry, & Psychology*, 9 (2): pp. 141–153

Ogden, T. (1989) *The Primitive Edge of Experience* (Northvale, NJ: Jason Aronson)

Ogden, T. (1992) 'The Dialectically Constituted/Decentered Subject of Psychoanalysis. I: The Freudian Subject', *International Journal of Psychoanalysis*, 73, 613–626

Ogden, T. (1995) 'Aliveness and Deadness of the Transference and Countertransference', *International Journal of Psychoanalysis*, 76, 695–710

Ogden, T. (1999) *Reverie and Interpretation: Sensing Something Human* (London, UK: Karnac Books)

Ogden, T. (2001) 'Reading Winnicott', *The Psychoanalytic Quarterly*, 70 (2): pp. 299–323

Ogden, T. (2004) *Projective Identification and Psychotherapeutic Technique* (Lanham, MD: Rowman & Littlefield Publishers, Inc)

Ogden, T. (2004a) 'On Holding and Containing, Being and Dreaming', *International Journal of Psychoanalysis*, 85 (6): pp. 1349–1364

Ogden, T. (2010) 'Why Read Fairbairn?' *International Journal of Psychoanalysis*, 91 (1): pp. 101–118

Olds, D. D. (2006) 'Identification: Psychoanalytic and Biological Perspectives', *Journal of the American Psychoanalytic Association*, 54 (1): pp. 17–46

Olson, T. *et al.* (2011) 'Addressing and Interpreting Defense Mechanisms in Psychotherapy: General Considerations', *Psychiatry: Interpersonal and Biological Processes*, 74 (2): pp. 142–165

Oram, K. (2000) 'A Transitional Space: Involving Parents in the Play Therapy of Their Children', *Journal of Infant, Child, and Adolescent Psychotherapy*, 1 (4): pp. 79–98

Orange, D. M. (2002) 'There Is No Outside: Empathy and Authenticity in Psychoanalytic Process', *Psychoanalytic Psychology*, 19 (4): pp. 686–700

Orange, D. M. (2008) 'Recognition as: Intersubjective Vulnerability in the Psychoanalytic Dialogue', *International Journal of Psychoanalytic Self Psychology*, 3 (2): pp. 178–194

Orange, D. M. (2010) *Thinking for Clinicians: Philosophical Resources for Contemporary Psychoanalysis and the Humanistic Psychotherapies* (London, UK: Routledge)

Ornstein, P. (2011) 'The Centrality of Empathy in Psychoanalysis', *Psychoanalytic Inquiry*, 31 (5): pp. 437–447

Panksepp, J. (2003) 'Feeling the Pain of Social Loss', *Science*, 302 (5643): pp. 237–239

Parens, H. (1975) 'Parenthood as a Developmental Phase', *Journal of the American Psychoanalytic Association*, 23 (1): pp. 154–165

Parker, I. (2010) *Lacanian Psychoanalysis: Revolutions in Subjectivity* (London, UK: Routledge)

Pavón-Cuéllar, D. (2010) *From the Conscious Interior to an Exterior Unconscious: Lacan, Discourse Analysis, and Social Psychology* (London, UK: Karnac Books)

Pavón-Cuéllar, D. (2014) 'Extimacy' in T. Teo (ed.), *Encyclopedia of Critical Psychology* (New York, NY: Springer), pp. 951–955

Pedder, J. R. (1979) 'Transitional Space in Psychotherapy and Theatre', *British Journal of Medical Psychology*, 52 (4): pp. 377–384

Perry, J. C. and Bond, M. (2012) 'Change in Defense Mechanisms during Long-Term Dynamic Psychotherapy and Five-Year Outcome', *American Journal of Psychiatry*, 169 (9): pp. 916–925

Phillips, A. (2007) *Winnicott* (London, UK: Penguin)

Phillips, D. A. and Shonkoff, J. P. (eds) (2000) *From Neurons to Neighborhoods: The Science of Early Childhood Development* (Washington, DC: National Academies Press)

Pigman, G. (1995) 'Freud and the History of Empathy', *International Journal of Psychoanalysis*, 76, 237–256

Piketty, T. (2014) *Capital in the Twenty-First Century* (Arthur Goldhammer, Trans.) (Cambridge, MA: Belknap Press)

Pile, S. (2009) 'Topographies of the Body-and-Mind: Skin Ego, Body Ego, and the Film "Memento"', *Subjectivity*, 27 (1): pp. 134–154

Pines, M. (1984) 'Reflections on Mirroring', *International Review of Psychoanalysis*, 11 (1): pp. 27–42

Pollak, T. (2009) 'The "Body–Container": A New Perspective on the "Body–Ego"', *International Journal of Psychoanalysis*, 90 (3): pp. 487–506

Polledri, P. (2003) 'Envy Revisited', *British Journal of Psychotherapy*, 20 (2): pp. 195–218

Popper, K. S. (1945) *The Open Society and Its Enemies* (London, UK: Routledge & Kegan Paul)

Prinz, J. (2004) 'Which Emotions Are Basic?' in D. Evans and Pierre Cruse (eds), *Emotion, Evolution, and Rationality* (Oxford, UK: Oxford University Press), pp. 69–88

Racker, H. (1957) 'The Meanings and Uses of Countertransference', *The Psychoanalytic Quarterly*, 26 (3): pp. 303–357

Rasmussen, B. and Salhani, D. (2010) 'A Contemporary Kleinian Contribution to Understanding Racism', *Social Service Review*, 84 (3): pp. 491–513

Ratcliffe, M. (2005) 'The Feeling of Being', *Journal of Consciousness Studies*, 12 (8–10): pp. 45–63

Ratcliffe, M. (2012) 'Phenomenology as a Form of Empathy', *Inquiry*, 55 (5): pp. 473–495

Ravitz, P. *et al.* (2010) 'Adult Attachment Measures: A 25-Year Review', *Journal of Psychosomatic Research*, 69 (4): pp. 419–432

Reik, T. (1948) *Listening with the Third Ear: The Inner Experience of a Psychoanalyst* (New York, NY: Grove Press)

Reiner, A. (2009) *The Quest for Conscience and the Birth of the Mind* (London, UK: Karnac Books)

Reiser, M. (1984) *Mind, Brain, Body: Towards a Convergence of Psychoanalysis and Neurobiology* (New York, NY: Basic Books)

Reynolds, D. (2003) 'Mindful Parenting: A Group Approach to Enhancing Reflective Capacity in Parents and Infants', *Journal of Child Psychotherapy*, 29 (3): pp. 357–374

Riccardo, S. (2003) *Unconscious Phantasy* (London, UK: Karnac Books)

Richard, A. (2012) 'The Wounded Healer: Can We Do Better Than Survive as Therapist?' *International Journal of Psychoanalytic Self Psychology*, 7 (1): pp. 131–138

Richards, A. and Willick, M. (eds) (2013) *Psychoanalysis: The Science of Mental Conflict* (New York, NY: Routledge)

Richards, B. (2000) 'The Anatomy of Envy', *Psychoanalytic Studies*, 2 (1): pp. 65–76

Ricoeur, P. (2012) *On Psychoanalysis* (Cambridge, UK: Polity Press)

Roazen, P. (1992) *Freud and His Followers* (New York, NY: Da Capo Press)

Robinson, P. A. (1993) *Freud and His Critics* (Berkeley, CA: University of California Press)

Roesler, C. (2010) *Analytische Psychologie Heute: Der Aktuelle Stand der Forschung zur Psychologie C. G. Jungs* (in German) (Basel, Switzerland: Karger Verlag)

Roesler, C. (2006) 'A Narratological Methodology for Identifying Archetypal Story Patterns in Autobiographical Narratives', *Journal of Analytical Psychology*, 51 (4): pp. 574–586

Roof, J. (1996) 'A Verdict on the Paternal Function: Law, the Paternal Metaphor, and Paternity Law' in W. Apollon and R. Feldstein (eds), *Law Politics and Aesthetics* (Albany, NY: SUNY Press), pp. 101–126

Roose, S. P. and Glick, R. A. (eds) (2013) *Anxiety as Symptom and Signal* (Hillsdale, NJ: Analytic Press)

Rose, H. and Rose, S. (2010) *Alas Poor Darwin: Arguments against Evolutionary Psychology* (New York, NY: Random House)

Rose, H. and Rose, S. (2013) *Genes, Cells and Brains: The Promethean Promises of the New Biology* (London, UK: Verso Books)

Rose, J. (2005) *Sexuality in the Field of Vision* (London, UK: Verso Books)

Rose, N. (2013) 'The Human Sciences in a Biological Age', *Theory, Culture & Society*, 30 (1): pp. 3–34

Rose, S. (2006) *The 21st-Century Brain: Explaining, Mending and Manipulating the Mind* (New York, NY: Random House)

Rosenbaum, B. (2003) 'The Unconscious: How Does It Speak to Us Today?' *The Scandinavian Psychoanalytic Review*, 26 (1): pp. 31–40

Rusbridger, R. (2012) 'Affects in Melanie Klein', *International Journal of Psychoanalysis*, 93 (1): pp. 139–150

Ross, A. (2007) *The Rest Is Noise: Listening to the Twentieth Century* (New York, NY: Palgrave Macmillan)

Roth, P. and Lemma, A. (eds) (2008) *Envy and Gratitude Revisited* (London, UK: Karnac Books)

Rovainen, C. M. and Yan, Q. (1985) 'Sensory Responses of Dorsal Cells in the Lamprey Brain', *Journal of Comparative Physiology A*, 156 (2): pp. 181–183

Rubin, L. B. (1976) *Worlds of Pain: Life in the Working Class Family* (New York, NY: Basic Books)

Rubin, L. B. (1983) *Intimate Strangers: Men and Women Together* (New York, NY: Harper & Row)

Rushkoff, D. (2013) *Present Shock: When Everything Happens Now* (New York, NY: Penguin)

Rustin, M. (1991) *The Good Society and the Inner World: Psychoanalysis, Politics, and Culture* (London, UK: Verso Books)

Rustin, M. (2010) 'Varieties of Psychoanalytic Research', *Psychoanalytic Psychotherapy*, 24 (4): pp. 380–397

Ruti, M. (2008) 'The Fall of Fantasies: A Lacanian Reading of Lack', *Journal of the American Psychoanalytic Association*, 56 (2): pp. 483–508

Ryan, R. (2007) 'Motivation and Emotion: A New Look and Approach for Two Reemerging Fields', *Motivation and Emotion*, 31: pp. 1–3

Rycroft, C. (1968) *A Critical Dictionary of Psychoanalysis* (London, UK: Thomas Nelson & Sons)

Sabbadini, A. (2011) 'Cameras, Mirrors, and the Bridge Space: A Winnicottian Lens on Cinema', *Projections*, 5 (1): pp. 17–30

Sackett, D. L. *et al.* (1996) 'Evidence Based Medicine: What It Is and What It Isn't', *British Medical Journal*, 312 (7023): p. 71

Safran, J. (2000) *Therapeutic Alliance* (New York, NY: John Wiley & Sons)

Safran, J. (2012) *Psychoanalysis and Psychoanalytic Therapies* (Washington, DC: American Psychological Association)

Safran, J. and Muran, J. (1996) 'The Resolution of Ruptures in the Therapeutic Alliance', *Journal of Consulting and Clinical Psychology*, 64 (3): p. 447

Safran, J. and Muran, J. (2000) *Negotiating the Therapeutic Alliance: A Relational Treatment Guide* (New York, NY: Guilford Press)

Safran, J. and Muran, J. (2006) 'Has the Concept of the Therapeutic Alliance Outlived Its Usefulness?' *Psychotherapy: Theory, Research, Practice, Training*, 43 (3): pp. 286–291

Safran, J., Muran, J. and Eubanks-Carter, C. (2011) 'Repairing Alliance Ruptures', *Psychotherapy*, 48 (1): p. 80

Sagan, O. (2008) 'Playgrounds, Studios and Hiding Places: Emotional Exchange in Creative Learning Spaces', *Art, Design & Communication in Higher Education*, 6 (3): pp. 173–186

Salamon, G. (2010) *Assuming a Body: Transgender Theory and Rhetorics of Materiality* (New York, NY: Columbia University Press)

Sandler, J. (ed.) (2012) *Projection, Identification, Projective Identification* (London, UK: Karnac Books)

Sandler, J. and Sandler, A. (1998) *Internal Objects Revisited* (London, UK: Karnac Books)

Sandler, J., Fonagy, P. and Person, E. S. (eds) (2012) *Freud's on Narcissism: An Introduction* (London, UK: Karnac Books)

Sandler, P. C. (2009) *A Clinical Application of Bion's Concepts: Dreaming, Transformation, Containment and Change* (London, UK: Karnac Books)

Sands, S. (2008) 'The Concept of Multiple Self States: Clinical Advantages', *International Journal of Psychoanalytic Self Psychology*, 4 (1): pp. 122–124

Sarkar, J. and Adshead, G. (2006) 'Personality Disorders as Disorganization of Attachment and Affect Regulation', *Advances in Psychiatric Treatment*, 12: pp. 297–305

Sayer, A. (2005) 'Class, Moral Worth and Recognition', *Sociology*, 39 (5): pp. 947–963

Sayers, J. (1998) *Boy Crazy: Remembering Adolescence, Therapies and Dreams* (London, UK: Routledge)

Sayers, J. (2000) *Kleinians: Psychoanalysis Inside Out* (London, UK: Polity Press)

Schafer, R. (1999) 'Recentering Psychoanalysis: From Heinz Hartmann to the Contemporary British Kleinians', *Psychoanalytic Psychology*, 16 (3): p. 339

Schafer, R. (2005) 'Listening in Psychoanalysis', *Narrative*, 13 (3): pp. 271–280

Schlegel, A. and Hewlett, B. L. (2011) 'Contributions of Anthropology to the Study of Adolescence', *Journal of Research on Adolescence*, 21 (1): pp. 281–289

Schlegel, R. and Hicks, J. (2011) 'The True Self and Psychological Health: Emerging Evidence and Future Directions', *Social and Personality Psychology Compass*, 5 (12): pp. 989–1003

Schlegel, R. *et al.* (2009) 'Thine Own Self: True Self-Concept Accessibility and Meaning in Life', *Journal of Personality and Social Psychology*, 96 (2): pp. 473–490

Schore, A. N. (2001) 'Effects of a Secure Attachment Relationship on Right Brain Development, Affect Regulation, and Infant Mental Health', *Infant Mental Health Journal*, 22 (1–2): pp. 7–66

Schore, A. N. (2003) *Affect Dysregulation and Disorders of the Self* (New York, NY: W. W. Norton & Company)

Schore, A. N. (2003a) *Affect Regulation and the Repair of the Self* (New York: W.W. Norton & Company)

Schore, A. N. (2005) 'Back to Basics Attachment, Affect Regulation, and the Developing Right Brain: Linking Developmental Neuroscience to Pediatrics', *Pediatrics in Review*, 26 (6): pp. 204–217

Schore, A. N. (2009) 'Relational Trauma and the Developing Right Brain', *Annals of the New York Academy of Sciences*, 1159 (1): pp. 189–203

Schore, J. R. and Schore, A. N. (2008) 'Modern Attachment Theory: The Central Role of Affect Regulation in Development and Treatment', *Clinical Social Work Journal*, 36 (1): pp. 9–20

Schorkse, C. E. (1980) *Fin-de-siècle Vienna* (New York, NY: Knopf)

Schwaber, E. (1981) 'Empathy: A Mode of Analytic Listening', *Psychoanalytical Inquiry*, 1 (3): pp. 357–392

Schwartz, C. (1988) 'Ambivalence: Its Relationship to Narcissism and Superego Development', *Psychoanalytic Review*, 76 (4): pp. 511–527

Segal, H. (1964) *Introduction to the Work of Melanie Klein* (London, UK: Heinemann)

Segal, H. (2013) 'The Psychoanalytic Approach to the Treatment of Psychotic Patients' in D. Bell (ed.), *Living on the Border: Psychotic Processes in the Individual, the Couple and the Group* (London, UK: Karnac Books), Chapter 1

Semi, A. (2007) *The Conscious in Psychoanalysis* (London, UK: Karnac Books)

Shaver, P. and Mikulincer, M. (2005) 'Attachment Theory and Research: Resurrection of the Psychodynamic Approach to Personality', *Journal of Research in Personality*, 39 (1): pp. 22–45

Shaw, J. (2014) 'Psychotic and Non-Psychotic Perceptions of Reality', *Journal of Child Psychotherapy*, 40 (1): pp. 73–89

Shea, M., Stout, R. and Yen, S. (2004) 'Associations in the Course of Personality Disorders and Axis I Disorders Over Time', *Journal of Abnormal Psychology*, 113: pp. 499–508

Shedler, J. (2010) 'The Efficacy of Psychodynamic Psychotherapy', *American Psychologist*, 65 (2): pp. 98–109

Shedler, J. (2013) Available at http://www.psychologytoday.com/blog/psychologically-minded/201311/psychodynamic-therapy-101

Shedler, J. and Westen, D. (2004) 'Dimensions of Personality Pathology: An Alternative to the Five-Factor Model', *American Journal of Psychiatry*, 161 (10): pp. 1743–1754

Shengold, L. (1974) 'The Metaphor of the Mirror', *Journal of the American Psychoanalytic Association*, 22: pp. 97–115

Singh, K. (1996) *Guilt (Ideas in Psychoanalysis)* (London, UK: Icon Books)

Siskind, D. (1997) *Working with Parents: Establishing the Essential Alliance in Child Psychotherapy and Consultation* (New York, NY: Jason Aronson)

Skocpol, T. (1992) *Protecting Soldiers and Mothers* (Cambridge, MA: Belknap Press of Harvard University Press)

Smetana, J. G., Campione-Barr, N. and Metzger, A. (2006) 'Adolescent Development in Interpersonal and Societal Contexts', *Annual Review of Psychology*, 57: pp. 255–284

Smith, A., Msetfi, R. and Golding, L. (2010) 'Client Self Rated Adult Attachment Patterns and the Therapeutic Alliance: A Systematic Review', *Clinical Psychology Review*, 30 (3): pp. 326–337

Smith, H. (2000) 'Countertransference, Conflictual Listening, and the Analytic Object Relationship', *Journal of the American Psychoanalytic Association*, 48 (1): pp. 95–128

Smith, H. (2005) 'Dialogues on Conflict: Toward an Integration of Methods', *The Psychoanalytic Quarterly*, 74 (1): pp. 327–363

Solms, M. (2012) 'Depression: A Neuropsychoanalytic Perspective', *International Forum of Psychoanalysis*, 21 (3–4): pp. 207–213

Solms, M. (2014) *The Neuropsychology of Dreams: A Clinico-Anatomical Study* (London, UK: Psychology Press)

Sotirova-Kohli, M. *et al.* (2013) 'Symbol/Meaning paired-associate recall: An "archetypal memory" advantage?' *Behavioral Sciences*, 3 (4): pp. 541–561

Spezzano, C. (1993) *Affect in Psychoanalysis: A Clinical Synthesis* (Hillsdale, NJ: Analytic Press)

Spiegel, D. and Cardena, E. (1991) 'Disintegrated Experience: The Dissociative Disorders Revisited', *Journal of Abnormal Psychology*, 100 (3): pp. 366–378

Spillius, E. B. (1994) 'Developments in Klein's Thinking', *Psychoanalytic Inquiry*, 14 (3): pp. 324–364

Sroufe, L A. (1996) *Emotional Development: The Organization of Emotional Life in the Early Years* (Cambridge, UK: Cambridge University Press)

Stanghellini, G. and Rosfort, R. (2013) *Emotions and Personhood: Exploring Fragility-Making Sense of Vulnerability* (Oxford, UK: Oxford University Press)

Steele, H., Steele, M. and Murphy, A. (2009) 'Use of the Adult Attachment Interview to Measure Process and Change in Psychotherapy', *Psychotherapy Research*, 19 (6): pp. 633–643

Stein, R. (1999) *Psychoanalytic Theories of Affect* (London, UK: Karnac Books)

Steiner, J. (1979) 'The Border between the Paranoid-Schizoid and the Depressive Positions in the Borderline Patient', *British Journal of Medical Psychology*, 52 (4): pp. 385–391

Steiner, J. (1993) *Psychic Retreats: Pathological Organizations in Psychotic, Neurotic and Borderline Patients* (New York, NY: Routledge)

Steiner, J. (1994) 'Patient-Centered and Analyst-Centered Interpretations: Some Implications of Containment and Countertransference', *Psychoanalytic Inquiry*, 14 (3): pp. 406–422

Sterba, R. (1934) 'The Fate of the Ego in Analytic Therapy', *International Journal of Psychoanalysis*, 15: pp. 117–126

Stern, A. (1938) 'Psychoanalytic Investigation and Therapy in the Borderline Group of Neuroses', *Psychoanalytic Quarterly*, 7: pp. 467–489

Stern, D. (1997) *Unformulated Experience: From Dissociation to Imagination in Psychoanalysis* (Hillsdale, NJ: Analytic Press)

Stern, D. (2004) 'The Eye Sees Itself: Dissociation, Enactment, and the Achievement of Conflict', *Contemporary Psychoanalysis*, 40 (2): pp. 197–238

Stern, D. N. (1998) *The Interpersonal World of the Infant: A View from Psychoanalysis and Developmental Psychology* (London, UK: Karnac Books)

Stern, D. N. (2009) *The First Relationship: Infant and Mother* (Cambridge, MA: Harvard University Press)

Stevens, A. (2006) *The Archetypes* (London, UK: Psychology Press)

Stevens, A. (2013) *Archetype: A Natural History of the Self* (London, UK: Routledge)

Stewart-Steinberg, S. (2012) *Impious Fidelity: Anna Freud, Psychoanalysis, Politics* (Ithaca, NY: Cornell University Press)

Stolorow, R. (2011) 'Toward Greater Authenticity: From Shame to Existential Guilt, Anxiety, and Grief', *International Journal of Psychoanalytic Self Psychology*, 6 (2): pp. 285–287

Stolorow, R., Brandchaft, B. and Atwood, G. (1987) *Psychoanalytic Treatment: An Intersubjective Approach* (Hillsdale, NJ: The Analytic Press)

Strongman, K. T. (1995) 'Theories of Anxiety', *New Zealand Journal of Psychology*, 24 (2): pp. 4–10

Suler, J. R. (1980) 'Primary Process Thinking and Creativity', *Psychological Bulletin*, 88 (1): pp. 144–165

Sullivan, H. S. (1953) *Interpersonal Theory of Psychiatry* (New York, NY: W. W. Norton & Company)

Sullivan, H. S. (1973) *Clinical Studies in Psychiatry* (Vol. 2) (New York, NY: W. W. Norton & Company)

Sullivan, R. E. (2005) 'Social Theory, Psychoanalysis, and Racism', *Contemporary Sociology: A Journal of Reviews*, 34 (2): pp. 139–140

Sussman, S. and Arnett, J. J. (2014) 'Emerging Adulthood: Developmental Period Facilitative of the Addictions', *Evaluation & the Health Professions*. Published online. DOI: 10.1177/0163278714521812

Sweet, A. (2012) 'Internal Objects and Self-Destructive Behaviours: A Clinical Case Highlighting Dissociation, Splitting and the Role of the Primitive Super-Ego in the Addictions', *The Scandinavian Psychoanalytic Review*, 35 (2): pp. 116–126

Symington, J. and Symington, N. (1996) *The Clinical Thinking of Wilfred Bion* (London, UK: Routledge)

Tan, R. (2006) 'Racism and Similarity: Paranoid-Schizoid Structures Revisited' in R. Moodley and S. Palmer (eds), *Race, Culture and Psychotherapy: Critical Perspectives in Multicultural Practice* (New York, NY: Routledge), pp. 119–129

Tangney, J. and Dearing, R. (2003) *Shame and Guilt* (New York, NY: Guilford Press)

Target, M. and Fonagy, P. (1996) 'Playing with Reality: II. the Development of Psychic Reality from a Theoretical Perspective', *International Journal of Psychoanalysis*, 77 (3): pp. 459–479

Tauber, A. I. (2010) *Freud, the Reluctant Philosopher* (Princeton, NJ: Princeton University Press)

Taylor, C. (1989) *Sources of the Self: The Making of the Modern Identity* (Cambridge, MA: Harvard University Press)

Thorne, A., McLean, K. C. and Lawrence, A. M. (2004) 'When Remembering Is Not Enough: Reflecting on Self-Defining Memories in Late Adolescence', *Journal of Personality*, 72 (3): pp. 513–542

Tomkins, S. (1995) 'What Are Affects?' in E. K. Sedgwick and A. Frank (eds), *Shame and Its Sisters: A Silvan Tomkins Reader* (Durham, NC: Duke University Press), pp. 33–74

Torsti, M. (1998) 'On Motherhood', *The Scandinavian Psychoanalytic Review*, 21 (1): pp. 53–76

Tracy, J., Robins, R. and Tangney, J. (eds) (2007) *The Self-Conscious Emotions: Theory and Research* (New York, NY: Guilford Press)

Tsiantis, J. (ed.) (2000) *Work with Parents: Psychoanalytic Psychotherapy with Children and Adolescents* (London, UK: Karnac Books)

Turkle, S. (2012) *Alone Together: Why We Expect More from Technology and Less from Each Other* (New York, NY: Basic Books)

Turnbull, O. and Solms, M. (2007) 'Awareness, Desire, and False Beliefs: Freud in the Light of Modern Neuropsychology', *Cortex*, 43 (8): pp. 1083–1090

Turner, T. (1980) 'The Social Skin' in J. Cherfas and R. Levin (eds), *Not Work Alone: A Cross-Cultural View of Activities Superfluous to Survival* (Thousand Oaks, CA: Sage Publications), pp. 112–140

Turner, V. (1969) *The Ritual Process* (Chicago, IL: Aldine)

Vaillant, G. (1992) *Ego Mechanisms of Defense: A Guide for Clinicians and Researchers* (New York, NY: American Psychiatric Publishing)

Vanheule S. (2011) *The Subject of Psychosis: A Lacanian Perspective* (London, UK: Palgrave)

Venter, J. C. *et al.* (2001) 'The Sequence of the Human Genome', *Science*, 291 (5507): pp. 1304–1351

Verhaeghe, P. (2004) *On Being Normal and Other Disorders: A Manual for Clinical Psychodiagnostics* (New York, NY: Other Press)

Verhaeghe, P. (2011) *Love in a Time of Loneliness* (London, NY: Karnac Books)

Verhaeghe, P. and Vanheule, S. (2005) 'Actual Neurosis and PTSD: The Impact of the Other', *Psychoanalytic Psychology*, 22 (4): pp. 493–507

Vygotsky, L. S. (1962) *Thought and Language* (Cambridge, MA: MIT Press)

Vygotsky, L. S. (1978) *Mind in Society: The Development of Higher Psychological Processes*. (ed. M. Cole, V. Johnson, S. Scribner and E. Souberman) (Cambridge, MA: Harvard University Press)

Wallerstein, R. (2002) 'The Growth and Transformation of American Ego Psychology', *Journal of the American Psychoanalytic Association*, 50 (1): pp. 135–168

Waska, R. (2002) *Primitive Experiences of Loss: Working with the Paranoid-Schizoid Patient* (London, UK: Karnac Books)

Watson, P. J., Little, T. and Biderman, M. D. (1992) 'Narcissism and Parenting Styles', *Psychoanalytic Psychology*, 9 (2): pp. 231–244

Weideman, A. (2012) 'Positivism and Postpositivism', *The Encyclopedia of Applied Linguistics*. DOI: 10.1002/9781405198431.wbeal0920

Weinberg, H. (2007) 'So What Is This Social Unconscious Anyway?' *Group Analysis*, 40 (3): pp. 307–322

Weisbrode, K. (2012) *On Ambivalence: The Problems and Pleasures of Having It Both Ways* (Cambridge, MA: MIT Press)

Wertz, F. (1993) 'The Phenomenology of Sigmund Freud', *Journal of Phenomenological Psychology*, 24 (2): pp. 101–129

West, M. (2010) 'Envy and Difference', *Journal of Analytical Psychology*, 55 (4): pp. 459–484

Westen, D. (1998) 'The Scientific Legacy of Sigmund Freud: Toward a Psychodynamically Informed Psychological Science', *Psychological Bulletin*, 124: pp. 252–283

Westen, D. and Weinberger, J. (2004) 'When Clinical Description Becomes Statistical Prediction', *American Psychologist*, 59 (7): pp. 595–613

Westen, D. and Weinberger, J. (2005) 'In Praise of Clinical Judgment: Meehl's Forgotten Legacy', *Journal of Clinical Psychology*, 61 (10): pp. 1257–1276

Whitebook, J. (1996) *Perversion and Utopia: A Study in Psychoanalysis and Critical Theory* (Boston, MA: MIT Press)

Will, D. (1980) 'Psychoanalysis as a Human Science', *British Journal of Medical Psychology*, 53 (3): pp. 201–211

Will, D. (1985) 'Psychoanalysis and the New Philosophy of Science', *The International Review of Psychoanalysis*, 13 (2): pp. 163–173

Williams, S. J. (2003) *Medicine and the Body* (London, UK: Sage Publications)

Winnicott, D. W. (1949) 'Hate in the Counter-Transference', *International Journal of Psychoanalysis*, 30: pp. 69–74

Winnicott, D. W. (1953) 'Transitional Objects and Transitional Phenomena', *International Journal of Psychoanalysis*, 34: pp. 89–97

Winnicott, D. W. (1958a) *Collected Papers: Through Paediatrics to Psycho-Analysis* (London, UK: Tavistock)

Winnicott, D. W. (1958b) 'Primary Maternal Preoccupation' in D. W. Winnicott (ed.), *Collected Papers: Through Paediatrics to Psycho-Analysis* (London, UK: Tavistock), pp. 300–305

Winnicott, D. W. (1965) 'The Development of the Capacity for Concern' in D. W. Winnicott (ed.), *The Maturational Process and the Facilitating Environment: Studies in the Theory of Emotional Development* (London, UK: Hogarth Press and the Institute of Psycho-Analysis), pp. 73–82

Winnicott, D. W. (1971) *Playing and Reality* (London, UK: Tavistock)

Winnicott, D. W. (1974) 'The Fear of Breakdown', *International Review of Psychoanalysis*, 1: pp. 103–107

Winnicott, D. W. (1992) *The Child, the Family, and the Outside World* (New York, NY: Da Capo Press)

Wong, P. (1999) 'Anxiety, Signal Anxiety, and Unconscious Anticipation: Neuroscientific Evidence for an Unconscious Signal Function in Humans', *Journal of the American Psychoanalytic Association*, 47 (3): pp. 817–841

Woods, M. Z. and Pretorius, I. M. (eds) (2011) *Parents and Toddlers in Groups: A Psychoanalytic Developmental Approach* (London, UK: Routledge)

Wurmser, L. (1994) *The Mask of Shame* (New York, NY: Jason Aronson)

Wurmser, L. and Jarass, H. (eds) (2011) *Jealousy and Envy: New Views about Two Powerful Feelings* (New York, NY: Taylor & Francis)

Yates, C. (2000) 'Masculinity and Good Enough Jealousy', *Psychoanalytic Studies*, 2 (1): pp. 77–88

Young-Bruehl, E. (1994) *Anna Freud* (New York, NY: W. W. Norton & Company)

Young-Bruehl, E. (1998) *The Anatomy of Prejudices* (Cambridge, MA: Harvard University Press)

Zachar, P. (2000) 'Psychiatric Disorders Are Not Natural Kinds', *Philosophy, Psychiatry, & Psychology*, 7 (3): pp. 167–182

Zahavi, D. (2008) 'Simulation, Projection and Empathy', *Consciousness and Cognition*, 17 (2): pp. 514–522

Zahran, S. K. A. E. K. (2011) 'Type of Parental Socialization across Cultures a Psychoanalysis Review', *Psychology*, 2 (5): pp. 526–534

Zanarini, M. *et al.* (2003) 'The Longitudinal Course of Borderline Psychopathology: 6-Year Prospective Follow-Up of the Phenomenology of Borderline Personality Disorder', *American Journal of Psychiatry*, 160 (2): pp. 274–283

Zepf, S. (2011) 'The Relations between Language, Consciousness, the Preconscious, and the Unconscious', *The Scandinavian Psychoanalytic Review*, 34 (1): pp. 50–61

Zerubavel, N. and Wright, M. O. D. (2012) 'The Dilemma of the Wounded Healer', *Psychotherapy*, 49 (4): pp. 482–491

Žižek, S. (1992) *Enjoy Your Symptom! Jacques Lacan in Hollywood* (London, UK: Routledge)

Žižek, S. (2006) *How to Read Lacan* (London, UK: Granta)

index